GROWING
FOR
MARKET

Section authors: Donald O. Cunnion
                            David Schonberg
  Contributors: Jennifer Hamburg, David Hull, Len Kucinski, Sharon
                            MacLatchie, Jim Ritchie, Ellin Stein, Catherine Taggett,
                            Netta and Howard Thompson, Charlotte Waldron, and
                            Marion Wilbur.
  Photography: Ken Clauser, Carl Doney, T. L. Gettings, John Hamil,
                            Ace Hoffman Studios, Paul Kagan, Mitch Mandel,
                            University of North Carolina Sea Grant College Program,
                            Pennsylvania Department of Agriculture, Jim Ritchie,
                            David Schonberg, Sally Shenk, and Roger B. Yepsen, Jr.

GROWING FOR MARKET

**A guide to producing and marketing
vegetables, fruit, honey, herbs,
beef, cheese, mushrooms, wine,
woolen goods, and more.**

Edited by
Roger B. Yepsen, Jr.

 Rodale Press,
Emmaus, Pa.

2 4 6 8 10 9 7 5 3 1

Printed in the United States of America on recycled paper, containing a high percentage of de-inked fiber.

Library of Congress Cataloging in Publication Data
Main entry under title:
Growing for market.
   Includes index.
    1. Farm produce—Marketing.   2. Direct selling.
I. Yepsen, Roger B.
S571.G76   338.1   78–18527
ISBN 0–87857–233–3

Contents

Introduction

Section Three:

A SEASON IN THE LIFE OF DAVID SCHONBERG • *David Schonberg*

Section Four: _____

SPECIALTIES

Section Five: _____

Introduction

IT MIGHT NOT appear so from the modest title of this book, but *Growing for Market* is riding the crest of a trend—a move towards both direct marketing and self-employment that is quietly gaining momentum.

Direct marketing involves producer and consumer, with little or no help or interference from middlemen. Increasingly, truck farmers, cheese makers, fishermen, and orchardists are getting together with customers outside the supermarket and shopping mall. They meet at roadside stands, over wooden tables at farmers' markets, and at pick-your-own orchards. Shoppers are learning that the biggest, brightest supermarket imaginable cannot offer fresher food than the grower who was out picking in the fields a few hours before. And producers find they can get a better price from the consumer than they can from a wholesaler.

Direct marketing is nothing new, of course. Neither is self-employment, which can be thought of as a direct means of marketing your time and skills: an employer is much like the middleman. But large faceless corporations, like Brave New World supermarkets, are not ideal places to carry on life's work—especially for the free-spirited people who forgo the security of a regimented day and week and year. And so it is with the people in the chapters that follow. They have dipped a toe into self-employment, and report here that the water's fine.

R.B.Y.

DIRECT MARKETING

Ace Hoffman Studios

Take off your gloves and meet the consumer.

One

1: What is direct marketing?

D IRECT MARKETING IS the simplest and least costly method of selling—the producer dealing directly with the consumer, with no middlemen in between. It's the original method of buying and selling.

As civilization developed, people began producing things other than food. These people were obliged to obtain their food from others. They went to a grower to buy or barter. Or the grower came to them.

Towns and cities sprang up. The first middleman appeared. He bought from the producer and sold to the consumer, an arrangement that made things more convenient for both producer and consumer. As urban areas expanded, other changes took place in order to get food from its place of origin to its final destination. Soon we had terminal markets, brokers, commission merchants, and wholesalers. All these created the need for sophisticated transportation and distribution facilities. The marketing system reached its present complex status— and its present number of middlemen.

While cheap energy, cheap transportation, and cheap labor were available, few consumers complained about the system. Food might not be as fresh as when it came directly from the producer, but it was relatively cheap. Consumers were willing to pay for built-in maid services in buying their food, getting it prewashed, pretrimmed, prepackaged, and precooked. This convenience meant less work in the kitchen.

Then came the blow-off. Inflation hit. Suddenly, food ceased to be a bargain. Today, food prices are far above levels of just a few years ago and all indications are they will go still higher.

One answer, of course, is to find ways to cut through the costly conventional marketing system and its many middlemen. This means reverting, at least to some extent, to the original marketing concept— direct relations with the producer.

Interestingly, producers also have become unhappy with the marketing system. They have been caught in a cost–price squeeze, with production costs shooting up faster than the price they get for what they have to sell. In many cases, small producers have been forced out of the wholesale marketplace because of the huge volumes of standard quality demanded by the corporate supermarket chains. They just don't want to bother with a lot of little guys.

So direct marketing is off and running in all parts of the country. Each year sees more and more consumers buying direct from producers. At the same time, more and more producers are getting into direct marketing as a means of survival.

No one knows at this time just how many producers are selling direct, or how many consumers are buying direct. We may have a better idea after some research is conducted under the Direct Marketing Act of 1976, passed by Congress to encourage more direct marketing.

Morris S. Fabian, associate marketing specialist at Rutgers University, New Brunswick, New Jersey, pooled some miscellaneous statistics and came up with the observation that there are over 5,000 direct marketing facilities in six northeastern states alone—Connecticut, New Jersey, New York, Pennsylvania, Massachusetts, and Rhode Island. He figured total sales at about $220 million annually.

Pennsylvania alone sells about $50 million worth of farm output via the direct marketing method every year, according to estimates made by the Pennsylvania Department of Agriculture and the Pennsylvania State University Extension Service. A recent University of Minnesota study indicated that nearly half of all households in that state buys some food directly from the producer. The figures go from as high as 59 percent for rural nonfarm families to 35.6 percent for city families.

You can get some idea of the potential profitability of growing produce for direct sale by considering the difference between what the farmer gets selling wholesale and what the consumer pays at the supermarket. The difference is known among economists as the farm–retail price spread—and it's a spread that's been widening for some time.

Recently, for instance, the spread on fresh tomatoes was 28.4 cents a pound out of a retail price of 48.2 cents. That means the producer got only 19.8 cents wholesale. Potatoes that sold for $1.36 for a ten-pound bag brought the farmer only 44.4 cents wholesale. You'll note that the spread in each case was greater than the original price to the grower.

The spread is no mysterious thing. It represents the many added costs that take place as a commodity moves through the marketing channel. The spread covers the costs of transportation, overhead, taxes, profits, and a heafty chunk for labor: farm workers, truck drivers, packing house workers, wholesale distributor help, and retail store employees. Actually, labor accounts for over half of all marketing costs; on the average, marketing charges account for about 50 cents of every dollar the consumer spends at the supermarket for fruits and vegetables.

A part of the trend toward direct selling has been the consumer's move back to good, wholesome food—food that is fresh and tasty. And many shoppers prefer food that hasn't been in contact with chemicals.

In the supermarket, too often the perishable food is many days away from the original source, having gone from producer to terminal market to wholesaler's warehouse to one supermarket's storage room, and then out into the store itself, where it may sit a couple of days before being sold. Even if properly handled and kept at optimum temperature, which isn't always the case, the stuff has lost a lot of its original goodness.

Why do consumers like to buy perishables direct from the grower? In several recent surveys, quality and freshness (which often are related) head the list of reasons. Interestingly, friendliness gets high marks—an important point to remember since this could be another reason why many consumers are becoming disenchanted with big chain supermarkets. Reasonable prices also are mentioned; however, most direct buyers don't appear to worry too much about how cheap the prices are as long as the quality is what they want.

2: Meeting the consumer

THERE ARE SEVERAL methods of direct selling. You may want to select one or several. For most growers, the simplest form of direct marketing is the roadside stand.

Roadside selling.

In setting up a roadside stand, plan to sell a fairly broad variety of items. The consumer who takes the trouble to drive out to your place wants the trip to be worthwhile. And the more you sell to a single customer, the more profitable it is for you—if you figure all your unit costs for help, advertising and promotion, and so on.

For a roadside structure you can start out with a simple lean-to building. From there, expand with your business. Many established operators have found that one of the most practical and versatile designs incorporates overhead doors, like a multiple garage. With the doors up, your market is wide open to the outdoors, offering an inviting appearance to consumers and permitting unhampered foot traffic. With the doors down, you are protected from bad weather and can operate into late fall, or even year around if you want to. Some growers have put existing structures to use, including old barns.

A walk-in cooler can be very useful, permitting you to pick early in the morning (even sweet corn) and keep the produce cool and fresh for the entire day. It even allows you to keep many unsold items in good condition until the next day, instead of having to toss them out. You may be able to get plans for a walk-in cooler from your county agent. However, some agricultural engineers suggest the best bet is to get a ready-made cooler. You can erect it yourself.

When choosing a location for your roadside establishment, you should plan on providing ample parking space off the road. Don't worry too much if your place is located off the beaten path: a high-speed, heavily traveled highway can present a disadvantage, as many drivers won't want to stop. One successful Pennsylvania roadside market operator is on the wrong side of town on a road difficult to locate. But he has brought the public to his door with smart advertising, promotion and merchandising—and you can too, without it costing an arm and a leg.

Some operators rent land on a main road because they feel their farms are too far out of the way. But that brings about logistic problems in moving commodities from your remote growing area. In addition, it helps to locate your roadside market close to your production area for the reason that customers like to see that you grow what you sell. Even though you may not normally grow near where you plan to have a stand, you may find it good merchandising to plant an acre or two alongside or behind your outlet.

Try to make your market attractive, eye appealing, and appetizing. Keep it painted. Keep the grounds neat. A little landscaping does wonders; annuals such as petunias can do a great job of creating a pleasing atmosphere.

If you have a closed-in establishment, make sure there is plenty of light inside. Here again, try for pleasing displays. You'll find more ideas under *Merchandising* in Chapter 3, "Marketing."

Your county extension service should be able to get you plans for roadside stand construction.

Pick-your-own, the ultimate in self-service, ties in neatly with a roadside stand. You sell at a lower price, but save on harvesting and sales labor. Some supervision of pickers is required, but generally this is a minimal thing, according to many growers.

Pick-your-own.

Pick-your-own (PYO) is a natural adjunct to the roadside market. Don't worry about PYO hurting your stand business, as most operators would assure you. While some customers like to go out into the field or orchard to pick, others prefer to buy at a counter. Besides, you'll be selling crops at the stand that you don't make available via PYO.

Customers think of PYO as a day in the country, communing with nature. And they enjoy saving money, of course. Strawberries generally have proved the most popular and profitable commodity for PYO. However, many things can be sold this way, both fruits and vegetables. Root crops can be a problem, of course, but there is at least

one potato grower who runs his digger over the field and then lets the customers pick the spuds off the ground. Another grower gathers the potatoes into a pile in the field and lets the customers pick and choose.

Some operators have worked out elaborate systems for traffic control in the fields. Others don't worry about it at all, and simply make sure the pickers stick to the designated areas. In some cases, pickers are allowed to drive their cars right out into the field or orchard. In others, arrangements are made for central parking, with the pickers hauled to the site on a flatbed wagon or some other vehicle.

Some operators permit pickers to bring their own containers. Others insist that only containers furnished by them be used. But most operators have come to the conclusion that the best way to sell is by weight, not volume. Selling by weight saves arguments about just how full is full, and keeps customers contented.

Children running around in the field can be a problem. One PYO operator solved this by imposing a minimum quantity each person in the field will be charged for, including kids—a hard-boiled approach, maybe, but it saves a lot of wear and tear. In some cases enclosed play yards are provided for the small fry.

How much do customers waste and damage in a PYO setup? Some growers complain about broken branches and trampled crops. Others just shrug their shoulders and say it's all part of the cost of doing business this way. More than one operator has had to go into PYO, ignoring the damage, because seasonal help is so hard to find.

One especially interesting note about PYO that keeps many growers happy is that most customers will pick and pay for stuff they wouldn't give a second look at the supermarket, as far as color, shape, and size are concerned. After all, they picked the crop themselves and are mighty proud of it.

Farmers' market.

A third choice is the public farmers' market. Such markets date far back in history, and now are enjoying a whole new wave of popularity, providing a way to move a lot of stuff in a hurry. They are located at sites readily available to throngs of customers. If no such market exists in your area you probably could get one started with the help of other growers. Or, the next best thing is a one-grower market; some individual growers rent a bit of open space in the downtown business section or in a shopping center parking lot, and sell off the tailgates of their trucks.

Some cities and towns have permanent retail farmers' markets that operate the year around. Unfortunately, many of the tenants of such markets are non-growers who buy their stuff at the nearest produce wholesale center. In some cases stall space is available to legitimate growers on a seasonal basis, but the so-called hucksters often get preference because they can sell the year around.

The fastest-growing type of public market right now is the open-air or tailgate market. Some of these are owned and operated by growers who have formed cooperatives to buy land and erect rooflike shelters over their stands. Sometimes an entrepreneur opens such a market on his own land and rents space on a day-to-day basis. In other cases, markets are organized by the local chamber of commerce as a means of attracting consumers back downtown. The Wilkes-Barre, Pennsylvania, farmers' market was opened in 1974, and now does business on 17 Thursdays through the warm months. An estimated 5,000 shoppers patronize the market, and the city merchants say that their business has gone up ten percent as a direct result.

Farmers' market, Wilkes-Barre, Pennsylvania   *Ace Hoffman Studios*

Everything sold must be grown by the farmer or handcrafted by the craftsperson. The city's Office for Community Development charges a season fee of $150 per stall for farmers. Handcraft dealers pay $5 per day. The fees help cover wages for extra employees hired for maintenance and promotion expenses. A survey showed that approximately 500 acres of farmland had been cultivated by area growers specifically in preparation for the market.

Some open-air markets, especially those controlled by producers, are limited to farmers who grow commercially. Backyard growers are barred either by the simple means of a fairly substantial membership fee, or by renting space on an annual basis. The commercial growers reason they must sell at a price that reflects production costs and other expenses in order to realize a profit. They fear backyard gardeners will wreck the price structure by selling at giveaway prices, since whatever they get for their surplus is gravy: they don't need it to live on.

In some parts of the country, space for small growers or backyard gardeners has been set up on the grounds of big wholesale farmers' markets. Another innovation is the operation often called a garden market, set up expressly for the sale of surplus home garden stuff. These frequently are sponsored by a local service club or other organization encouraging home gardening or community gardens. Only a small fee is charged—just enough to cover rental charges, if any, and perhaps the services of a traffic officer.

Some open-air markets operate without any sort of protection from sun or rain. Sellers compensate by using umbrellas or awnings. Once well-established, some markets erect a rooflike arrangement on posts for protection against the elements.

Fairgrounds buildings can serve as good sites. So can abandoned railroad stations, which often have platforms with roofs. Often a local government or private firm will provide an unused warehouse. It's just a question of exploring all the possibilities.

If you and some other growers decide to start up your own farmers' market, help may be available from your county extension agent or the marketing division of your state department of agriculture. Manuals have been published by some experiment stations and state departments. But no two markets operate exactly the same way, and no amount of outside help can tell you everything about consumer shopping habits and other variables.

Experience shows that it's best to work at a farmers' market at least twice a week, unless you have other outlets for what you are growing. The fruit and vegetables come along too fast for a weekly operation.

A market open to all growers who come along may be the most democratic way of operating. But here again, experience has shown that a market with too many sellers for the number of potential customers can result in great waste and little profit. No one sells enough to make the effort worthwhile and a lot of stuff must be thrown out because there's more than the customers can buy.

If you are planning to organize a market, think in terms of what Madison Avenue calls the product mix: seek as much diversification as possible. Some markets have found it highly beneficial to have at least one meat purveyer, as well as a couple of people selling baked goods, crafts, and so on. A person selling hot dogs, french fries, and hot and cold drinks will be well patronized by both buyers and sellers.

Look into insurance protection against liability claims. Someone may fall and get hurt and blame negligence on the part of a seller or the group operating the market.

A market manager is a must. This person is responsible for handling all the details of operating the market, and for settling problems and controversies on the spot. Such a manager, of course, follows a general policy laid down by the group running the market.

Other growers, especially organic, have built up a fair business selling produce to nearby restaurants, hotels, and even local grocery stores. Others sell door-to-door, but this seems like a hard way to make a buck. If you go in for certain specialty items, such as herbs or processed foods, you might find an outlet via mail order.

The last few years have seen a major effort to bring consumer food cooperatives and buying clubs into direct contact with growers. Some success has been achieved in states where food co-ops are going enterprises. This is especially true in cases involving organic growers. Unlike the traditional forms of direct marketing in which there is a one-to-one relationship between grower and consumer, the food co-op arrangement offers an opportunity for one grower or a group of growers to sell to a group of consumers. For the grower this means moving large quantities at one time and usually at slightly better prices than he'd get via conventional wholesale channels.

Don't feel obliged to settle for any one method of direct selling. A combination of two or more may be the answer to generating the volume of sales you feel you require.

3: Marketing

Location.

Must you be located close to a city or the suburbs in order to have a successful direct selling operation? In most cases the answer is no. In the first place, rural people can be good customers. In a multi-county survey made in the western part of New York State, Cornell University researchers found that a high percentage of farm, rural nonfarm, and small village residents reported making purchases at roadside markets, public farmers' markets, and via pick-your-own. Also, don't forget that tourists and campers can make good customers in remote locations.

It is possible to be located too far off the beaten path, of course. One Colorado organic apple grower is so remotely located he can sell only a small percentage of his crop direct; there just aren't more than a handful of permanent residents within traveling distance and tourists aren't very thick.

Your location can have a lot to do with deciding what form of direct marketing you engage in. The Minnesota study referred to earlier found that suburbanites are the most frequent users of roadside stands, while farmers' markets are most popular with city people. People living in rural areas are big on pick-your-own.

Mail order is the answer for some direct marketers located in remote areas, even for selling produce. Gift boxes of fancy fresh fruit have been made a paying proposition by some. But the most common foods sold by mail are processed items, including meat. Mail order also can be a good way to sell small foliage and flowering plants, bulbs, seeds, transplants, and nuts.

Mail order calls for an investment in advertising space and in packaging, plus the extra labor of making up the packages and taking them to the post office. (If you aren't too far out in the sticks, you may be able to get United Parcel Service, which picks up shipments right at your door.) Mail order also calls for skill in writing appealing ads and in the selection of publications that will reach the greatest number of potential customers at the lowest possible cost.

Pricing.

There is no single method of pricing the goods you produce, no matter what form of direct marketing you are involved in.

Many roadside operators charge just about the going supermarket price or slightly less. This pricing is used with items most in demand, such as sweet corn, tomatoes, cukes, lettuce, peppers, and onions. Such things as squash often are sold quite a bit cheaper than in the stores.

Nearly the same pricing formula will work at a public farmers' market. Prices are highest early in the season, then drift downward as more and more supply becomes available. This presents a good reason to try to put some of your produce on the market early.

Pick-your-own prices, of course, are lower than the others because no harvesting, handling, and transportation costs are involved. A survey of PYO operators on pricing yielded answers that ranged all the way from production cost plus ten percent to "all the traffic will bear." In many cases, PYO prices run about what the producer would get FOB wholesale, or slightly less. You should keep in mind that there is a certain amount of overhead cost in handling check-ins and check-outs, patrolling the fields, crop damage, and so on.

Few small growers really know their production and handling costs. So they depend on price comparisons—what the stores are getting and what other direct marketers are getting. But the really successful direct marketer makes it a point to know just what his costs are.

One truck farming family has figured what yield of corn per acre they need to make what profit at what price. They know, for instance, that they can make a decent profit on a yield of 750 dozen per acre at a retail price of 69.5 cents a dozen. If yield drops to 600 dozen the family knows it will just about break even at the same price. This family strives for a 33 percent markup over cost of production and harvest. That's a gross profit margin of 25 percent.

Which brings us to the difference between markup and margin: markups are figured on the cost; margins are figured on the selling price. Thus, a 100-percent markup means a 50-percent margin. Whichever word is used in the produce business, margin is usually the intended meaning.

Few experienced professional marketers use a uniform markup. Instead, they shoot for a predetermined overall gross margin and mark up individual items at various levels, depending on cost and demand. It takes a bit of know-how to make the overall gross come out where you want it, but wise pricing permits meeting competition and running low-margin specials.

Advertising and promotion.

If you plan to sell roadside or pick-your-own, advertising and promotion are something to think about. You have to let people know you're in business and where the business is located. More than that, you may find that you've got to lure people to your establishment, by one means or another.

Newspaper and radio advertising are most commonly used. So-called newspaper display space, one or two columns wide by several inches deep, often will do the job. Some marketers get first-rate results from the classified pages. Local radio stations have reasonable prices for spot commercials. You may find it productive to use both media.

For radio, consider a quick, newsy item plus your market name and location. Early in the season you might use something like: "Fresh picked sweet corn now is available at Blank's Roadside Market, located on Route 63 one mile east of Podunk." Later on, you might change your ad: "Fresh sweet corn now only 69 cents a dozen at. . . ."

In newspaper ads you can list several items. All don't have to be specials, but specials are guaranteed traffic pullers—as supermarket operators learned a long time ago. Customers will come to buy your specials and leave with a armful of other things as well.

Advertising experience has proved that descriptive adjectives, such as fresh, sweet, juicy, tangy, crisp, and plump, do have customer appeal, whether the customers are aware of it or not.

Radio is an excellent way of getting out quick word to PYO customers. Be aware that newspapers may want several days' lead time on an ad. Many PYO operators send postcards to regular customers when various commodities are ready to pick.

Special events can be an important element in promotion. The following ideas have worked well. Rent a pony or two and hire a couple of boys to lead the animals for free rides. Or use a hay-covered flatbed wagon, drawn by horse or tractor, for trips around your farm. You might try a corn roast: to promote early sales, cut up corn ears into one-inch pieces and serve on toothpicks. Free samples are especially effective in stimulating watermelon sales. Everybody likes something for free. Size and value don't matter.

Advertising can be tricky with PYO since such operations are highly dependent on the weather. You may advertise on Wednesday that strawberries will be reading for picking on the weekend, only to have it rain Saturday and Sunday. Experience shows you'll need to advertise again in a couple of days to remind the folks that the strawberries are still out there waiting.

Remind customers to come and buy in quantity for canning or freezing. Offer quantity prices, of course.

If you are involved in a public farmers' market you won't need to do individual advertising. But be sure the group running the market does a good job of it. Newspaper and radio are both effective. But also think about signs displayed on the back of local buses and tacked up in public places.

Price specials work great as a means of attracting customers to a public market. The idea is to get several sellers to agree in advance to offer something at a special price. Just make sure that the special is in large enough quantity to supply all, or most, of the customers who will demand it. Otherwise, you'll have some very unhappy people—who may not come back.

Merchandising.

Merchandising covers a wide range of activities. It covers what you sell and how you sell it. Promotions are part of merchandising. So is publicity. However, there are some other elements you'll find valuable to know about.

Eye appeal is important to good merchandising. Make your displays attractive. Keep your stand, whether at roadside or at a public farmers' market, neat and tidy. Be sure you and your help also are neat and tidy.

Mass displays are known to have greater sales appeal than just a few samples. Customers usually don't want to see your produce displayed the way it is at the supermarket: pre-packaging can be a real drawback. One potato grower moved very few potatoes at a farmers' market while he had them packed in 10- and 25-pound bags; when he dumped them out in a pile on the table next to a heap of open containers, sales immediately soared.

Sell quality stuff. Throw out anything you yourself wouldn't want to buy. Sell clean produce, even if that means washing it.

Treat customers cordially and courteously. Be friendly and helpful. But don't be pushy. Let the customer pick and choose, unless he or she asks for your help. Give honest answers to questions about variety and when the crop was picked.

If a customer complains about the quality of an item, apologize and replace it without an argument. You may win the argument, but likely at the price of losing a customer, and this is important in a business that depends in large part upon return customers. Some operators find that as high as three-fourths of their sales are to regular customers, whether at a farmers' market or at a roadside stand. Customer loyalty runs high, once established.

Should you display prices or not? There are two schools of thought on this. Some operators feel that marked prices save them the bother of quoting prices to shoppers. Those who don't show prices contend it forces the customer to ask, thus opening the way for the seller to point out the merits of the item.

Multiple-unit sales work well. Show the price for two or three pounds or bunches rather than the price for just one. Try selling sweet corn at so much for 14 ears instead of 12, for instance.

Regulatory matters.

Before you go too far in getting organized for a roadside stand, pick-your-own operation, or new farmers' market, be sure to check on governmental rules and regulations—local, county and state.

Zoning restrictions may dictate the type of structure you can use for a roadside market, as well as its size and location. There may be restrictions on size and location of signs, as well as location and size of parking facilities.

If you hire help, you may be required to meet certain rules on washup and toilet facilities. You also should check into child labor laws, minimum wages, and workmen's and unemployment compensation.

Then there's the matter of conforming to various weights and measures requirements for legal containers and approved scales. You'll want to check into personal comprehensive liability insurance coverage for protection against possible injury to customers and help. And don't forget to keep accurate financial records for income tax purposes.

Handling personnel.

Experienced direct marketers find it pays to train sales people in handling produce as well as customers. If the clerks don't know already, they should be told that many fruits and vegetables bruise easily, spoil quickly in the sun, and suffer from intense heat.

Sales people should know as much as possible about the commodities being sold. In the case of apples, for instance, see that they are equipped with the names of the varieties, whether they are sweet or tart, and what varieties are best suited for cooking or eating out of hand.

Many customers want to know how to prepare foods they are not well acquainted with. They also like to hear about a different way to prepare something they use regularly.

If a customer complains about the quality of an apple or a string bean, the sales person should replace it without question and do so in a manner that indicates concern for the customer's happiness.

If you have several sales people you may want to consider having all customers go through one cashier. This puts the responsibility of handling cash on one person rather than several.

Sales volume expanders.

Since you have a fixed overhead, you may want to consider expanding sales volume by carrying more than just fruits and vegetables as a way of assuring a reasonable net profit at the end of the year.

Homemade honey has proved a good item with many direct marketers. So has honey from nearby suppliers. In some areas it is possible to get commercially prepared jams and jellies packaged with your own label.

Home-baked goods such as bread, rolls and pies do well for many operators. Fudge made in a commercial machine sells well in most areas. So does peanut butter freshly made in a commercial-scale grinder.

Bedding plants are a natural in spring and early summer, and some operators have a good thing going with dried weeds for floral arrangements. You can gather your own or buy them commercially.

If you decide to operate a roadside market year around, you may wind up with a combination specialty food and gift shop. Local crafts sell well and you probably can handle them on a consignment basis rather than buying them outright.

4: Roadside stands

A ROADSIDE STAND IS close to the source of supply and can be attended by members of the family without leaving home base. It can involve only a very small investment, or none at all. Old boards on boxes have gotten some people started. Others have sold from a flatbed wagon parked at the edge of the road. You can go from there as business expands. One New Jersey grower started off selling 4 acres of vegetables from an old wagon parked under some shady trees. Today he grows 100 acres of vegetables for direct sale.

Roadside stands can be operated successfully under a wide variety of situations. The Department of Agricultural Economics at Cornell University recently studied three roadside markets in three different locales in New York State. One was located on a rural road in the suburbs of a city of 250,000. Another was located five miles from a small city of 30,000 souls. The third was out in a rural area but on a

A small, attractive roadside stand   Pa. Dept. of Agriculture

main highway. The market located near the small city operates only 3½ months a year, but has an annual gross of about $28,000. The rural stand on a main highway is open 8 months and grosses about $25,000. The suburban area operator would not disclose his sales figures, but he has a stand about seven times larger than the other two and a parking area five times larger. You can draw your own conclusions about his gross.

The average distance traveled by consumers to reach these stands is 4.9 miles. From the rural stand on a main highway the average distance is 6.3 miles, but it's not uncommon for customers to travel much greater distances.

As with similar surveys, the Cornell study showed that customers rated quality and freshness as the principal reasons for buying at these stands. Price rated below convenience and friendliness. The importance of quality, freshness and friendliness stands out sharply when you learn that most of the customers at roadside stands are "repeaters," shopping at the stands an average of once a week.

In their concluding observations, the Cornell researchers made this interesting point: "Each market had its own image in the eyes of the customers. It appears there is no one 'right' image for a successful roadside market, but rather each market manager must fit his market to his capabilities and the customers in his market area."

Don Cunnion, former director of marketing for the Pennsylvania Department of Agriculture, cites the example of four growers in that state who gross over a million dollars a year through quite different types of stands, operated under different conditions. Two are located on the outer suburban areas of a metropolitan area. Another is on the edge of a small college town, seven miles from a city of 75,000. The fourth is located in a rural area about five miles from a town of 16,000 and on a well-traveled two-lane highway.

Each of these markets differs from the other. Each has a different product mix and different type of customer. Each has its own distinctive physical setup and appearance. One makes a specialty of milk in plastic bags, beef and potatoes. Another stresses vegetables and bedding and houseplants. Another is very big in berries and fruit. The fourth carries a big line of fruits and vegetables, but also handles specialty items such as candied apples and dried weeds for flower arrangements. But they all have one thing in common—a sharp sense of management and merchandising.

Getting started.

Don't worry if your place is located off on a side road. You can bring the customers to you with advertising and promotion and by offering quality merchandise at the right price.

The Colemans of Maine feature organic vegetables at a roadside stand located seven miles off a secondary road. There is no nearby town of any size, but summer vacationers have proved to be excellent customers. A woman in rural upstate New York depends largely on customers traveling from New York City to summer cottages in the mountains. There are organic growers operating roadside stands in all parts of the country, near cities and out in rural areas. Some are small and gross just a couple of hundred dollars a year. Others have sizable operations and their gross is in the thousands.

Some operators have rented land on a main road because they felt their farms were too far out of the way. But this brings up logistic problems in moving commodities back and forth from the home base. Experienced marketers find it helps to locate the sales area close to the production area for more than just convenience—customers like to see that you grow what you sell. Even though you may not normally grow stuff near where you plan to put your stand, you may find it is good merchandising to plant some things in a visible spot. A woman operator located on a high-speed highway in New Jersey goes out of her way to plant sweet corn along the highway across from her stand. She says it helps attract customers who might otherwise shoot on by.

As suggested earlier, you can get started in roadside selling with only a card table under a tree or with a couple of planks laid across boxes. But such a setup never will bring in any serious money. Many consumers won't stop at such rinky-dink arrangements, feeling you aren't going to have the quality they want. In other words, you have a poor image.

A simple lean-to structure, nicely painted and well-stocked, often will be enough to inspire confidence in the mind of the nearby resident or the passing motorist. Do-it-yourself plans for structures of this and other types of roadside stands are available through your county extension agent. If he doesn't have them on hand, he can get them for you. The charge, if any, will be very nominal.

One of the most practical and versatile buildings for a moderate-sized operation looks like a multi-car garage with overhead doors. With the doors up, your market is wide open to the outdoors, permit-

Market with overhead doors

ting easy access and presenting an inviting appearance to the public. With the doors down, you are protected from the weather, permitting operation into late fall, or even year around if you are so inclined. Plans for these structures also are available from your county agent.

Many growers going in for direct marketing have put existing structures to use. Ordinary barns have been converted at moderate cost. It's really just a case of using some imagination.

In many cases, structures are expanded as business expands. One grower has been adding on a section almost every year, as money be-

A converted barn

comes available. His most recent project was to tack on a plastic greenhouse which he uses for both plant propagation and as a sales area.

Visits to established roadside stands will give you plenty of ideas. Most of the operators will be happy to take the time to tell you about the plusses and minuses of their structures and provide whatever cost figures they have.

No matter how small you start out, you'll have to give some thought to how readily motorists can turn off the road to your place. And you'll need to provide adequate parking space. Information from the University of Delaware suggests 15 parking spaces for every 100 cars you expect in a day. A minimum space width of eight feet is recommended for each car, and you must allow some space for turning.

All the experts agree—try to make your market attractive, eye appealing and appetizing. Keep it painted or stained. Maintain the grounds and mow the grass. A little landscaping with flowers and shrubs will do wonders. If you have a closed-in establishment, make sure there's plenty of light inside.

Since quality and freshness are the two principal reasons customers prefer to buy from roadside stands, it's a good idea to give considerable thought to maintaining these virtues in what you sell. The hot sun can knock quality into a cocked hat in practically no time at all. So can just plain heat and humidity. Shading your produce will help. So will using fans if you have a closed-in market. Spraying water over produce occasionally helps. Many established retail marketers turn to refrigeration to help keep their produce, eggs, meat, and dairy products in prime condition.

The University of Wisconsin's guidelines for roadside market operators suggest that sweet corn held at no higher than 70°F (21°C) for one day will change half its sugar to starch. In contrast, sweet corn held under refrigeration at 32°F (0°C) will lose only about 5 percent of its sugar in 24 hours. Temperatures up to 40 or 50°F (4 or 10°C) will hold most produce in satisfactory condition for three or four days.

A popular form of refrigeration for roadside markets is a walk-in cooler. You can build your own or buy a pre-built unit. Some are available with two temperature ranges since research has found that some produce holds best at 35 to 40°F (2 to 4°C) and some best at 55 to 60°F (13 to 16°C). You can get detailed information on coolers from your county extension service. Plans for a walk-in two-temperature farm refrigerator have been developed by the USDA, and are likely available through the county extension agent for about two dollars a set.

Some growers feel they are better off with a prefab unit purchased from an area supplier. These usually are made up in sections and can be dismantled and moved if you change locations. But probably more important, the prefabs are carefully engineered for the utmost efficiency, considering insulation, compressor size, and the critical balance between temperature and humidity. Such a unit is apt to be more accurate than one built from scratch. The prefab coolers come with detailed instructions for erection, so you can save the cost of labor. Prices vary by size and accessories. The Bally Case and Cooler Company of Bally, Pennsylvania, which claims to be the world's largest maker of this type of cooler, figures you ought to be able to buy a 175-cubic foot unit (4 feet wide, 6 feet long, 7 feet high) for about $2,500 to $3,000 installed, as of 1977.

A walk-in cooler will enable you to maintain a variety of produce close to the sales area, saving frequent trips to the fields or orchards to replenish supplies. It also will enable you to carry items overnight, and to handle items you do not grow yourself and can get only every couple of days.

Some roadside operators have acquired used cooler display cases of the kind grocery stores use. These detract somewhat from the rustic appearance of a stand, but work well to keep highly perishable items in good condition.

Roadside market organizations.

Once you become established as a roadside operator you may find it worthwhile to join an association of such operators. Many states have what are typically called certified roadside market associations. Often sponsored by the state farm bureau organization, these groups have a set of standards governing both the physical setup of the members' markets and a code of ethics for their operation. Size is usually not a factor, just as long as you are seriously in business and produce a substantial amount of what you sell.

These associations provide many benefits. An inspection service is customary, first to check whether you qualify for membership and, second, to see that you continue to maintain prescribed standards. Unlike some government inspectors, these association inspectors are there to help you do a better job. They can point out shortcomings of which you are unaware and suggest remedies, perhaps passing along helpful hints they pick up from other members.

The associations often provide cooperative buying services for such things as containers, point-of-sale advertising material, and recipe leaflets. Such cooperative buying can help hold down your costs. The associations also are involved in promotional activities to make consumers more aware of the virtues of buying at roadside stands, especially those of association members. The New Jersey Roadside Marketing Association has an active promotion program involving shopping malls, where a small stand is set up and typical roadside items are sold, giving consumers an idea of what they can expect at a regular stand.

To learn whether your state has a roadside market organization, check with the county extension service or state department of agriculture. Membership fees vary depending on services rendered. Ohio, for instance, charges $30 for each month the market is open.

All indications are that sales at roadside markets are on a rising trend, especially for organically grown food. The University of Wisconsin goes out of its way to make this observation: "Increasing demand for the so-called organic foods should . . . result in increased sales of fresh fruit and vegetables and for those foods processed naturally." The Wisconsin report optimistically concludes that "all available evidence points to continued success for roadside marketing."

The interest among growers is demonstrated by the increasingly large number of men and women who turn out for roadside marketing conferences held annually in a number of states. If you are contemplating a stand, you could do worse than spend a couple of days attending one of these affairs. You'll get an earful and eyeful.

Roadside marketing conferences.

Conferences usually are sponsored by the state extension service, sometimes in conjunction with roadside marketing associations and state departments of agriculture. The agenda is structured to include the latest information on production and marketing techniques, but the backbone really is the marketers themselves. Individual marketers are selected to describe unique highlights of their operations, usually backed up with color slides.

It is truly amazing how creative and resourceful these people are. They are the leaders and the most articulate, of course, but their ideas are well worth listening to, looking at, and adapting to your own situation. One of the special events at the annual Pennsylvania–Maryland conference is the free-for-all contest to see who can come up with the most unusual merchandising idea. In addition to the scheduled events, there is plenty of time to meet and talk with individual marketers. Ideas are shared willingly on a personal basis as well as from the podium. Long-lasting friendships result.

A special feature of these conferences is the demonstration booths of suppliers of roadside market equipment and goods. You can look over various types of bags and containers, equipment for making fudge and peanut butter, and such sundry, but profitable, items as fancy baskets and inexpensive trinkets and novelties. You'll even find representatives of frozen pie companies because quite a few marketers have found it pays to sell fresh baked pies bought frozen and cooked in fast-heating ovens. The aroma does the selling for the pies.

At roadside marketing conferences you learn that experienced marketers find it wise to train sales people in handling produce as well as customers, whether your help be family members or hired folks. Sales people must learn to be polite and solicitous with customers, selling without being pushy. They should know as much as possible about the commodities they sell: the variety names and how foods can be prepared for the table.

A cardinal rule is this: If a customer complains about the quality of an apple or a snap bean, the seller should replace it without question and do so in a manner that indicates concern for the customer's happiness.

5: Pick-your-own

LETTING CUSTOMERS HARVEST their own fruits and vegetables is likely the fastest-growing type of direct marketing. Bill Courter, University of Illinois specialist, recently made a tour of PYO operations across the United States and Canada, and came to the conclusion that this form of direct marketing has a very bright future indeed.

High labor costs, as well as a scarcity of labor, have been a major reason for commercial growers to turn to PYO. Then there's the matter of the cost—price squeeze in the conventional marketplace: higher production costs all along the line, coupled with wholesale prices, don't leave room for a decent profit. PYO appears to be at least part of the answer for many commercial growers.

Many consumers think PYO is one of the greatest ideas since the wheel. They buy prime-ripened produce and get it at a highly attractive price. Besides that, they get a day communing with nature in the country. As one PYO operator has pointed out: "We're doing more than selling produce at an attractive price. We're selling a form of recreation, a day of pleasure and serenity, a day of accomplishment, a

feeling of well-being." Many of his customers come with the whole family and picnic basket and stay all day.

Growers have made the interesting observation that many customers don't seem to fuss about the cosmetic appearance of what they pick. They soon learn that the fact that an apple or peach is slightly misshapen or off color has little to do with its flavor and goodness. As a result they pick and take home stuff that would cause complaining if it had been purchased at a supermarket.

Pick-your-own is not a new idea, by any means. It's just an idea whose time has come. Cherries were being sold PYO in Wisconsin as far back as 1928 according to the University of Illinois' Bill Courter. A Pennsylvania grower, Ken Youngs, also was selling cherries way back in the same year.

Courter says over 90 percent of the strawberries being grown in Illinois now are being sold PYO. Other strong PYO items in the Midwest, Courter found, are blueberries, raspberries, blackberries, apples, and peaches. But very few vegetables were being sold this way in the middle part of the country when he made his check. In the East, however, vegetables are becoming a strong PYO item.

Strawberries generally lead the field when it comes to PYO, no matter where you go. They seem to suit best both the grower and the consumer. And they're mighty profitable for the grower. Herbert Hoopes of Maryland started with a half-acre in 1962. By 1976 he had expanded to seven acres and was grossing $30,000. He says his total out-of-pocket investment amounted to $8,500. Another Maryland grower, Ron Sowell, decided to get into PYO strawberries and leaped off with a ten-acre planting. The ambitious start paid off, and he's very happy with his big gamble.

Most experienced hands recommend starting small when it comes to strawberries. They figure you ought to be able to sell 8,000 to 10,000 pounds an acre via PYO. The average sale per customer has been estimated by some growers at between 20 and 30 pounds.

Studies made at the University of Maryland indicate you can expect to put in about 63 man-hours per acre with strawberries sold PYO. The study also shows profits from PYO strawberries should be about double what you'd get with paid pickers. The rate of return per dollar invested, not counting interest rates on loans or mortgaged land, was figured at 22.8 cents for paid harvest and 48.7 cents for PYO—quite a difference.

PYO has been tried for just about every kind of crop. Bob Hodge of Pennsylvania has tried PYO for peaches, apples, pears, strawberries, rhubarb, raspberries, sweet corn, tomatoes, eggplant, and grapes. His big PYO effort, though, is on strawberries, 30 acres of them. Root and tuber crops suggest problems, of course, but one potato grower runs a digger over his field and then lets the customers pick the spuds right off the ground. Another grower gathers the potatoes into a pile in the field and lets the customers pick and choose.

In a survey made by the University of Illinois Extension Service, the most popular tree fruits mentioned by PYO customers were peaches, apples and cherries. Raspberries, blackberries and blueberries ranked tops in their category. Leading the list for vegetables were tomatoes, green beans, corn, peas, and watermelon. A survey made by Cornell University in western New York State brought similar responses. Strawberries, apples, tomatoes, blueberries, cherries, and raspberries were the PYO favorites. Except for apples, most of the stuff was picked for preserving.

In Minnesota, asparagus and tomatoes have been found to be the most common vegetables for PYO, according to the University of Minnesota. Just as the asparagus season ends in June, the strawberry season is coming in to help keep the customers returning into the summer.

The University of Illinois survey showed that 79 of the PYO customers interviewed travel up to 50 miles to reach their favorite PYO operation. Ten percent travel over 100 miles. And about half of the customers said they live in small towns, under 5,000 population. When asked what they like most about PYO, 75 percent said quality and about two-thirds said price. More than 10 percent said they like PYO for the recreation it offers.

A number of organic growers have gotten into PYO. David Hull (Chapter 40) of Warwick, New York, does very well. He grows 40 acres of apples and sells them all PYO, except for the culls that go into cider. Hull opens his whole orchard of five varieties to the public, offering both standard and semi-dwarf trees, with the standards pruned back to 16 feet for picking convenience. Hull bars the use of ladders, and instead rents pole pickers to his customers at 75 cents each. He throws in a three-quarter-bushel bag.

An innovative kind of guy, Hull also has tried renting trees to consumers. The idea has worked so well he plans to continue. The setup works to everybody's advantage. A family rents a tree for the year, presently at $25. Hull takes care of pruning and any other labor involved during the growing season. The renting family has the privilege of coming out to view the tree at any time, perhaps picnicking under it. At harvest time, the family does its own picking. Depending on the year, the tree may yield anywhere from 5 to 20 bushels, Hull says. In some cases several families share the rental and harvest of one tree.

Hull maintains a large parking lot, covering between three and four acres, and hauls the pickers to the orchard on a flatbed wagon pulled by tractor. He finds children no problem, allowing them to accompany their parents into the orchard. Families may picnic in the orchard if they wish.

Like many other direct marketers, Hull has found that since he has what the retail profession calls "traffic" coming to his place, he might as well sell other things besides apples. So he offers bedding plants, cut flowers and mums, all grown in his fiberglass greenhouse.

Robert Burrell, an organic grower in Colorado, manages to sell some cherries via PYO even though he is quite isolated. In his own words he is located "250 miles and three mountain passes from the nearest city of over 40,000," but in 1976 sold two tons of cherries PYO at 26 cents a pound. Cherries were selling at 39 cents in area stores.

Here's a summary of some suggestions made by PYO operators at a recent direct marketing conference.

Set up controlled access to your operation. Try to arrange for customers to come into your place on one lane and out another. Fence in your fields, if economically feasible. Establish a general parking lot and transport customers to the picking area, or let them walk to it.

Establish check-out areas where produce can be weighed or counted and the money collected. If you have a lot of customers, try using two or more check-outs. Experienced operators say customers get a bit turned-off by having to wait in line too long, especially at the end of a hot day with their kids getting fussy.

Establish a few simple rules and regulations for customer conduct and post them in conspicuous places.

Provide supervision for each picking area. The supervisors can explain to the customers what to pick and how to pick it.

Whether you allow young children into the picking areas is pretty much a matter of personal preference. Some operators absolutely forbid children under school age. Others try to keep out everyone under high school age. On the opposite side, there are operators like David Hull who feel letting the kids help pick and scramble around is part of the cost of doing business—and besides, the kids are tomorrow's customers.

To make sure customers pick enough to at least pay for the cost of overhead, there are operators who set a minimum quantity that may be picked. Some set a minimum for each person in the party, kids and all. They figure this helps reduce the small fry invasion.

Some operators permit customers to bring their own containers. This can cause problems because the containers vary so much in size. Pouring stuff out onto a scale and then back again can be a nuisance. You may want to think about providing containers. Such hardy items as apples, green beans, sweet corn, and even tomatoes can be transferred to a plastic bag if the customer doesn't want to pay for the container you supply.

Nearly all operators, judging from comments at direct marketing conferences, have come around to selling many things by weight instead of volume. It saves a lot of argument about how full is full. Still, there are operations that sell by volume at which the sales people scoop off what they regard as excess before letting the customer check out. They say the customers seldom put up a fuss.

PYO operators who permit pickers to drive their cars right out into the picking area sometimes have a problem with pilferage—pickers hiding produce in the trunk of their car before going to the check-out, for example. Operators who allow cars usually require customers to open the trunks of their cars for inspection. But most customers are honest, agreed most growers at a recent direct marketing conference. The degree of honesty and cooperation with the grower's ground rules appear to be in direct relationship to the size of the community the customers come from. Problems are greatest for growers close to highly populated areas.

6: Public farmers' market

THE PUBLIC FARMERS' markets discussed here are places where a group of growers are gathered together to sell directly to the consumer. This distinction is made here to prevent confusion between this type of market and the wholesale farmers' market found in some sections of the country. While some wholesale farmers' markets may also sell retail, those covered here are retail only.

Farmers' markets take many forms. Some cities and towns have permanent markets that operate the year around. Unfortunately, this type of market often attracts a large number of so-called hawkers or hucksters who get their produce at the nearest wholesale distribution center. Except for such things as eggs, meat and processed foods, growers in the northern part of the country sell their own produce only for a few months. As a result, only a few producers can take advantage of a market stall 12 months of the year. Some community farmers' markets operate only seasonally.

Markets are either sponsored by the local government, entrepreneurs or the growers themselves.

The fastest-growing type of market at present is the open-air or tailgate market, as this is the quickest and least expensive way to get a market started. Such markets can be located on a vacant lot in town or out in the country along a highway. A paved area serves best, but you'll find markets on packed earth, crushed stone or mowed fields. Markets of this type generally operate a couple of days a week; unless the participating growers have other outlets a minimum of two sales days is needed to take care of the maturing produce; nature just won't wait for the convenience of the growers.

Some markets, especially those controlled by farmers, are limited to commercial growers. Backyard gardeners with excess produce are barred by the simple means of a fairly substantial membership fee, or by renting space on an annual basis. The commercial growers reason they must sell at a price that reflects production costs and other expenses and still leaves room for a profit. Backyard gardeners, they fear, will wreck the price structure by selling at dirt-cheap prices, since whatever they get for their surplus is pure gravy. The backyarders don't live on the income they take home.

But the trend to more home gardening has seen the development of a market that accommodates the little guys, too. Such markets can be held in a relatively small area since most participants can sell their limited stash of tomatoes, cukes or snap beans off a card table or the back of a station wagon. Consumers stand to find real bargains at these markets. And the growers may pick up enough cash to pay for their seed. Everyone goes home happy.

If you are planning on selling a fairly substantial amount of stuff you'll want to consider participating in a setup that operates regularly (at least through the summer months) and offers adequate space for both the sellers and the customers. Ample parking space is very important, too.

First, look around for a going market that has an opening for you. Dale Hurliman of Beavertown, Pennsylvania, sells organic cider and apples at a long established farmers' market he located in the nearby borough of Lewisburg; the Milt Cunninghams live in Jerome, Idaho, and sell organic fruit and vegetables at a market in Twin Falls which is sponsored by the local YMCA and YWCA. You may be surprised to find markets in your area that didn't exist just a couple of years ago. If you don't know where to start, try checking area chambers of commerce or your county extension service.

Organizing a market.

The mayor of Pittsburgh became excited by the idea of helping inner city folks get fresher produce, and the city sponsored a tailgate market on a municipal rehabilitation site, paving a vacant lot and putting in lights. The market operates two nights a week, with growers from the surrounding area paying a small fee for the use of the facilities. This market is likely unique in that most of the parking space for customers is located in a high-rise municipal garage across the street from the sales area.

The Pennsylvania Department of Agriculture decided a good way to encourage the formation of public farmers' markets would be to set up a demonstration model on its huge State Farm Show parking lot in Harrisburg, the state capital. A marketing specialist was assigned the task of putting the market in motion. With the aid of nearby county agents he contacted some 50 growers for an organization meeting.

The idea of a tailgate market on the parking lot was explained. No state funds would go into the project. The services of the marketing specialist would be provided free. Farmers would pay a modest rental fee for the use of the space, as well as any costs for advertising and promotion. The growers formed an association to run the market, electing officers and drawing up by-laws and regulations. They put up $50 each to cover advance expenses, including advertising and promotion, and liability insurance. Further funds for promotion and the hiring of a traffic controller came out of the fees charged each operating day.

The market was an outstanding success from the start. The market operates on Tuesdays and Fridays, as these days were most convenient for most of the growers, some of whom also sell at other markets. Tuesday generally is not much of a marketing day, but customers were lured in satisfactory numbers by the use of advertised specials.

The market completed its second year in 1976 and now appears to be an on-going enterprise. In the first year, total sales per market day per seller ranged from $200 to $900. One husband-and-wife team reported total sales for the season at nearly $15,000. Organically grown items did well for several sellers. The market now has a full-time manager.

One of the keys to the success of the market has been consistent advertising via radio and newspapers. To start the season, the association also buys a week's space on the back of local buses.

A definitive study on retail farmers' markets in New York State, done in 1975 by the Department of Agricultural Economics at Cornell University, produced some interesting findings. First, the study showed that a variety of organizations sponsor the markets in New York State. They include municipalities, chambers of commerce or related business groups, community action or resource development programs, and agricultural marketing associations (farmer-owned co-ops). Some of the markets open in June with the coming of strawberries, rhubarb, asparagus, and radishes. The others open with the ripening of the first sweet corn and tomatoes, the most popular of items. Markets oriented mostly to fresh vegetables close by September 30. Others, especially those with apples, stay open into late October or early November.

Most of the New York State markets open in the morning, according to the study. Fees range from $2 to $5 per day for a 10- or 12-foot-wide selling space into which a car or truck can be backed. While some of the markets allow non-growers to sell, this usually was with the provision that they be charged a substantially higher fee. Of the 25 markets on which financial data was available, 10 reported a balance in the treasury at the end of the year, 5 broke even, and 10 wound up in the red. The basic goal of all was to break even or perhaps have some money left to start up the following year. A balance in the treasury also can provide the where-with-all to make improvements, such as paving the sales area or adding lights.

A centralized location in a populated area was characteristic of all the markets in the Cornell study. Seventeen were found in downtown shopping areas, of cities large and small. Four were located in suburban malls. In Buffalo, Rochester and Syracuse—all large cities—the retail farmers' market was an adjunct to the wholesale produce market.

Offerings covered a wide range. Fruits and vegetables, flowers, eggs, honey, maple products, and herbs were the major items. Also on sale were cheese and homemade baked goods. Some markets permitted arts and crafts to be sold. Reported sales by market sellers varied from $20 to $400 a day. (Over one-half of the sellers interviewed said they also had a roadside stand.)

The idea of a small market at a toll road rest stop was tried on the New York State Thruway in 1976 and proved moderately successful. Two farmers were involved, but one dropped out after a few weeks. The remaining farmer's gross sales ranged from $200 to $600 a day in the period covering July and August when traffic was heavy, but dropped to as low as $50 a day after Labor Day. Plans call for trying the idea at other locations on this road, which is the state's major east-west highway.

In Vermont, the Natural Organic Farmers Association (NOFA) is responsible for stimulating interest in farmers' markets. The NOFA people rented space in vacant stores in some places and used open air sites in others. At first they tried markets made up of both organic growers and crafts people. But Bob Houriet, one of the NOFA leaders, says they finally came to the conclusion that it would be best to operate these functions at separate markets.

Several farmers' markets are operated in West Virginia by the state's Department of Agriculture, in cooperation with farmers' cooperative associations. Money for establishing the enclosed markets was provided by the state legislature. Staffing is by marketing specialists attached to the Department of Agriculture's Bureau of Markets.

The West Virginia markets operate on the consignment or old commission—merchant plan. Growers of any size can bring in any amount of produce, as little as a single basket, and have it sold for them at the market. A small commission is deducted to cover overhead costs. These markets started out as public auctions, then started wholesaling to brokers, supermarkets, hotels, and restaurants. Now, however, consumers are encouraged to come in and buy direct in any quantity. Besides produce, they can now get eggs and a wide variety of processed foods.

Eight new farmers' markets came into being in the state of Washington during 1974 and 1975 and more are being encouraged by the Hunger Action Center, funded by the Community Services Administration, a federal agency. The center provided seed money for the launching of some of the markets, and it has served as a co-sponsor for a Farmers' Market Workshop.

Open-air markets are popping up even in New York City. An operation known as Greenmarket opened up on a lot at 59th Street and Second Avenue under the sponsorship of the Council on the Environment of New York City, a non-profit group. It was so successful that similar markets were organized farther downtown and in Brooklyn.

In Honolulu, the city government sponsored a program that has resulted in 21 weekly markets located in low-income areas. Because of the climate, these markets can be kept supplied with local produce the year around.

No one knows just how many farmers' markets there are in the United States at the moment, but the number must be in the thousands. Pennsylvania alone has well over 100 as a result of the recent surge. A recent report showed that Canada has more than 100, most of them in Ontario and Quebec.

Farmers' markets always have been popular in Pennsylvania, particularly in the central-eastern part of the state where there is a heavy concentration of German-descended Pennsylvania Dutch. A survey by Jim Toothman, marketing professor for the Pennsylvania Extension Service, located some 80 markets that have been in operation for many years. Some are farmer-owned cooperatives, two of them in existence for over 50 years. But most are operated as private enterprises in large, permanent buildings. Some of these markets have as many as 75 stalls operating year around. Meat, eggs and poultry are big at most of these markets.

A market open to all growers may be a democratic institution, but experience has shown that too many sellers for the number of potential customers can result in great waste and little or no profit; no one sells enough to make the effort worthwhile.

If you and other growers want to start up your own market, you should be able to get help from the county extension service or the marketing division of your state department of agriculture. Several states publish booklets on the subject, and these may be of help.

How a Parking Lot Became a Successful Farmers' Market is published by the Pennsylvania Department of Agriculture and is available at no cost through the Department's Bureau of Markets, Harrisburg, Pennsylvania 17121.

The *Farmers' Market Organizer's Handbook* resulted from material developed at the workshop sponsored by the Hunger Action Center in Washington State. You can get a copy by writing Hunger Action Center, The Evergreen State College, Olympia, Washington 98505.

Planning Farmers' Markets in Vermont is valuable no matter where you live. It is available through Elizabeth Humstone, Charlotte, Vermont 05445. There will be a modest charge.

Then there is *Organizing Farmers' Markets,* an inexpensive booklet published by the Natural Organic Farmers Association of Vermont. Write to NOFA, RD 1, Box 30, Hardwick, Vermont 05843.

When planning to organize a farmers' market, think in terms of what Madison Avenue calls the product mix: Try to involve an array of producers who will provide a good cross-section of vegetables, fruits and berries. But don't stop there. Try also for sellers of meat, eggs, baked goods, home preserves, and bedding plants. A vendor handling hot dogs, french fries and hot and cold drinks will be patronized by both buyers and sellers.

A market manager is a must, whether he is one of the sellers who agrees to take on the job or someone hired from the outside. A retired person can fill the bill very well. The market manager is responsible for handling all the details of operating the market and for settling problems on the spot. He sounds the opening bell, sees that only qualified sellers occupy the spaces, collects the market day fees, handles advertising and promotion, and pays any bills. Such a manager, of course, follows a general policy laid down by the group running the market.

How large a customer potential do you need to start a market? The Cornell study referred to earlier came to the conclusion that the trading area should have a population of at least 10,000. It's important to understand that a trading area can cover several square miles and include several local communities. Some successful markets are located out in open country between population centers.

The Cornell study also notes that patronage at markets drops off substantially in rainy weather, whether or not shelter is available, and suggests an investment in a roof or shed may not be profitable. However, it is a fact that most permanent markets do provide some sort of shelter from wilting sun and from occasional showers. At some completely open markets, the sellers install beach umbrellas. An interesting variation is a tarp attached to the side or roof of a truck that rolls out like an awning. For this setup a seller needs to rent two of the normal stall spaces and park his truck sideways. But, then, two or more spaces are not at all uncommon for sellers with a lot to sell. The extra space also increases display area and, thus, sales opportunities.

7: Forming a cooperative

ANY GROUP OF growers, large or small, can form an agricultural cooperative similar to the kind that has enabled many commercial growers to compete successfully in the marketplace. Co-ops can be set up for all sorts of purposes, including buying, selling and processing.

One public farmers' market incorporated under Pennsylvania's agricultural cooperative law is the Scranton Night Market co-op. This organization is over 50 years old, and has its own chunk of land in an industrial area of the city. A roof shields the sales stands, and the sales area is paved. An annual membership fee is charged to cover operating expenses.

In California, a number of roadside stand operators have formed cooperatives for the purpose of pooling resources for advertising and promotional purposes, as well as for coordination of supplies. One of the most elaborate (and apparently, successful) cooperatives involving organic growers is the Farmers' Organic Group (FOG) located in Sonoma County, California. FOG works through a volunteer coordinator to facilitate marketing the members' produce. Information on available items is called in weekly to the coordinator, who maintains contacts with a wide range of buyers, including a non-profit distribution operation set up to service cooperative food stores and food buying clubs. Sue Shirley Weisman, a member of FOG, says the members cooperatively plan their crops in order to reduce duplication and to better meet the needs of buyers.

FOG also provides for cooperative buying of seed and soil amendments, the sharing of equipment, and group problem solving. FOG has 14 member farms and all are required to be certified as 100 percent organic. Some members sell at a farmers' market in Santa Rosa and one belongs to a 49-er trail group, through which members jointly promote their retail operations by such means as brochures and maps. Weisman herself reports selling about 65 percent of her output, mostly vegetables, through FOG. She sells the remainder at the farm or to a restaurant.

Members of the Natural Organic Farmers Association of Vermont coordinate their growing activities, but sell individually. Members sell to food cooperatives, sometimes under contract, and to restaurants, as well as at farmers' markets. The group is not formally organized as a cooperative.

Attempts at forming farmer cooperatives go far back in history, but the movement in the United States got its big impetus from the Capper-Volstead Act of 1922, federal legislation that established a favorable climate for cooperatives and set up operating principles and legal procedures.

Actually, the so-called Rochdale principles generally are conceded to be the cornerstone of the modern farm cooperative setup. Included in the present-day co-ops are the Rochdale principles of open membership, democratic control, and political and religious neutrality.

Purchasing co-ops.

These provide for group purchasing of production goods and supplies for members. The objective, of course, is to effect savings by buying "wholesale."

Marketing co-ops.

These are organizations through which members sell what they produce. These co-ops can vary greatly in how they function. Some merely bargain for the best possible price for members. Others sell for members on a commission basis, or even buy the product from members for re-sale.

You're aware of some of the largest of these marketing co-ops: Sunkist oranges, Sun-maid raisins, Diamond walnuts, and Ocean Spray cranberries. There are other co-op brand names of regional importance.

Processing co-ops.

These co-ops process their members' output, whether it be fruit, vegetables or milk. They are in direct competition with privately owned processing enterprises and many do very well. Some have grown into huge, corporation-type operations, offering a wide variety of items and covering multi-state areas. Some sell both wholesale and retail. At least one farmer-owned co-op operates a chain of supermarkets, and at one time owned 51 percent of the stock in a regional airline.

The key to success in any co-op is dedication on the part of the members and good management. Some marketing co-ops have failed because members didn't play fair, selling their best stuff through a private broker and letting the co-op have the left-overs. But poor management appears to be the major cause of failure. In some cases members couldn't see paying a good manager a salary that might surpass their own net income. Other co-ops have failed because the members tried to call the shots for management on a day-to-day basis, instead of laying down overall policies and leaving it up to management to follow them. The major problem seems to lie in proper balancing: hiring competent management, laying down policy guidelines, then watching to see that management properly carries out its function.

One large dairy co-op, engaged in the business of marketing its members' milk as fluid, cheese and ice cream, nearly went down the drain because management bamboozled the board of directors, made up of farmer members. Management made some bad, high-investment decisions and then doctored the books to cover up. The complex, highly documented proposals to expand were duly presented by management at board meetings, along with balance sheets, profit-and-loss statements and the like. But the farmer directors either didn't or couldn't analyze them properly. At least some of the members may have been highly competent managers of their own farms, but they weren't corporation management experts with sufficient background to understand the complexities of a multi-million dollar enterprise. What's more, many were too tired at evening board meetings to be mentally alert. It's pretty easy to doze off at 8:00 or 9:00 after a big dinner and after putting in a day that begins shortly after dawn—particularly when someone is rattling off hundreds of box car figures intermixed with big business jargon.

In the case of this cooperative, one remedial suggestion was that the farmer members of the board hire their own experts to sit with them and offer suggestions and advice. These experts would be responsible to the members, not to hired management.

If you form a co-op you aren't likely to run into the described situation—at least for awhile. However, the point still holds that you give serious consideration to supplying the best possible management personnel, whether from among your own members or from outside, and then keep your eye on them.

The first contact about forming a co-op can be your county agent. If he isn't too well posted, ask him for the name of the co-op specialist at the state university. If that doesn't work, you can always contact the Farmers' Cooperative Service, USDA, Washington, DC 20250. They're a helpful group.

Of course, you are not obliged to be formally organized to operate as a cooperative. Any group can get together and form an association and operate it on the Rochdale principles. Many groups start this way and, if successful, go the formal route later.

The drawback to being unincorporated as a co-op is that each individual member becomes liable for any incurred debts or judgments awarded by a court. When you are incorporated, the co-op itself is liable, to the extent of its assets. Individual members are not liable, unless they want to be.

There are certain fees attached to getting incorporated as a co-op. Usually the services of a lawyer are recommended. But the paper work can be done by anyone who wants to take the trouble to learn the ropes.

RUNNING THE BUSINESS

Decide what sells, and then learn how to market it.

Two

8: What can you sell?

IN ANSWERING THIS question, first consideration probably should be given to what you are growing or making now, especially those things you do particularly well. Most everyone has a specialty or two, and many successful direct marketers have built their reputations on a couple of featured items.

If you plan to sell produce you'll want to make sure you feature those crops most in demand. This will vary by sections of the country, but in many areas the top vegetable sellers include sweet corn, tomatoes, lettuce, peppers, peas, potatoes, green beans, cucumbers, and squash. Tree fruits usually sell well, especially apples, peaches, pears, plums, and sweet and sour cherries. Nectarines are a good possibility. All kinds of berries are good sellers.

A Cornell University study showed that in New York State fruit sales predominated at pick-your-own operations, with vegetable sales more prevalent at roadside markets and public farmers' markets. Cornell found that the more frequently purchased fruits and vegetables at pick-your-own operations were, in order, strawberries, apples, tomatoes, blueberries, cherries, and raspberries; at roadside stands, corn, apples, peaches, tomatoes, squash, lettuce, and potatoes; and at farmers' markets, corn, apples, lettuce, potatoes, tomatoes, squash, peaches, and cucumbers.

Many direct marketers of produce try to have a wide variety of vegetables available, including some off-beat types not usually found in the local supermarkets. They may not sell a lot of these specialties, but there are customers who are on the lookout for them and will stay to buy other things you have for sale. What vegetables are considered off-beat types? These vary by sections of the country, of course, but a few that come to mind include Jerusalem artichoke, kohlrabi, spaghetti

45

squash, swiss chard, and Oriental vegetables.

It goes without saying that organically grown produce has a built-in clientele. While the number of people who seek it may not represent a large percent of the total market potential, there can be enough of them to absorb much of what you have to sell. And, it would appear, the demand for organic produce is growing every day. If your quality is all it should be and the price is right, the general public will buy your organic output even though they don't care much one way or the other how it is grown; some organic growers report that most of the sales are to folks for whom the adjective "organic" means little.

Berries can be the most profitable of all produce, and are proven customer attracters. Some roadside operators have found that strawberries can mean the difference between profit and loss for a season. Don't overlook the brambles, especially red and black raspberries and blackberries. These are seldom found in the supermarkets anymore, as they're too perishable. But customers will eagerly buy them, almost without regard to price.

The Funk family of Millersville, Pennsylvania, realized a net profit of $2,061 an acre from red raspberries recently, selling them at 80 cents a pint retail. The Funks, a father-and-son team, are commercial growers noted for their meticulous record keeping, so you can trust their figures. You may not be able to duplicate their profit margin, but you can come awfully close with proper management. The Funks found black raspberries not quite as profitable as red. The same year they made so much money on red raspberries, they realized only $670.57 an acre from blacks, paying to have them picked and retailing at $1.20 a quart. They nearly doubled their profit on black raspberries, however, when they sold them pick-your-own, getting 82 cents a quart.

One great thing you have going for you by selling direct is that you can provide perishables at the peak of perfection. Commercial growers who sell wholesale have to pick many crops before they are fully ripe so they can stand the journey from farm to wholesale warehouse to retail store. Vine-ripened tomatoes are a good case in point. Even so-called nearby tomatoes sold in the stores usually are picked in the "pink" stage so they can stand up to the next several days. Real tomato fanciers insist there is nothing like a perfectly vine-ripened tomato for top flavor. You can provide it.

Profitable sidelines.

There is no need to limit your sales to fruits and vegetables, of course. Eggs, dairy products and meat are good sellers. In Minnesota it was found that eggs are the most popular item in direct food sales, followed by meat, vegetables and poultry, in that order.

Houseplants and bedding plants have been taken on by many roadside marketers because they can be highly profitable. The normal markup appears to be about 100 percent. That's a 50 percent profit margin. Potted foliage and flowering plants can be kept around the stand for a long time, if properly handled. Bedding plants have a shorter sales period and you must move them fast if you want to get maximum profit out of them.

Some marketers grow their own bedding plants in cold frames or hotbeds, as well as greenhouses. Or you can buy them from a commercial grower for re-sale. This often is the custom with houseplants, which can be purchased in various sizes, and may be the best way to start with houseplants. Later you can try rooting cuttings of some items, such as geraniums. Potted hanging plants have become a hot item for some marketers.

Quite a few organic growers have found that plants are money makers. Linda Wey of Dewitt, Michigan, grows a wide variety of herbs in her 12-by-24-foot greenhouse, built of redwood and covered with fiberglass. She's also added dried flowers to her repertoire and has drummed up a good business making these into arrangements for weddings. To help promote her business she gives talks to garden clubs within a 100-mile radius of her home. She also takes plants to flower shows as a way of building a reputation.

Organic greenhouse grower Gilbert J. Calta, Valley City, Ohio, sells bedding plants, houseplants, herbs, and geraniums. He has 1,400 square feet of greenhouses, which he says he built from odds and ends. Calta is located two miles outside the village of Valley City and is a half-hour from Cleveland. He says his customers come from a radius of 75 miles, enticed by antiques, gift items, and sheep as well as plants.

Selling potted herbs by mail has become a big thing at the Yankee Peddler Herb Farm, an organic operation of the Coouse family located in Brenham, Texas. Judy Coouse recalls that herb growing started out as a hobby, but soon became a business, with mail-order selling beginning in 1973. Besides shipping live plants, they also sell seed and dried tea herbs. The Coouses have three home-built fiberglass greenhouses covering 2,500 square feet.

In Jerome, Idaho, Milt Cunningham sells not only organic vegetables, fruit and berries via PYO and at a farmers' market, but has added potting soil and eggs to his lineup. The potting soil is made up of compost, worm castings, bone meal, and chicken manure, and is sold in two- and five-pound bags. Milt sells both brown and white eggs, plus low-cholesterol eggs from Araucana hens. Customers drive as far as 25 miles to buy their brown eggs. The Cunningham family has built up their organic produce business over some 20 years.

Organic apple grower Dale Hurliman of Beavertown, Pennsylvania, has built a sizable business selling his own brand of cider vinegar. He sells some of it retail at a farmers' market, but the business has become so large he now wholesales, mostly through Erewon, to health food stores from Boston to Washington. He uses no preservatives and says he can't keep up with the expanding demand. Here again, Hurliman doesn't stop with selling one line. He also sells dressed poultry, piglets and goats. Most of the dressed poultry goes to a food cooperative.

Wilton Jaffee has developed a unique mail-order business—he sells organic, certified seed potatoes from Aspen, Colorado.

Another versatile organic grower is Earl Lawrence. In addition to selling vegetables from a roadside stand and from the tailgate of his truck in downtown Rocky Mount, Virginia, Lawrence sells grains to a food cooperative in Washington, D.C. He also handles honey, eggs and pigs. Robert Burrell of Colorado sells many of his organic apples as juice which he pasteurizes and bottles himself. He plans to sell raw cider as a way of avoiding pasteurization.

A thriving mail-order business has been developed at Snowhill Farm, owned and operated in Chester County, Pennsylvania, by Norman and Marjorie Aamodt. They specialize in shipping organic beef by both air and truck to customers all along the East Coast. The beef is packaged to include an assortment of cuts to meet the customer's desires. Mrs. Aamodt says their beef grades out high choice to prime and commands a price accordingly.

A group of organic growers in Wisconsin have formed a co-op to sell sprouts to food cooperatives, health food stores and restaurants.

In Pennsylvania, apple schnitz brings in extra revenue for many roadside market operators. Schnitz is sliced, dried apples, originally prepared by the Pennsylvania Dutch for conversion into pies, pudding, and other goodies during the winter. It can be made from either sweet or tart apples. The frugal Pennsylvania Dutch usually make their schnitz out of drops—off-color or misshapen apples which have a limited fresh market. The apples are cut into slices and dried. Some still are being dried in range ovens, but more and more schnitzers now do their drying in modern electric food dehydrators.

Does schnitz differ from conventional dried apples? Well, it usually looks different—more shriveled. And it tastes a good deal better, in the opinion of many. Some, at least, is drier than commercially dried apples, an impression that was confirmed by sending samples to a food laboratory. Maybe that's partly why they taste better. Schnitz sold at roadside stands usually is purchased as snacks. Tourists buy it to munch as they travel along.

Another good seller is apple butter, typically made by stewing apples with cider and spices. A few operators also sell peach and plum butters.

Home-baked goods such as bread, rolls, pies, cakes, and sticky buns do well for many operators. If your neighbors are smitten with your baked goods, chances are the public will be just as favorably inclined. Homemade candy is a natural. So is freshly ground peanut butter. Honey is an old favorite for direct sales.

A nationwide survey done a few years ago by the University of Delaware found that items processed on the farm brought the highest profits in direct marketing. Cider was the best seller of the preserved items studied. Others with large sales volume included apple butter, hard cheese, cottage cheese, baked goods, honey, pickles, relishes, and such preserves as jams and jellies. Poultry, cut flowers, potted plants, and eggs were other popular items that turned up in the survey.

In all preserved food items you have a big edge going for you over the commercial products. You don't have to put in preservatives and other additives the commercial processors use to extend shelf life and improve appearances. Your customers will be happy and healthier for it.

Marketing crafts.

The making and selling of handcrafted goods may not seem central to a book on growing and marketing produce, but the two topics are similar. Both truck gardening and cottage industries reintroduce something to the marketplace that customers have missed: quality that reflects a real live person's skill and attention. A hand-turned pot has as much over the mass-produced item as a garden-fresh tomato has over the flavorless supermarket facsimile.

Another similarity between crafts and truck gardening is their suitability for part-time income. You needn't leave home for either; alternative markets exist, and the investment of capital is usually as modest as need be.

In a study on marketing channels for crafts in Tennessee, it was found that more than half of the craftspeople surveyed had annual incomes of less than $1,000. Most crafts were marketed through commercial retail outlets (typically craftshops) and craft fairs. All of those reporting annual incomes of over $10,000 attended craft fairs. Few sold their wares on contract or through catalogs.

9:   Costs and returns

NATURALLY ENOUGH, a burning question to be asked about various crops for direct marketing is "How much is it going to cost me to grow and how much profit can I expect to get out of it?"

Nobody, but nobody, can lay down facts and figures that will apply to each individual grower. There are too many variables: climate, soil, individual ability, and the local marketing situation. Obviously, some guidelines are needed to help make decisions one way or another.

Specific caveats must be kept in mind as you read the financial summaries that follow. "Net return" here means return to labor, land and management. In a large-scale market-gardening business, labor is mostly hired, and in any event is considered a cost deductible from income for tax purposes. But small farmers often feel that their own labor, the money their labor earns, is their profit, and indeed it often is the only profit. If you want to figure what business "profit" there might be in the enterprise models that follow, you can deduct from the return to labor and land the number of hours given as necessary for the operation at whatever wage rate you think your time is worth.

Secondly, this method ignores land cost, which is a considerable cost in business farming. Land cost can be calculated as the price you would pay to rent your land per acre, or the amount that you could rent out your land for, or what the money would return to you in interest if you sold the land and banked the proceeds. Land cost hasn't been deducted because in the typical small-scale part-time gardening situation, the land is being paid for (or hopefully has been paid for) out of earnings. It is part of a family's home which they will have and enjoy whether they farm the land or not. But you can make your own land–cost deduction if you want to.

Costs given here are mostly operating costs—cash yearly outlays per acre—though fixed machinery costs have been figured in, too. To calculate fertilizer costs for organic growers, you'll find estimates, since no university study seems to exist. Because organic manures and comparable fertilizers vary widely in nutrient content and availability, assessing a cost is extremely difficult. If you haul manure from your own barn, the cost for your nitrogen, potash, and trace elements may be very small—as will your cost for N and K from plowed-down alfalfa which you have harvested the year before for hay. On the other hand, your cost for raw phosphate will be as high as (or higher than) the chemical grower's costs for superphosphate. If you have to purchase organic fertilizers such as bone meal, soybean meal, blood meal, and meat scraps, your cost per acre will be considerably higher than the chemical grower's cost—at least in the early years before you have built up organic matter and a healthy biological life in your soil.

The following figures assume a situation where you have your own manure or can get it or a similar fertilizer free for the hauling nearby. (Homesteader-writer Gene Logsdon believes this is at present the only situation where an organic grower can make a *profitable* income.) The hauling cost of $10 per acre for a 15-ton-per-acre application of manure (or equivalent in sludge, leaves, shredded bark, etc.) is updated from some old data from Cornell. A yearly cost of $40 per acre has been figured for rock phosphate. You will have to adjust these figures according to your own experience and needs. You may need to buy additional potash, or less phosphate. Or your town might haul leaves to you for nothing.

A similar situation prevails with pesticide applications. Don't think that because you are organic you won't have pest problems, even though they may diminish as you achieve ecological balance in your garden. Even if you only hand-pick tomato worms, that's going to cost you time. If you use *Bacillus thuringiensis* on your cabbages, it will cost you as much as the more violent insecticides. Rotenone is not cheap. Biological controls are relatively low-cost (compared to chemicals) but they're not free. So the cost assigned to pest control is about half the cost of chemicals.

You will save by not using herbicides, but this means cultivating mulching for weeds more often; so the savings won't be quite as considerable.

In any event, you'll see here approximate chemical costs as given by the universities to serve as a comparison if nothing else. Organic costs may be lower than chemical, and then again sometimes they are higher.

Strawberries.

Probably the very best cash crop for homesteaders and small truck farmers is strawberries. This versatile fruit reaches full production its second year from planting, comes in varieties adapted to almost all regions of the United States, and commonly grosses $2,000 per acre— much more than that on high yields. The limiting factor is labor: a homesteading couple will do well to handle a quarter acre, if they intend to do all the picking themselves. Yet master organic grower Ken Morgan of Deerwood, Minnesota, says he grosses as much as $5,000 per quarter acre, selling both berries and plants. This seems unbelievable unless you've heard that California growers can harvest over 40,000 pounds of strawberries per acre.

Here's how costs and returns are averaged in agricultural research computations, in which selling plants is not figured. You could have much higher returns than those below—yields of 9,000 quarts for example.

Costs per acre, 1976

Plants $57

Fertilizer

> 15 tons of manure per acre from your own barn,
> along with legumes in rotation and other or-
> ganic practices; hauling and application $10

> Unrefined phosphate

>> half ton per acre per year $40

Lime . . . .$ 4

Organic control for possible insects
  and fungal disease $40

Fixed machinery cost $30

Machine operation cost $45

Mulch, containers and other miscellaneous
  expenses $300

Chemicals

> Nitrogen: 25¢/lb. x 50 lbs. $12.50
> Phosphorus: 20¢/lb. x 100 lbs. $20
> Potash: 10¢/lb. x 100 lbs. $10
> Pesticides $43

Total *(chemical fertilizers and pesticides not included)* $526

Gross return: average yield 6,000 qts.

> @ 60¢ per qt. $3,600

Costs . . . . − 526

Return to labor, land and management $3,074

• But you will put in 100 hours of labor per acre plus the labor of
  picking. If not a pick-your-own operation, figure 4 minutes to
  pick a quart (or more) or 400 hours to pick 6,000 quarts, for a
  total effort of 500 hours per acre.

- Irrigation and frost protection might cost $250 per acre.

- It takes about three tons of straw to mulch an acre of strawberries, says Ohio State. Kentucky measures it as 60 bales per acre.

- North Carolina says it takes 10 hours to remove blooms from one acre of strawberries, 22 hours to hoe and control runners the first year, and 30 hours to do the same the second year after harvest, per acre.

A part-timer might plan only a quarter-acre patch to harvest with family labor and shoot for an organic yield of 8,000 quarts per acre, or 2,000 quarts per quarter-acre of very high-quality, non-irrigated (they'll taste better) but heavily mulched berries. A larger operation probably would mean pick-your-own selling. Don't overlook the possibility of selling plants or fall berries.

Raspberries.

Raspberries take a little longer to get into full production and are more regional in nature—they grow better in the North than the South. But since raspberries are very difficult to ship, a local grower seldom has competition from large shippers. Because of good fall-bearing varieties like Heritage, the season can be stretched out considerably longer than with strawberries, another advantage to the small grower who needs to spread his labor over a longer period. The following computation, from the University of Kentucky, works on a very conservative yield. Good management would insure a considerably higher gross return.

Costs per acre, 1976

Plants	$30
Fertilizer, same as for strawberries (organic)	$50
Organic pest control	$20

    (a guess; some growers have needed none in 10 years)

Machinery operation $45

Fixed machine costs $28

Mulch, containers, stakes, wire, misc. $300

Total $473

Yield: 3,200 pts. per acre

@ 60¢ per pt. $1,920

Costs . . . . – 473

Return to land, labor and management $1,447

- You will need to put in 100 hours of labor *plus* picking. It takes less than an hour to pick 12 pints or 260 hours per acre, for a total of around 360 hours per acre.

- If you stake and tie your canes, figure another week's work.

- On fall-bearing crops, grown only for the fall crop, you can eliminate all hand-pruning. Simply mow and shred canes after fall harvest.

- You may be able to sell plants too—you'll have plenty you have to grub out, anyway. The above computation roughly fits blackberries and black raspberries. You probably will not have near the demand for blackberries.

Tomatoes.

Most growers of choice tomatoes for retail or wholesale stake their plants, which seems to produce fruit sufficiently better to warrant the expense and labor. It is far easier to pick staked tomatoes, and the fruits are protected from rot and slugs.

Most computations on hand-harvested, garden crop tomatoes specify stake-grown plants. If you grow yours on mulch, adjust cost accordingly. Yields on staked tomatoes seem to vary widely. In the mountain areas of North Carolina, a yield of 40,000 pounds per acre is used to figure costs and returns, while on the coastal plains of the same state, yields average 16,000 pounds. Organic growers can produce at a better rate, especially on a small (say quarter-acre) well-tended patch.

Costs per acre, 1976

Plants $40

Fertilizer:

> Organic, same costs as in previous crops $50

> But if chemicals are used, figure anywhere from $115 per acre for NPK (Kentucky) to $200 for those huge North Carolina mountain yields.

Pest control: Chemical, from $100 (Kentucky) to over $200 (North Carolina). Organic, perhaps $100, though often tomatoes can be grown without any problems at all, if rotated with other crops. Figure 4 hours of labor for patrolling and hand-picking tomato worms (tobacco hornworms) . . .$100

Lime, if necessary $4

Machinery operating costs $45

Machinery fixed costs $40

Truck hauling and marketing (if applicable) $285

Stakes, ties, other expenses $375

Total $939

Yield: 16,000 lbs. per acre

> @20¢ per lb. $3,200

> Costs . . . .− 939

Return to labor, land and management $2,261

- As you can plainly see, tomatoes are an excellent cash crop and easier to pick than strawberries. The catch is that you will have a harder time selling *all* your tomato production at a good price than you will strawberries.

- If you have to buy your organic fertilizer in the form of blood meal, soybean meal, bone meal, or any of the legitimate NPK label-analyzed organic fertilizers, figure anywhere from $150 to $300, depending on how much N and K you decide to add. (Price on most meal is very high at this writing.)

- Labor requirements are high—650 to 800 hours per acre—but are spread over a long season.

- You should be able to get more than 20 cents per pound for quality tomatoes, but you may get less toward the end of the season. You need 4,500 stakes per acre, says Kentucky; 6,000 says North Carolina, where they grow plants in denser stands.

- North Carolina figures 375 hours for hand-harvesting an acre, and 25 hours for setting stakes and stringing. If you mulch instead of staking, you'll want at least as much straw as for strawberries—3 tons per acre, or more.

Sweet corn.

Contrary to general opinion, sweet corn is not a big money-maker per acre, but then it does not require a great deal of hand labor. Operating expenses run as high as $500 per acre by Ohio State calculations to only half that in Kentucky, which gives you some idea of the variation in figuring costs. Since corn is somewhat a norm for the cultivation of crops in this country, the following figures from Ohio State will serve you well to get a general idea of the costs of commercial grain farming.

Costs, 1976

Plowing	$10
Fitting (2 times)	$10

Planting $6

Cultivation (3 times) $15

Spraying, if not organic, or perhaps organic if applying a liquid
    seaweed or the like (per application) $3

Hauling $10

Total $54

- The chemical grower may spray sweet corn 8 times. He also has a pesticide bill (herbicides and insecticides) of $32 per acre and a fertilizer bill of $58. You can figure on spending about $50 to $60 for your organic nutrients, too. Marketing supplies and costs may run $335 per acre, says Ohio State, but perhaps less for a small roadside stand.

- On a commercial level, return to labor, land and management for sweet corn comes to $245 (Ohio) with yield at 1,000 dozen ears per acre and a price of 70 cents per dozen. Kentucky figures 1,200 dozen at 60 cents each, and a return to land, labor and management of $448. North Carolina figures are wholesale, pricing the corn at $2.60 a crate (five dozen per crate) with a return to land, labor and management at a low figure of $116 per acre.

Summer squash.

Oddly enough, squash ranks high on the list of cash returns per acre. That's because yields are usually good. (Zucchinis are more prolific than rabbits.) But the fellows juggling those numbers do not take into account that you very well might not sell all those zucchinis before they grow into small logs. In a list of vegetables marketed as pick-your-own, New Mexico State University puts the highest net return per acre on summer squash at $1,370—and that was back in 1973.

By comparison, tomatoes were rated at $657.66 per acre, okra at $57, chilis at $304.87, cucumbers at $725, eggplant $37.75, sweet corn $127, and watermelon at $385.

North Carolina figures a return to land, labor and management of $465.10 for squash after a charge of $225 per acre is made for custom harvest. You could pick some or part of that if you harvest yourself. Yield is figured at 300 bushels per acre at a price of $3.50 per bushel for a gross value of $1,050. Georgia says that with a 250-bushel yield, you have a return to land, labor and management of $546.66 per acre when the price is $5 per bushel. The same source points out that if you harvest only 100 bushels per acre, you barely break even.

Commercially grown squash requires a lot of pest control. Be sure you can control cucumber beetles, squash bugs and borers before you launch into squash.

There are other crops that might interest you for extra cash. Kentucky says that cane sorghum, for sorghum syrup, should produce 150 gallons per acre. At $8 per gallon, that's $1,200. Cost of production runs $268.25 plus $42 fixed machinery costs. Return to land, labor and management is around $900. But figure 60 hours or more of hard work.

Bell peppers? This is a good one for organic growers because disease and insect problems are not as critical. Figure 300 bushels per acre at a price of $5.50 or a gross of $1,650, says Louisiana, with a total cash cost of only $350.26. That's not bad.

Cabbage is hard to sell if cabbage worms have gotten to it, but now organic growers have *Bacillus thuringiensis,* an approved bacterial insecticide, to help them around this roadblock. Figure a gross income of $1,500 per acre as a possibility, says Kentucky, on a yield of 25,000 pounds and an average price of 6 cents per pound. This will give you a return to land, labor and management of around $900, but you won't want to handle a whole acre by hand with just family labor. That's a mighty lot of lifting and cutting.

Muskmelons.

Two studies from Nebraska provide the kind of data rarely available for homesteaders on returns for muskmelons. Both studies were done on a small-gardening scale and so reflect better the situation most organic growers are in. In the first, the gardener, as a part-time project, raised muskmelons, sweet corn, tomatoes and watermelons on less than an acre of ground and *netted* $602 with 130 hours of labor. Almost all of this profit came from less than a half-acre of muskmelons—$475, paying $6 an hour. Summed up the gardener, "I can easily see a person making a net profit of $1,000 an acre on muskmelons if yields and markets were reasonably good."

The other study involved a project of growing one acre of melons, the results of which are, again, more pertinent to small growers than the per-acre rate statistics of large growers. Donald W. Mierau made the planting in 1974 at Henderson, Nebraska, and kept exact figures on all his costs. He used every modern method at his command, including irrigation and chemical rather than organic culture; but the breakdown of his costs and sales can be very helpful to any small grower in showing both the complexity of costs in growing even on a small scale, and the possibility of a good profit.

Costs for producing and selling one acre of muskmelons, 1974. *(Would be higher now, but so would selling price.)*

1½ qts. Treflan for weeds $10.15

> (substitute two additional mechanical cultivations for organic acre, which will cost about $6)

2 cases of Jiffy's-7's $54.90

7,000 ft. trickle irrigation tubes $140.00

8,000 ft. black plastic mulch $160.00

Freight for two above items $23.47

1 pound Sevin $2.25

> (organic substitute, $5 worth of rotenone)

Machinery rental, irrigation water, and misc. $50.00

2 ounces of seed $20.00

2 bags vermiculite $6.16

100 lbs. dry fertilizer $7.07

> (Very low amount by most standards. Price today for that amount would be about double. Figure organic costs as in preceding examples.)

35 plastic trays $12.25

Rent on one acre of land $60.00

Total $546.25

Fixed Costs

1 hand sprayer $12.88

Main irrigation lines $102.48

Freight for above item $8.00

1 tulip bulb planter $5.49

      (for making planting holes through plastic)

Fittings and valves $52.77

Total $181.62

Divided over 5 years $36.32

TOTAL GROWING COSTS $582.57

Marketing Costs
Mileage cost for selling

      @ 10¢ per mile $75.00

Gas for selling $35.00

Sales tax paid to state $18.68

Trailer overhead $20.00

TOTAL SELLING COSTS $148.68

TOTAL COSTS $731.25

INCOME yield of 22,946 lbs. of fruit

    Sold to grocers $1,813.06

    Sold to restaurants $32.00

    Sold retail $747.31

Total $2,592.37

NET PROFIT *(return to labor and management)* $1,861.12

Labor required, hours

Preparing land 8
Seeding flats 10
Weeding garden 20
Laying plastic and irrigation equipment 25
Transplanting melon plants 25
Spraying plants 22
Picking melons 70
Hauling melons to market 50

230 hours

(Or a wage of about $8 per hour)

Comments Mierau: "Where else can a person invest $600 and expect to receive back four times as much in a half-year?"

Other crops.

Here are a few more selected figures for various crops, giving a figure for return to labor, land management.

Sweet potatoes (Louisiana) $514

Snap beans (Virginia) . . . . .about $1,000

It takes 30 minutes to pick a bushel of snap beans, and you should get 200 bushels per acre. You can pick pole beans faster, but you have the cost and labor of the poles to add on. Average returns are about the same. But pole beans, a good grower, can produce 500 bushels per acre.

Ornamental corn (Virginia) . . . . .about $300

That's if you figure the ears at 5 cents apiece, say Virginia. If you tie into bunches of three and sell for 25 cents, you will increase profit (and labor) greatly.

Irish potatoes (Virginia) 1976 . . . . .about $2,000

It takes about 32 hours to plow out an acre of potatoes with an old potato plow, then pick up the potatoes.

Trellised cucumbers (Virginia) 1976 . . . . .about $2,000

A real good one if you can control the cucumber beetle. You need $400 worth of posts and $60 worth of No. 9 trellis wire, says Charlie O'Dell, extension specialist in Virginia, plus $80 worth of binder twine. You should be able to pick a bushel of cucumbers every 15 minutes and get 500 bushels per acre.

Halloween pumpkins (1976) $2,000

If you get them all sold for a dollar each, you've got yourself a winner. You've also got yourself 451 hours of labor, says O'Dell. An acre should produce 2,400 pumpkins to load, haul and unload and maybe load and unload again.

Onions (Utah) 1973 . . . . .about $500

On yield of 350 cwt per acre

Blueberries (Tennessee) 1973 . . . . .about $1,100

On yield of 6,000 pints per acre

For the beginner or the sideline grower, even an acre is probably too much of one crop to try at first. One of the best models is the "mini-farm plan" developed by the Tennessee Valley Authority for very small farms and nonfarm income. This plan encourages production in units of less than one-acre patches. For example, TVA sees a homestead of three acres producing perhaps $1,000 net cash income ($614 in 1974 when the study was made) in addition to family food, with the land used as follows: .2 acre in sweet corn, .3 acre in tomatoes, .1 acre in snap beans, .1 acre in sweet potatoes, .1 acre in watermelons, and 2.2 acres in ladino–fescue clover supporting a beef cow and calf.

The mini-farm plan, which could have many, many variations, is a good one for homesteaders. Work with not more than a quarter-acre of any one vegetable or fruit, rotate these plots whenever possible with legume pastures, and use part of the pasture hay for livestock of some kind. Work into a plan gradually, as you discover what the limits of your labor are, so that the spare time you want to spend on food production is fully used, but not overextended. As these tabulations indicate, you can eventually build an income of $5,000 or more from a homestead as small as 5 acres or even less, because as you gain experience, you will learn how to beat cost and yield averages given here considerably.

10: Governmental regulations

BEFORE YOU GO too far in getting organized for a roadside stand, pick-your-own operation, or new public farmers' market, be sure to check on governmental regulations—local, county and state.

Zoning restrictions may dictate the type of structure you can use for a roadside market, as well as its size and location. You may be required to locate your stand so many feet back from the road. In addition, there can be restrictions on location and size of your parking area, as well as the location and size of any signs you may want to put up. These usually are local (township or village) government restrictions. Your village or town clerk can provide the information you need. Some townships have no restrictions of any kind for direct selling out in the country.

In the case of establishing a public farmers' market, most townships, villages, cities, and boroughs (or whatever the local government bodies are called in your area) will have some sort of regulations. And the operators of local food stores may well see to it that local officials enforce them.

Then there's the matter of conforming to weights and measures laws. You'll probably be required to get your scale checked and approved. Also you'd best be sure that you are using legal dry and liquid measures if you plan to sell by the peck, bushel, pint, or quart. Before you buy bags, baskets, or other containers that are supposed to hold a certain amount, first get the assurance of your supplier that they conform to local or state requirements.

Pennsylvania Department of Agriculture's former Director of Marketing, Don Cunnion, recalls a couple of roadside marketers who got into trouble with the county weights and measures inspector through no fault of their own. They had purchased apple bags that were supposed to hold a half-bushel but did not conform to recently changed local requirements. A new requirement was that the container must hold its stated amount when filled level to the top. Heretofore, the inspectors had allowed the bag to be heaped to make the half-bushel.

But don't get up-tight about regulatory matters. Most inspectors are pretty nice guys who will tell you what is wrong and how to correct it. Next time they come around, though, make sure you are doing things right.

Besides those mentioned, there also are inspectors who may want to check on health and sanitation matters. Some localities require a certificate from the health department for persons handling food. If you hire help, you may be required to meet certain rules on wash-up and toilet facilities. You'll also want to check on such things as child labor laws, minimum wage rates, workmen's and unemployment compensation; these often apply differently to growers who sell as compared with regular store operators.

In Cunnion's contacts through the country, he has learned that most regulatory agencies take into account the fact that direct marketing historically has had its own methods of selling. These are largely honored, even though they may not conform strictly to rules and regulations on the books for supermarkets. In one state, for example, supermarkets must sell apples only by weight or count (such in an overwrap tray). Roadside marketers, however, are allowed to sell apples in dry measure containers, such as a peck or bushel.

Some small direct marketers sell by count or container as a means of getting around the problem of approved scales. Tomatoes, for example, are sold in a quart berry box holding about five tomatoes. Other items sold this way are lima beans, shell peas, green beans, and peppers. Marketers also sell in large quantities, of course—half-pecks and pecks, for example. Supermarkets sell summer squash at so much a pound. Direct marketers usually charge by the size.

If you decide to give an official grade label to anything, such as U.S. No. 1 or U.S. Fancy, you'd best be sure the stuff really is in grade. Most states have laws to cover this—and inspectors to enforce them. The best way around this trouble is not to designate any official grade. Most direct marketers follow this line. They may sell apples and potatoes at different prices depending on general quality and size, but they let the prices speak for themselves. Or, they use such general terminology as good, better and best. Most consumers who buy direct from producers don't seem to give a hoot about grade designations. They do their own grading with their eyes, or by pinching. They are interested in their own standards of quality, not the government's.

As far as Don Cunnion is aware, no governmental bodies require liability insurance for those going into direct marketing. "But experienced operators tell me it's a darned good thing for peace of mine. You can be liable for so many kinds of injuries and property damage: somebody trips over a box at your stand, someone falls out of a tree at your pick-your-own orchard, or a customer's car gets damaged by hitting a bump in a parking area."

11: Pricing

WHAT TO CHARGE for what? That's the burning question for every direct marketer. Pricing is one of the most important tools in marketing. It can make you or break you.

Agricultural economists are of limited help. They can learnedly discuss markups based on production costs, including every conceivable expense, including value of land, real estate taxes, interest on loans, and wear and tear on equipment. While this method is perfectly correct, many small growers really have no idea of what their costs amount to. They may keep track of out-of-pocket costs, but it's the intangibles, the less noticeable costs, that often aren't considered.

If you keep good records and really know your production costs, then you may want to consider that, on the average, a supermarket will shoot for an over-all profit margin of 30 to 35 percent on its fresh product. That means a markup of about 50 percent over what the stuff cost delivered to the back door.

Before going further, let's straighten out what appears to be a very confusing point in pricing—margins versus markups. Sometimes these terms are used interchangeably in the marketplace. However, there is a distinct difference. Markups are figured on the cost of the product, while margins are figured on the selling price. Thus, a 100 percent markup means a 50 percent margin. For example, if an item costs you one dollar to grow or make and you sell it for $2, this would be a markup of 100 percent. However, the margin would be 50 percent, since $1 is 50 percent of $2. The food trade generally talks in terms of margins, although the word markup sometimes is used synonymously. One reason for using margins may be that the figure is lower than that for markups: a 33 percent margin sounds better than a 50 percent markup.

The fact that a supermarket may shoot for an overall margin of, say, 31 percent for produce doesn't mean that every item reflects that figure. Depending on competition and availability, margins will vary on individual items. The margin on a particular item can drop to zero or thereabouts if offered as a special. When that happens, the prices on other items usually are adjusted to take up the slack to come out with the desired overall margin.

For the direct marketer, production costs probably will have a modest effect on what he can charge for things he grows. He must consider the competition, checking going prices at the local retail stores and at any other direct marketing operations nearby. This is especially true for roadside markets and at public farmers' markets.

For roadside markets and at farmers' markets, growers often charge a little bit below the supermarket price for most items. Super-market price specials are ignored. For things of especially good quality, it often is possible to charge more than the going price. Just how much more will depend on trial and error until you learn how many of your customers are looking for super quality and are willing to pay for it.

The University of Delaware manual on pick-your-own operations offers observations on pricing that fit any kind of direct marketing. It suggests a markup based on costs and a relationship to what others are charging. The markup should also reflect the quality of both the physical setup of the selling operation and the merchandise itself. In answer to those marketers who would charge all the traffic will bear, the Delaware booklet says the trouble with this tack is that it can result in widely fluctuating prices as the supply and demand changes. The booklet suggests the answer lies in finding a price that is fair to both producer and consumer.

Most observers agree that the price of an item shouldn't be changed too often. The University of Kentucky handbook on roadside markets notes that people expect rather stable prices at such places, and that dissatisfaction can develop when people start comparing price variations at a stand from one day to another.

There are many ways of getting around changes in supply and demand without constantly changing basic unit prices. One is to offer "two for" and "three for" specials. The unit price remains at, say 50 cents, but the multiple price comes out two for 95 cents or three for $1.25. Another way is to increase the number of units being offered at the regular price: 15 ears of corn instead of 12, for instance.

You can count on getting the highest prices early in the season (a good argument for taking risks with early plantings). As supplies become more abundant, prices drift downward. Some sellers don't let them drift down below a pre-determined point. Others will sell very cheaply just to move the stuff. Occasionally growers will actually sell at a slight loss rather than leave things in the field. They chalk up such losses against keeping customers happy by providing the always-loved bargain.

It is amazing how prices can vary from one marketing area to another. At a recent roadside marketing conference, one sweet corn grower reported selling his corn as high as 15 to 25 cents an ear early in the season, but never below $1.35 a dozen. He figured his average price for the season was $1.50 a dozen—year after year. Another grower from another state said he maintains a flat rate of 10 cents an ear all season. He gets rid of surpluses by selling cheaper in bulk for freezing—a gunny sack full, which doesn't relate directly to his 10 cents an ear. Still another grower said he can get only 90 to 95 cents a dozen and throws in an extra ear. A fourth grower said he regularly gets $1.39 a dozen. A lot depends, of course, on how many other people are selling corn in your locale. Most growers at the conference who got a chance to speak up said they felt it best not to change prices too often. They mentioned using such devices as "clean-up specials," "evening specials" and multiple pricing as a means of making a distinction with their regular pricing policy.

The meticulous record-keeping Funk family of Pennsylvania knows right down to the nickel what sweet corn costs them to grow and what they must sell it for at their roadside markets to make a profit. The family knew, in 1976, that it could make a decent profit on a yield of 750 dozen an acre if the retail price was 69.5 cents a dozen. But if the yield dropped to 600 dozen per acre, the 69.5 cents price would only just about break even. Note: the family strives for an overall 33 percent markup over cost of production. That's a gross profit margin of 25 percent. They may not hit this figure every day they sell sweet corn, for instance, but that's the way they try to make it come out for the season.

When it comes to pick-your-own pricing you are more on your own than if figuring for a roadside stand or farmers' market—unless, of course, you've got some PYO competition nearby. Marketing specialist Don Cunnion surveyed a batch of PYO operators for pricing strategies, and got answers that ranged all the way from "production costs plus 10 percent" to "all the traffic will bear." In some cases, PYO prices were about what the grower would get in the wholesale market. More often they were above wholesale, but below retail. It was pointed out that even though the buyers are providing the harvesting labor, there are still such overhead costs as handling check-ins and check-outs, providing parking space and patrolling it, patrolling the fields, advertising, and damage to crops and to trees in case of orchards. Some operators told Cunnion they were selling recreation and country atmosphere, commodities they felt were worth something in dollars and cents.

Some growers—sellers have found that in times of heavy supply it works well to do a better grading job for their standard selling setup and then push the remainder as "specials" or "seconds." At least one fastidious marketer Cunnion talked to refuses to compromise and sells his second-rate stuff to street vendors rather than to his customers.

So far we've been talking about produce. For processed foods the pricing can be much more stable. Customers expect to pay more for

homemade bread, pastries, jams, jellies, and the like than they pay at
the supermarket. Most marketers set a price for what they've got to sell
and then just leave it there, raising it only to reflect higher ingredient
costs.

12: Spreading the word

Y OU'VE HEARD THE old saw about the mousetrap: if you build a
better one the world will beat a path to your door. Maybe. But
first the world has got to know who's got the better mousetrap and
where they can get it. That's where advertising comes in.

If you plan to sell roadside or via pick-your-own, give some
thought to advertising your operation. Advertising for public farmers'
markets is a group effort usually handled by the market manager. Most
direct marketers utilize one or a combination of four advertising media:
newspapers, radio, direct mail, and road signs. Some depend only on
word-of-mouth, which is a lot cheaper, of course, but can be slow and
undependable. It also can be negative as well as positive, while you
control what is said in paid advertising.

The University of Delaware suggests direct marketers evaluate
each advertising medium in regard to cost, ability to achieve what you
want, and ability to reach the buyers you want to reach. In other
words, utilize the advertising that's most efficient for you.

Among organic growers Don Cunnion has talked with, newspaper
advertising is the most widely used, with road signs a close second.
Other forms included direct mail and price specials. One operator mentioned using the Yellow Pages. A fair number of organic growers said
they depend only on word-of-mouth.

David Hull (Chapter 40), organic grower of Warwick, New
York, utilizes both newspaper ads and radio spots to sell his PYO apples and his herbs, cut flowers and mums. He buys newspaper display
advertising and tapes his own radio spots. For him, the newspaper ads
are more effective.

In Auburn, California, Keith Anderson uses classified newspaper ads to push his organic cherries, sold both at his roadside stand and via PYO. Gilbert Calta, who sells organically grown bedding plants out of Valley City, Ohio, says he finds classified ads cheaper and more effective than display. He advertises on holidays and when his stuff is in heavy supply. The Yankee Peddler Herb Farm, Brenham, Texas, uses a wide variety of advertising techniques since it sells both at the farm and via mail order. Their lineup includes road signs, newspaper ads, radio spots, garden magazine classified ads, and direct mail. Linda Wey, of DeWitt, Michigan, advertises her herbs and dried flowers by means of both display and classified ads in nearby city newspapers.

As noted, newspapers offer two types of advertising—display and classified. Display is sold by the column inch (number of columns wide times the number of inches deep) and costs more than classified since you are using more space and can, in some cases, specify position, such as a spot on the food page. Classified ads usually are sold by the word. Classified headings such as "Articles for Sale" have a higher readership than you might expect. If there are a number of direct marketers in your area, your newspaper may even have a special classified category for them.

Some marketers use a standard type of newspaper ad, one which simply identifies the market by name, where it is located, and what it sells, such as vegetables, fruits, berries, and preserves. Other marketers run timely ads which may note that strawberries are now ready and how much they cost. Still others use price specials to lure customers, usually on items that are in heavy supply; specials are guaranteed traffic pullers, as supermarket operators learned long ago.

Radio advertising is sold by time spots, anywhere from ten seconds and up. Usually it is necessary to run a number of spots in a single day if you want to reach a significant number of listeners. Unlike a newspaper, which usually hangs around the house for a day (or longer, if it is a weekly) and can be picked up at any time and read, a radio spot is a fleeting thing.

The radio station sales people will help you write your spot and the announcer will read it. Or you can tape your own spot if you feel you'd like to give it a more personal touch. Some direct marketers are very good at this. Don Cunnion knows one who sponsors a weather report and gets directly into the act by means of an open telephone line with the station. He and the announcer banter a bit, but the marketer manages to get in some hard sell.

For radio, consider a quick, newsy item plus your market name and location. Early in the season you may want to use something like: "Fresh-picked sweet corn now is available at Smith's Roadside Market, located on Route 63 one mile east of Hamilton." Later on, as the sweet corn season advances, you could switch to: "Fresh sweet corn now only 69 cents a dozen at. . . ." Or "eighteen ears of sweet corn for the price of 12 at. . . ."

Radio is an excellent way to get word out quickly to PYO customers. Sometimes newspapers want several days' lead time on an ad, making it impractical for operators to account for a PYO crop that's ready early, a crop running late, or rain interference.

Among marketers who use direct mail advertising, some do just one mailing at the start of the season. Others do periodic mailings when various crops are available, or to push specials for preserving. Direct mail requires a list of names and addresses, which is usually built up over the years as customers are asked to register. Keeping a mailing list up to date requires a certain amount of tedious work, but it pays off in savings on printing costs and postage to people who no longer are potential customers.

While road signs get a high rating from direct marketers, there can be problems with local restrictions on such signs. This seems to be a growing thing. Some communities limit signs to a certain size and to specific locations. You'll just have to go along with what is allowed.

Television advertising may have the greatest impact, but it is pretty costly both in preparation and in air time. Few direct marketers use it.

Experience with advertising, no matter what kind, has consistently proven that descriptive adjectives do sell. Such adjectives as fresh, sweet, juicy, tangy, crisp, and plump have customer appeal, whether the customer is aware of it or not. You'll do well to use them often.

What does newspaper and radio advertising cost? This will vary greatly, mostly by the size of the circulation of the newspaper or the listening audience of the radio station. The greater the circulation or listening audience, the higher the rate for space or time. However, the cost of reaching each thousand readers or listeners goes down as the number of thousands reached goes up.

The direct marketer usually is concerned with what the total ad or spot is going to cost and whether it will reach his potential customers. That's where the local newspaper or nearby radio station comes in. They usually cover just about the area of the countryside from which you can expect to draw most of your customers. If you have more than one local or area newspaper or radio station, you can get detailed information on their respective coverages from the advertising department. Ask for the "rate card" and circulation data on reader or listener characteristics: where they live, income level and size of family. Also ask how much of the total population they reach in the circulation area.

To give you some idea of newspaper advertising costs, one local daily that circulates in an area of 60,000 people has a circulation of 19,000. It charges 30 cents per agate line for display advertising. At 14 agate lines per inch, that converts to $4.20 an inch for an ad one column wide. For an ad measuring two inches deep by two columns wide the cost would be four times $4.20 or $16.80. That's for a one-time insertion. You can get lower rates by ordering multiple insertions or by contracting for a minimum number of agate lines per month or year.

A radio station in the same town claims it reaches a population area of over 186,000. But a listening audience figure for a radio station is not as exact as newspaper's circulation figures. Size and nature of the listening audience usually is determined by telephone surveys to a selected sample of families in the listening area. A sampling by this station showed that, of those families sampled, about one third were listening to the station from 7 A.M. to 9 A.M., about the same number from 11 A.M. to noon. Listening between 4 P.M. and 6 P.M. dropped to about 20 percent. In each instance, the number of women listeners outnumbered the men by about two to one—a good point for a direct marketer.

Based on these figures, the radio station charges $10.50 for a one-time, one-minute commercial. The rate drops to $7.50 if you contract for 156 times. However, if you contract for 10 one-minute spots to be used within a period of seven days, the rate per spot is $8.50. This drops to $5.50 per spot for 60 times in seven days. The rate for a 30-second spot is 75 percent of the one-minute charge.

How much should you spend on advertising? That's a question on which you can get little agreement, even from people selling similar products under similar conditions to similar people. As noted earlier in this chapter, there are some direct marketers who spend nothing at all on advertising; others spend quite a bit. The amount varies from situation to situation. If you are just starting in business you'll probably want to spend enough to let people know you have something to sell and would like to sell it to them. This is what the pros call the "pioneering" stage and usually requires a larger investment than called for once you get established. Many established, successful direct marketers say that about 1 to 3 percent of gross sales have gone to their budgets for all forms of advertising. A couple marketers put that figure at 5 percent.

If you are involved with a public farmers' market, you won't have to think about individual advertising. But be sure whoever is running the market does a good job. Newspapers and radio are both good here. Also worth considering are signs displayed on local buses and tacked up in public places. Price specials in advertising work well as a means of attracting customers to a farmers' market. The idea is to get several sellers to agree in advance to offer something at a special price for that day. A single commodity may be offered, or several. Just make sure whatever is on special is in large enough quantity to supply all, or most, of the customers who want to buy it. Otherwise, you'll have some pretty unhappy people who may not come again.

13: Merchandising

MERCHANDISING, AS DISCUSSED here, covers how you sell what you have to sell. Top priority in merchandising by a direct marketer must be an emphasis on quality, since that is the principal reason people give for buying direct from the producer.

Naturally, you must try to come up with quality products to begin with. But everything you grow won't meet good standards. You'll have to do some weeding out, some grading. Many direct marketers do a first-rate job of grading their produce. This doesn't necessarily mean they try to meet official USDA grade standards; they just toss out what they themselves wouldn't want to buy. Many put the second-rate stuff off to one side and sell it at a discount price, calling it "seconds" or otherwise making it clear that this produce is not representative of the seller's standard of quality.

Eye appeal is important. Smart operators wash their produce if it has gotten dusty or mud-spattered. But there's no need to polish things, such as apples. Buyers don't expect that kind of finish on an item they buy at a grower's stand.

Make displays attractive. For some reason, mass displays have real pulling power. The supermarkets learned this long ago. A market seller with his display area piled high will outsell the guy next door who puts out only a few kinds of the same kinds of things. Perhaps this is because the buyer has more from which to pick and choose.

An attractive roadside stand gives the passing motorist the confidence to stop. An operator in southern New Jersey told a direct marketing conference that her attractive stand with large, colorful displays helped stop the fast-moving traffic that passes her place on the way to the seashore.

A hot sun is tough on produce, even if you have a roof over your stand. Many marketers spray their fruits and vegetables with water several times a day. Others used crushed ice.

Customers usually don't want to see your produce displayed the same way they see it in the supermarket. Prepackaging can be a real drawback. One potato grower moved few of his potatoes at a farmers' market when he had them prepackaged in 10- and 25-pound bags. When he dumped the potatoes out loose on the table and heaped up bushel and half-bushel open containers, his sales immediately soared.

Many direct marketers display their produce both in bulk on counters and in open containers on low benches or on the ground or floor. Containers run the gamut from wood to plastic and paper. For their container displays, some operators put the produce in open plastic bags which, in turn, are placed into an open basket. The customers can readily inspect the produce, but when it comes time to make a sale, the seller merely has to lift out the bag and hand it to the customer. Most customers don't want to pay the current high cost of wooden baskets.

In its suggestions to roadside stand operators, the University of

Kentucky suggests that sellers think in terms of larger container sizes than found in the supermarkets: quarts, pecks, half-bushels, and bushels. Traditionally, in many areas, direct marketers have used quart berry boxes to display units of such things as tomatoes, beans, peas, plums, and grapes.

Multiple unit pricing works for direct marketers just as well as it does for the supermarkets. This simply means offering a discount when the buyer takes more than one unit, such as one pound, one quart, one bunch. For example: Beets, 50 cents a bunch, two bunches for 90 cents, five bunches for $2.00. This kind of pricing enables you to maintain the basic unit price throughout the season if you wish, but it helps move more stuff in time of heavy supply.

Should you display prices or not? Some shoppers prefer to see prices and do their own comparison shopping. For the direct marketer, open pricing allows them more independence, as they don't have to hover over the customer. On the other hand, operators who do not display prices say this obliges the customers to ask, opening the way for the seller to point out the merits of the item.

Many marketers do more than just show price. On the price card, or on a separate card, they tell the variety and even provide information on how the items may be eaten, such as raw, cooked, or in pie or pudding. Varietal names seem to be most important for tree fruits such as apples, peaches, plums, and pears. Varieties of vegetables have less meaning for many customers. Seldom does a shopper come across varietal names for green beans, sweet corn, or tomatoes. Most squash is identified by type—acorn, zucchini, butternut—but seldom by the name of the strain. The same goes for such items as Japanese cucumbers, pole beans, and snow (sugar) peas.

Handling customers may not be part of merchandising, but it certainly is an important part of selling. A veteran direct marketer gave these words of advice on handling customers: "Treat them cordially and courteously. Be friendly and helpful; don't be pushy. Let the customer pick and choose and don't interfere until your help is asked for. Customers want honest answers to questions about variety and how to use an item, when it was picked, and whether or not it was organically grown."

If a customer complains about the quality of an item, apologize and replace it without argument. As the long-time marketer said: "You may think you have won the argument, but you most certainly will lose the customer." In this regard it is important to remember that most of your business will be with repeat customers. Repeat business can account for as much as three-quarters of your sales. Only contented customers come back. Customer loyalty runs high, once established. A chap who has been selling at a farmers' market for over 20 years says that he has customers who will wait until he has what they want, rather than buy it at the next stand.

14: Promotion and publicity

THE MOST SUCCESSFUL direct marketers are good promoters. For some, promoting has been a means of survival, as they were too far off the beaten path to succeed by just opening up and waiting for customers to drop in.

When the Funks of Pennsylvania decided to switch from selling at farmers' markets to operating a roadside stand, family members came face to face with the fact that they were located on the wrong side of town, and most of the traffic went in and out of town on other roads. They set up a steady advertising program, supported with a whole flock of promotions. At one time they offered free donkey rides to children of customers. Another time, when sweet corn was in heavy supply, they handed out free roasted ears, buttered and salted. They cooked up a scheme whereby lucky winners of a free produce item were called out every hour. They often hand out samples of apple cider, an inexpensive gesture that results in heavy sales of cider. During melon season they hold their Melon Ball, a festive event with a melon queen, fashion show and special contests with prizes of—what else?—melons. Since going in for bedding plants and houseplants, the Funks have started a plant-of-the-month club and during the winter conduct evening seminars on how to take care of houseplants. They make no money for the seminars themselves, but invariably sell a large number of plants after every session.

The Linvill family of Pennsylvania has helped build a large clientele for its roadside market by going in big for school children tours of the farm. They haul the kids around on wagons to see the animals and the orchards. They keep a variety of nonfarm animals, such as deer, for added interest. Invariably the kids get a glass of apple cider, an apple, or some other little token before they leave. Paul Linvill points out that this sort of promotion is not exactly cheap, but that after every tour they can expect an influx of new customers—namely, parents of the children who made the tour. The kids go home and tell their folks all about the place. The Linvills, like the Funks, maintain a variety of promotions. Because they sell a lot of dried flowers they hold classes in making dried flower arrangements, which has paid off with increased sales.

Still another Pennsylvania roadside marketer, John Rogers, has special days when he gives away an ice cream cone to each customer. He promotes homemade bread "made of Pennsylvania wheat, ground into flour in Pennsylvania, and baked in Pennsylvania."

Remember that free samples cost very little, especially when the stuff is in heavy supply and you may not be able to sell all of it anyway. Then, too, the value of such promotional samples are tax deductible—as are all types of advertising and promotional expenses.

Mrs. Genie DeCou of New Jersey helps make her roadside stand, located on a heavily traveled highway, more intriguing by featuring a large geodesic dome. She also has ducks and small animals such as goats running about. She holds pumpkin decorating contests. She even encourages children to bring in their surplus kittens to be given to people who might be looking for a pet. Tours are conducted for some 10,000 school children a year.

Gail and Paul McPherson of Pennsylvania found they had a problem when they decided to direct market some of their peaches. As Gail says, they were the fifth direct marketing operation on their road—and the last in line. They realized the need to do something that would get customers to drive past the other places and choose theirs. They developed promotions. Their big promotion is a Peach Blossom Festival which has become something of a community fair. They invite in local arts and crafts people, but require that each of them feature one item having something to do with peaches. Gail developed a peach recipe book that is a good seller.

Up in Michigan, Linda Wey helps promote her organic greenhouse plant business by talking before garden clubs and taking plants to flower shows. She'll travel as far as 100 miles to make an appearance, knowing it will help bring customers.

Giveaway recipes are good promotional items. People love recipes and can hardly pass them up. It costs very little to have some typewritten recipes printed via offset on inexpensive paper. Printing in large number is the cheapest way, of course, and this is where cooperative efforts with other direct marketers can help. Some of the roadside stand associations print up hundreds of thousands of recipes on 3-by-5 cards for distribution by members. You can hand-stamp the name of your own place on the cards.

Write-ups in your local newspaper or interviews on radio and television stations fall into the category of unpaid promotions, although there can be some costs attached, such as travel, cost of materials used, and the like. But don't wait for the media to come to you. Try to figure out something newsy or unusual, or something in the human interest area. This might be the first strawberries or peaches of the season, funny-shaped squash, or your favorite recipes for cooking what you grow.

Publicity is a great promotional tool if you can learn how to use it properly. The Funks of Pennsylvania maintain close relations with a nearby TV station, suggesting agricultural ideas which may or may not involve themselves. When it's time for the first strawberries, for example, they contact the farm broadcaster of the station. As a result, they are asked to come in for an interview on the subject and to bring along some berries to be shown on the air. When the Funks do this they never fail to bring along a whole crate of berries, to be left behind for the benefit of the station personnel. It's not a bribe, but just a friendly gesture that the station people appreciate. Mrs. DeCou of New Jersey does a live show for a local radio station. Naturally, she gets opportunities to plug her roadside stand. Like the Funks, she also makes it a practice to tip off the media to possible agricultural stories, especially those related to direct marketing. As a result, her roadside stand or her husband's peach orchard often get involved.

Gail McPherson of Pennsylvania contributes a regular column to a local newspaper and thereby gets an opportunity to mention her promotions when the time is ripe.

Organic growing still is newsy enough to intrigue many media people, especially those involved with farming, gardening, foods, environment, and consumer protection. You may well find one or more people on the staff organically oriented. This wouldn't hurt a bit.

A SEASON IN THE LIFE
OF DAVID SCHONBERG

Truck farming in Minnesota's Lake Country.

David Schonberg at the wheel of his Reo flatbed

Three

15: A market gardener tells his story

*G*ROWING FOR MARKET is less a primer than a guided tour of three dozen or so operations, with an emphasis on marketing—meeting the customer through roadside stands, backdoor sales, farmer's markets, co-ops, pick-your-own operations, health food stores, mail order, and more.

Some direct marketers will be mentioned in passing; a few are profiled at some length. In the next few chapters, David Schonberg, a Minnesota truck farmer, introduces us to the trials and rewards of growing food for market.

Like many in Minnesota's lake country, he is of Scandinavian descent, and a sing-song Swedish lilt is noticeable as he talks. David and his family have been in business for eight years now, raising

Getting ready for the morning run into Alexandria

vegetables on 45 acres of land outside the town of Alexandria. Early each morning of the season, he and a hired hand or two pick cauliflower, corn, tomatoes, or melons, putting in half a day's labor by breakfast. It is a good time of day for David. He enjoys breathing the early morning air, watching the sun come up over the fields, and listening to the birds in the woods and in the tall slough grasses.

After a breakfast served up by his wife, Jean, he loads up two old Reo flatbed trucks for the trip to a shopping center parking lot on the outskirts of town. It's a struggle setting up as the constant dry wind from the Dakotas threatens to blow away signs, bags and tarps.

Everyone who stops receives David's full attention. He is helpful, solicitous, but not overbearing—a delicate balance, it seems, and yet an approach that's necessary to maximize sales. David seems genuinely interested in getting together customer and the best tomato or head of cauliflower in the pile.

At day's end he sits down to a meal of fresh garden produce, happy at the thought that 100 or 200 or 500 families in the community are enjoying the same wholesome, tasty food as his family.

In Chapters 16 through 24, David shares his experiences.

16: Going retail

" OUR OPERATION IS very small compared to the giant farming complexes that supply most of the fruits and vegetables to the local grocery stores. Production charts and graphs, offices and warehouses, and plenty of money for research and expansion are not part of our business.

We started out with only a few hundred dollars operating capital, an old pickup, an old Allis B tractor, and an eight-foot field cultivator; and we have even learned how to resurrect ancient farm machinery found rusting away among high weeds in old farm lots.

I first tried selling to supermarkets—without much success. It wasn't that the produce managers tried to make it hard, but sometimes a produce manager, no matter how hard he tries to accommodate a small grower's harvest, simply cannot take another 50 dozen ears of corn. Perhaps he has a shipment coming in from the South. Perhaps he gladly would take yours if he hadn't an order for corn with his warehouse. Or it could be that another gardener beat you to the market with his own corn. Stores may already be lined up for the season with a long-time supplier, and produce buyers might not want to jeopardize good relationships with them by buying locally.

It has been several years since I last tried to sell our sweet corn through a grocery store. The change came the year I had about three acres of corn to sell. It was good corn and we had worked for it. We were raising it on rented land. The previous renter had released the land in the fall, and in spring the melting snow revealed heavy windrows of oat straw from the last year's harvest. The soil looked good, however, and even though the field had not been worked in the fall and the windrowed straw would certainly give us trouble, I thought we could get a decent crop if we worked at it. Hardly had the snow disappeared, however, when I saw why the previous renter had let the land go—it was full of quack grass. Within a week, warm weather turned the field into a green carpet. It looked like a golf course. The landlord recommended Atrazine but I was resolved to do it without weed killers or not at all.

The weeks that followed were tough ones. My little John Deere digger, pulled by the Allis B, did a good job with the quack grass, pulling up piles of long healthy roots. But a good stand of quack is endless. I planted early in hopes that I could be one of the first in the area to get a harvest. But sweet corn does not grow fast in the early spring and quack grass does. As soon as the young corn was high enough to cultivate, my brother and I hooked a single-row, horse-drawn cultivator onto the Allis. I drove and my brother steered the cultivator over the corn. The ground was again quickly covered with more piles of quack roots, but a close look showed that the job still was not done. There was nothing left to do but give up or break out the hoes. Fortunately the two of us were young, but hoeing three acres of tough quack grass makes even a young person feel old in a short time.

We decided that if the fields weren't clean in a week the corn would be severely stunted. That meant a dozen long rows a day between the two of us. Six rows each. Two each before breakfast while the day was still fresh. Two more after breakfast followed by a break. The remaining two rows when we could—hopefully before mid-afternoon. Only by systematically budgeting our work for the week and disciplining our backs did we get the chore finished. Only by gingerly lying down on the ground would our aching backs begin to relax.

I survived and so did my sweet corn. I did hit the early market and did well with most of the field. The sweet corn market was flooded before the end of the season, and I tried going retail to sell the remaining ears as well as a good crop of tomatoes. I drove into town and scouted out likely locations to park a pickup and display my produce. I figured I needed a spot that was visible, accessible, well-traveled, and with parking space. A local businessman agreed to go along with my experiment in exchange for 10 percent of the sales.

On the first day I was up early picking melons and tomatoes and stacking them into an old pickup. I also tossed in a few head of cauliflower and some posterboard signs that my wife had painted up. Then I headed for town. I was worried that no one would stop, and thought how humiliating it would be to pick up my bushel baskets of tomatoes and melons at the end of the day and return home with my load. But I supposed it couldn't be much worse than the hassle I was having trying to sell wholesale. After all, I had made quite a few dry runs that way, too.

I felt very conspicuous pulling into my parking place on the northern end of town, turning the pickup around and backing it up to the roadside. What would all the local people think? Would they grin at the young farmer as they drove by?

I tacked my posterboard signs up a little way down the road in each direction and hurried back to the truck to display the baskets along the road, alternating baskets of red tomatoes with large mounds of yellow muskmelons. The grocery scale was leveled so that the hairline rested on zero. With my machete I opened a couple of muskmelons and propped the halves up against the other melons, facing them in the direction of upcoming traffic. Waiting for the first customer, I opened another and sampled it. Before long I had company—at least the bees knew I had something good to eat.

I don't remember any of my customers that first day, though I'm sure I have seen many of them countless times since. There were many faces, and the day was a success. I paid $3 to my kind business friend for letting me park on his lot, and went home with an empty truck and $25 in my pocket. People began to look for me on Wednesdays and Saturdays. Sales improved. Soon $50- and $60-days were not uncommon—more than I had taken home from grocery stores even though selling in quantity. Of course, I now spent the entire day selling whereas at a store the transaction could be completed in a few minutes.

The summer soon drew to a close, and the nights threatened to nip the vines; perhaps the realization that the season would soon be over brought more customers.

That was eight years ago. Now, instead of two days a week we sell six days a week. The business has increased from a few acres to 45 acres, though success and expansion has not been without its failures and frustrations. The old Allis is gone, and so is the John Deere digger.

The first day of every year is still like the first day eight years ago. I am apprehensive. Will people stop? Will I have a successful day? It is always gratifying to pull into our current location with our 2½-ton truck overflowing with fresh produce and find familiar faces already waiting for us.

A few extra rows for cash.

For the gardener whose bounty sates the family, overflows the larder, and feeds the neighborhood, thoughts naturally turn to selling the surplus. After all, gardening is no different than any other hobby that might be turned into a vocation. There are many parallels with crafts, woodworking, and animal husbandry.

In any of these areas, a certain proficiency is necessary before going commercial. Before you get carried away with big plans for a market gardening future, make sure you can grow a quality home garden. Cauliflower and tomatoes do not always turn out looking as cosmetically perfect as the seed packet photos, just as a first-time cabinetry project likely involves less-than-true lines and a laceration or two.

Try to grow marketable-quality produce for your own family, being intolerant of blemishes. If your tomatoes are still green at frost, the sweet corn patch produces only enough ears for one dinner, and the onions grow no bigger than golf balls, then perhaps you should work at the basics just a while longer before tilling the lawn.

A number of times over the years, I have kicked myself for going into a new area without adequate research and experimentation. One spring I decided to go into onions rather heavily, as they had sold well the year before: twelve thousand onion plants had grown up into beautiful, mild onions that went over big with our customers. So, the following spring we bought 14 cases of onion plants, with 4,000 to 6,000 plants per case, set them out with hired assistance. Help was hired to weed. The result was near disaster. We lost about two-thirds of the crop—all because several of the varieties weren't suited to Minnesota growing conditions.

I'm still pained by an experience of a recent season. Again, it was an example of moving optimistically, and naively, into something new—cauliflower. We set out 25,000 plants that had been carefully raised in our greenhouse and then hardened to outdoor temperatures. These were half a dozen strains of the snowball variety that had done well for us some years previously. I didn't know which strain we had purchased, and figured I'd have some insurance by selecting several. As it turned out, two of the strains, totalling 7,000 plants, died almost immediately after transplanting into the field, and one strain failed to mature before the season came to an end. The lesson? Start small and move cautiously.

Putting a price on your produce.

The natural tendency is to feel a little cheap about charging for your surplus produce, especially if the customer is a friend of yours. But anyone seriously interested in supplementing their income by selling the surplus from a large garden must learn to suppress some of their hobby gardening instincts and cultivate instead a marketing mentality.

The hobby gardener usually takes great delight in being able to surprise a neighbor or friend with a basket of vine-ripened muskmelons, still dripping and sticky at the stem end, or a box of tomatoes, or new potatoes, or a dozen ears of sweet corn. The reward is in seeing the look of surprise and delight on your friend's face. We all know this to be one of the joys of gardening—to be able to share something good from the garden with others without charge.

Raising a few extra rows for cash doesn't mean you can no longer give your friends and neighbors a treat now and then. But it does mean that, to the extent that you intend to make money on your garden, you are going to have to suppress those generous feelings and start charging for your product, even if the customer is a friend of yours. Eventually, almost *all* of your customers will be your friends. Furthermore, most friends and neighbors feel more comfortable when they can pay a reasonable price for something than when they are continually treated at your expense. Of course, if after the transaction is completed you wish to say thank you by tossing in an extra tomato or two, by all means, do so.

Don't fret if some produce goes to waste.

Another mental transition must accompany the hobby gardener as he puts in a few extra rows for cash: don't get upset if a few tomatoes or melons spoil on the vines. No one likes to see good food go to waste, least of all the one who raised it. While home gardeners will pick, deliver, and give away surplus vegetables rather than see them rot, this approach can frustrate a market gardener or even threaten his business. After doing all that can be profitably done to move your surplus, through specials and pick-your-own, you must simply let it go. If people are critical, remind them that you got more good food from your labor than they got from watering and mowing their lawns all summer. Taking a more philosophical point of view, you might mention that the seed you planted did what it was supposed to do. The soil did what it was supposed to do. You did what you intended to do. And that any leftover will simply become valuable fertilizer for next year's crop. **" "**

17: Marketing: the small grower's problem

" IT IS OFTEN easier to raise a product than to sell it. This is especially true for the small grower who is trying to get started.

Breaking into the market is apt to be tough. First of all, you are not yet known. No one has gotten into the habit of buying from you. Second, your operation is not yet big enough to attract attention. Your garden does not extend over acres and acres of field, you have no shop, no business vehicles, and no impressive displays of produce.

What are some of the ways to overcome the marketing problem? You may find the best and easiest way is to go through a grocery store produce buyer and move your produce wholesale. You might get into a marketing cooperative or a local farmers' market. Perhaps you can work out a route to local resorts, selling your vegetables to vacationers who had to leave their gardens behind when they came to the lake.

If you are situated on a fairly well-traveled road, work up a few neatly lettered posterboard signs, tack them up on a plywood backing, and set them out along the road. If you can work up a small display at the end of your driveway so much the better, provided it does not become the target of vandals.

One fall I parked a farm wagon on our property at a two-lane highway and let people serve themselves to watermelon. I learned to fasten the cash box down and to keep it locked, providing just a slot for the money. I checked on the load several times through the day, and brought it all home in the evening. We lost a few melons, but not as many as you might think, and we sold up to $40 a day worth. This is not the ideal means of marketing since a number of conscientious customers always seemed to feel uncomfortable about putting their money in a box and would drive on. But if you have the produce and no better way to market it, $15 or $20 or $40 a day through self-service with a small loss is better than losing it altogether for lack of market.

I have found the real secret to capturing a market, whether you are small or big, is in raising what I call a drawing crop—a crop which will get people to slam on their brakes when they see it and back up along the highway. It is the crop that shoppers will plan their shopping day around. It is the crop that people will buy as a treat for their friends. It is the crop whose price is seldom argued with. It is the crop that will earn you a dollar and then sell two dollars worth of other vegetables. We have two such crops in our business: sweet corn and muskmelons. A good display of either will catch the impulsive buyers, and a reputation for fresh, tasty sweet corn or vine-ripened muskmelons will bring the customers back for more. This is not to say that all of your marketing headaches will be over, but you will probably find that a good drawing crop will help you break into a market faster and easier than almost anything else you can do.

What drawing crop can you raise? Have you been able to raise large, attractive melons with good flavor? If so, perhaps this is your best crop to begin with.

If your strawberry crops have always done well, consider enlarging your strawberry bed. If you possess a knack for sweet corn and have enough land, try a few extra rows of a proven variety. Marketing is difficult enough with a proven crop. On your very first attempt at market gardening, go with a familiar crop. **"**

18: What makes a money crop?

" J UST GETTING SOMETHING to grow is not enough. To make money, your crop must sell. But not all crops that sell are money crops.

Pickles sell! What went wrong?

One of the items in demand in central Minnesota is pickling-size cucumbers, or "pickles," as we call them. People will buy a bushel at a time. And if it becomes general knowledge that you have pickles to sell, many bushels a day could probably be sold during the early part of the canning season. Many homemakers even ask for them late in the summer. This suggests a fairly steady demand for pickles all the way through to frost, and the more I thought about it, the more promising the pickle business seemed. Furthermore, a not-too-distant pickle factory would take any surplus, so I was assured of a market for every pickle we could raise. To make a long story short, we planted more than an acre of pickles, worked hard during the summer to bring the crop to harvest—and then let it go. We wasted our investment in the land. We wasted fuel and machinery life. Most of all, we lost many, many hours of hard work. What went wrong?

We found out that our pickle pickers could not pick fast enough to pay their own wages. I guaranteed them their wages, and then to give them a little incentive to pick faster, offered them a commission on sales as an option if they could do better that way. They couldn't. When I tried to increase the price of a bushel of small pickles to the point where they began to pay off, my customers balked. The factory was no help either, offering but 9 cents a pound for pickles scarcely larger in diameter than a lead pencil and only a couple of inches long. If they weighed $1/3$ ounce each it would take 48 to make a pound (9 cents worth) and a little better than a thousand pickles to pay one man's wages for one hour. This required a picking average throughout the day of better than one pickle every 4 seconds, just to pay the pickers their wages. (This did nothing to pay for the prior investment or to leave anything for the boss.) As the size increased, the price per pound dropped until the largest the factory took were worth only 1 cent or 2 cents per pound. This didn't even cover transportation costs. Obviously the only thing to do, even though we had a market for our product, was to drop the pickle business as quickly as possible.

It must not be concluded from this that pickle production is always a losing proposition. If the factory were next door and a man had a houseful of ambitious kids and a little land to spare, one can easily picture a very successful enterprise. A grower could also succeed with mechanical creepers and other equipment. The point is simply this: you can't make money if it doesn't sell; you can't always make money even if it does sell.

A look at some of the factors.

- In any given operation, if the production of the crop or the harvest of the crop is too time consuming to be profitable, either production and harvest methods will have to be improved or the crop will have to be dropped. This elementary observation is basic to any business. Often the solution is to invest in bigger and better machinery. Sometimes it's more expedient to simply look around for another way to invest your time.

- What is your land situation? Is land available and at what price? Some land is so expensive to own or to rent that only the most intensive crops could ever justify its use for agricultural purposes. Yet some of your most valuable crops are not always the ones that return the most per acre. Does the cost of your land allow you to raise such crops? Furthermore, you must determine if you have an economical way to till and cultivate larger acreages.

- What about insect pests? This is an important consideration for many crops. It becomes especially serious if you wish to limit pest control to natural methods. One of two things must be true if you are going to stay in business with a crop that normally encounters problems with insects: either your natural control for these pests must be as cheap to buy and as easy to use as the chemical pesticides, or else you must find a clientele willing to pay a premium for organically grown produce.

- Do you face a problem with larger predators such as rabbits, blackbirds, racoons, deer, or gophers? The difference between a successful harvest and an unsuccessful one might be the many melons which the field mice scarred up, or the many dozen ears of corn the blackbirds destroyed. Do you have a practical way of preventing this damage?

- Depending on the summer and the locality, the difference between success and failure for certain crops might be a single irrigation. How might irrigation affect your plans? Do you have water available? How much will it cost to put the water on your field? Does the crop justify the investment? Onions, for example, need plenty of moisture not only to develop size but for uniformity and flavor.

- Do you have an adequate growing season for a given crop? To lose a harvest to frost in the fall of the year is disastrous. A late spring freeze or an early summer hail storm are costly and disappointing, but to lose a crop after nursing it all the way through to harvest is the greatest kind of loss. One Labor Day weekend not long ago, I looked out over eight acres of frosted muskmelons. We lost an estimated 50 percent of our crop to frost that year. Can this sort of loss be absorbed in the long run, or would the fall frost damage be a fairly regular occurrence?

- What is the plant life of a given crop? Does it need to be harvested when it first becomes ready to harvest or can it remain on the plant for a lengthy period of time without losing its quality? The less time one has to harvest a crop, the more of a problem marketing becomes.

- What is the shelf life of the crop? Does it need to be sold the day it is picked or can it be carried over from one day or week to another without deterioration? The longer it can be held, the less pressing it is to locate an immediate market.

- Does the item need to be washed, trimmed, graded, weighed, counted, bundled, or packaged? Don't overlook this aspect of production. The work is not always over once the crop is harvested. Long hours may have to be invested in preparing a crop just when you think everything has been successfully completed. One of the advantages of the retail market is that much of this work is reduced or eliminated entirely. It makes little difference whether one shows up at the stand with the tomatoes packed in peach crates or peck baskets. For the sake of the display, maintain a fair degree of uniformity, but this does not mean buying costly, specially manufactured cases. Use whatever containers are available, and use them over and over. Neither must there be a standard weight or count in each container.

- Does the crop lend itself to your transportation facilities? In order for an item to be successful it must survive the hazards of transportation. In the case of especially heavy or bulky items, will there be any profit after you pay for the cost of shipping? Does it pay to haul a load of pumpkins 100 miles, for instance, if you get but 18 cents apiece? If they average nine pounds each, your total return for the entire season is two cents a pound. Two cents a pound hardly pays for the cost of transportation, not to mention your investment in raising the crop.

- Is there any way, unique to your operation, for you to convert what would normally be a real drawback in the production of a given crop into an advantage? If you can do something special with a crop, and can offer something unique to the area, you may have a money crop.

If you can get a steady stream of people to drive out to your farm to purchase swiss chard from you for a dollar a pound, you're in business. If you can grow mild radishes when all others in the area are hot, you may have yourself a valuable crop. If you can consistently get your muskmelons to mature when most melons in the area are lost to frost, you have a valuable crop. If you can get your tomatoes to ripen up two weeks before everyone else's, you have a valuable crop. If everyone's onions are destroyed by onion maggots and yours escape, you have a valuable crop.

So, the intriguing question is, are there any special features about your farm, your soil, your market, your location, that might possibly reduce the drawback to production on any given crop? This of course is what regional agriculture is all about. Every part of the country develops its own type of agriculture suited to its own conditions. On a smaller scale, that is precisely what a commercial gardener has to do. He has to look for ways to capitalize on the things which are favorable to his own operation.

In marketing your products, take advantage of anything unique going for you. Perhaps your uncle is the produce manager of a large grocery store in a nearby city. Talk to him. Maybe you can break into a profitable wholesale market. If your farm borders a busy highway, roadside marketing may be your best outlet. If a friend of yours runs a service station on a busy intersection and there is plenty of parking space available, talk to him. He may be eager to let you park an attractive truck on his property, figuring you might attract a few more people to his station. You could offer him a modest commission on sales or a bit of rent.

Is the lay of the land such that your field will warm up and dry off earlier in the spring than most other land in the area? A southeastern slope can often be planted a week or more before other people can get into their fields. If it is assured of adequate moisture during the growing season, that slope may push a crop of tomatoes, sweet corn or melons to market a week or two before others are ready. This is like getting your summer weather before it comes to your neighbors.

Do you have irrigation water readily available? Do you have a cheap source of good natural fertilizer in your neighborhood? Because of your situation on a hill or your close proximity to a large body of water, are you less vulnerable to frost than others might be? Be alert to ways in which a drawback can be converted into your advantage. **" "**

19:   Our choice of crops

" "ONE OF OUR most valuable crops is sweet corn. Almost everyone loves good sweet corn, and the price is good, especially at the start of the season. We find that our tillage and cultivation equipment are suited to raising corn. With a two-row corn planter and two-row tractor-mounted cultivator, one person can easily tend the 20 or 30 acres we need. Sweet corn does not return as much per acre as some crops, but because we have the land and the means to till the land, I plant a lot of it. Other growers may not fare well with corn if land is limited or if there is no practical means of tilling and cultivating a large acreage.

I have not had a great deal of trouble with insect pests on corn. Occasionally, however, a field does run into a little trouble. I have even had fishermen stop at the stand for free bait. Fortunately, wormy corn has been the exception rather than the rule. Organic growers troubled with corn worms may have to go through an entire field, perhaps more than once each season, and put a drop of mineral oil on each developing ear. In such a case it is important to determine if the market price and the demand actually justify this extra investment of labor.

Sweet corn is also a favorite food of blackbirds, skunks, raccoons, gophers, deer, and crows. While a farmer might not begrudge a little blackbird damage on the ends of his field corn, you can see how disastrous even a little damage can be to sweet corn. People are entirely more fussy than cattle. They simply will not buy corn if the tip of the ear has been shredded and a few kernels destroyed, or if a dried blackbird dropping mars the silk.

Raccoons and skunks take their share of our sweet corn, but our real problem is blackbirds. Blackbirds present a real threat throughout the Minnesota lake country. One Sunday we came home from church and went out to the field to pick a few ears for dinner. What had been a good field a few hours earlier was now hardly worth salvaging. The blackbirds had shredded the ends of nearly every ear of corn. A cloud of birds rose up from the field as I approached. Since that time, I have become more diligent with the shotgun.

Perhaps the greatest single drawback in sweet corn production is its perishability. You may have only one week to harvest and market a given field of sweet corn, and if the weather is exceptionally hot, this harvest period may be reduced to four or five days. To complicate the matter, changing weather conditions make it hard to judge in advance just when the field will be ready, which in turn makes it hard to tell the produce manager just when your supply will be in. He usually has to know what to order or what not to order from his warehouse at least a week in advance. If you tell him that your corn will be ready in seven days and then a period of cool rainy weather sets in, your corn may not be ready for two weeks. Or if you wait too long before giving notice, and then some hot weather moves in, your corn may be ready too soon.

Furthermore, once you pick your corn, it should be placed in a cooler or the hands of your customers right away. Sweet corn, as most people know, has a short shelf life. Although it will not look spoiled, it quickly loses flavor once picked. You may have purchased a dozen very fine looking roasting ears only to discover upon biting into them that there was no flavor. The problem is not usually the variety, but the length of time the ears have been off the stalk. So, for such perishable items as sweet corn, a market must be ready and waiting.

Because we sell through a roadside stand, the job of getting the corn from stalk to kettle is rather easy. I pick the corn in the morning (and often throughout the day) and run it into town in time for customers to fix it for lunch or supper. It was for this very reason that I experimented with the retail market in the first place—to reduce the problem of marketing highly perishable items. Yet even with a roadside stand I still contend with the short market life of sweet corn.

Because of its short market life, corn can only be made available all summer long through consecutive plantings. But, with consecutive plantings, differing varieties, changing weather conditions, unforeseen setbacks, and varying consumer demands, I find it difficult to guess two months in advance just when and how much to plant. The goal, of course, is to end up with the right amount of corn each day throughout the entire summer. During unseasonably hot weather I have watched corn ripen faster than it could be sold. A field was ready to go before the last one was but a quarter harvested. In two days a thousand dozen ears of corn would be too mature for fresh eating. In four days it would not even be fit for canning. I called long distance to a large chainstore warehouse. The produce buyer would gladly have taken it had he known of the supply a week earlier. But on such short notice he had to say no. I put a few ads over the radio for people to come and pick their own. While a number of people took advantage of a good deal, the main portion of the field eventually had to be tilled into the ground.

One of the pleasant bonuses of going retail is that you no longer need to count out five dozen ears of corn to the sack—sacking up corn isn't necessary. As the ears are harvested, they are dumped into the truck or trailer. Upon arrival at the stand, customers are invited to sort through the load and pick out the ears that suit their taste. Some go for mature ears; some go for the light ones. Except the culls, which are removed throughout the day, nothing even needs to be unloaded. So, this way of marketing can be a real time and labor saver for the grower.

Tomatoes are also an important crop at our roadside stand. Early in the season the demand for them is great and the price is excellent. Tomatoes must be started indoors in cooler climates if one hopes to hit the early market. And, this means greenhouse work and the job of transplanting. However, since we do not stake or prune the vines, we consider the work of raising tomatoes virtually over once they have been transplanted. Weeds are controlled with a tractor-mounted cultivator. Since our entire market is supplied by an acre of plants, the job of cultivation is finished in a matter of minutes.

Because tomatoes are one of the easiest crops to raise, and require less land than many others, we usually try to plant a little more than we anticipate needing. This provides greater volume at the start of the season when demand and price are greatest, even though at some point in the normal season the increasing production is likely to match and then exceed the demand. Eventually, even with selective picking and special canning discounts, production far outstrips a faltering tomato market, and a lot of tomatoes end up going to waste. This isn't too serious, however, if you have been able to raise the crop with only a small amount of labor. (The harder you struggle to raise a crop the less you can afford to let any part of it go to waste.)

The big job in tomato production is harvesting. This may sound strange to the home gardener who goes out to the garden and in a few minutes comes back with a half-bushel of tomatoes. The tough part is selection. The home gardener doesn't worry if his tomato has cracks in it, is a little grotesque in shape, or has a green shoulder, or a small stem puncture in it. But customers paying 30 cents or 40 cents a pound want tomatoes without blemishes. To satisfy the customer, harvesting becomes a bit time-consuming. For tomatoes, as for sweet corn, you needn't do any grading, counting, weighing, or packaging. Customers pick out the tomatoes they like. The ones they leave are sold separately for canning or juice.

Believe it or not, one of the main drawbacks with tomatoes is that they are almost too ideal a plant. The fruit is delicious and easy to raise. The vines are productive and require very little space. Consequently, nearly everyone plants a tomato vine or two. There may not be room for sweet corn and squash, but there is always room for tomatoes. And the few who don't have their own gardens usually have friends who do. So, even though the tomato season may last for a couple of months, the demand and the price are great only at the start of the season. The challenge is to have a tomato crop ready to go two or three weeks ahead of everyone else's.

Another valuable crop for us is the hamburger onion. Sitting by itself in a retail market it would not be that important, but a large hamburger onion is just the thing to place in a display alongside tomatoes and corn. Not everyone is successful in raising a nice onion. Some get small onions. Some get hot, strong onions. Some get none at all. Because of this, the market for a nice onion remains very good throughout the season. It does not drop off as does the market for tomatoes. In fact, towards fall people start buying onions in volume for storage.

Onions demand a considerable amount of work to raise, and you may run into trouble with onion maggots. Furthermore, onions often require irrigation. But there are several advantages which tend to offset these drawbacks. First of all, onions are highly productive. One single acre may yield several thousand dollars worth of produce—an important factor if land is scarce or costly, or if you must irrigate. In addition, one of the nicest features about an onion is that it is not highly perishable. Unlike sweet corn, which offers a period of only a week to harvest, an onion may be picked at any time throughout the summer for the fresh market.

Furthermore, what you don't sell today will keep until tomorrow, or the next day, or the next. When fall comes and the mature onion is ready for harvest, it is easily pulled and easily stored. Onions must be sold within a reasonable length of time or they will spoil, but the pressure to move them is not nearly as great as it is for other items.

Slicing cucumbers, like onions, are not a principal crop. But they are nice to set into the display, adding color and variety and often lending themselves to making friends. It costs very little to toss an extra cuke into your customers' shopping bags. They will appreciate the free produce and the kind gesture on your part.

The amount of land needed to supply cucumbers for market is very little, a plus feature for cucumber production. A disadvantage is that the vines have to be picked thoroughly approximately every third day, or the fruits will become too large. We simply pick a third of the patch each day.

One of our most valuable crops is the muskmelon. Like sweet corn and tomatoes in the early part of summer, the later muskmelon is in great demand. Not only does it bolster sales directly, but it contributes to sales indirectly. People stop when they see muskmelons even though they may not have been planning to do so. After they select their melon, it is not uncommon to see them pick up a few tomatoes, an onion, and some sweet corn or squash.

Muskmelons are not too difficult to raise. They take up space but the return per acre in a successful year is much greater than that of sweet corn. Harvest is strenuous but simple and easily pays for the time spent picking. For best flavor, melons have to be picked when they ripen and then sold promptly. This can be a drawback to melon production if you do not have a waiting market. A vine-ripened melon has to be handled and transported with care. For the direct marketer, this simply means drive carefully and don't stack the load too high.

When the weather turns a bit chilly in the fall and a little heat in the house feels good, homemakers start using their ovens again. That's the time of year baking squash is in demand. Baking squash (including acorn, buttercup and hubbard) may not be a fast-moving item like corn or muskmelons, but the demand is steady and there's little work involved raising it. A couple of acres of squash on good soil in a good year will produce tons and tons of fruit. Squash requires little effort to raise due to the fact that the young squash plants are vigorous, needing only one or two passes with the cultivator before they are able to be on their own. In a very weedy field it might be necessary to break out the hoe and clean around the plants by hand. This goes quickly, however, since there are relatively few plants per acre. Once the vines start to sprawl, squash can handle the weed competition pretty well by themselves. Another nice thing about baking squash is that they are easy to harvest and need not be sold immediately. A mature squash can be either picked for sale or left on the vine until a freeze threatens. It is an equally good keeper off the vine, going weeks and even months without spoiling. Squash come on strong when other items like tomatoes, slicing cucumbers and corn have tapered off, making it a valuable asset to late-season sales.

Green peppers are seldom a principal crop, but the demand is fairly good if the price is right, and peppers require very little work to raise and harvest. One very favorable feature of green pepper production is that the fruits need not be picked at any particular stage of their development. They may be picked when still rather small; or they may be allowed to grow until large. The bigger they are the better they sell. If some turn red, so much the better. Pepper plants are very sensitive to frost and to hard wind, but have few insect enemies. One drawback to pepper production is the temperamental nature of the crop. Some years, perhaps due to unfavorable weather conditions, very little fruit is produced. Since they are relatively easy to raise, however, an occasional failure to bear fruit is merely disappointing. One good year more than pays for a poor year.

Pumpkins of course are a late-season crop that comes in with the squash and cauliflower. A prominent display of colorful pumpkins is a nice drawing item. Sales may not be spectacular, but they are steady. Like squash, pumpkins are very easy to raise, very easy to harvest, and keep for a long time. They do require a fair amount of land, however, which for some could be a drawback. Where land is available though, this drawback may prove to your advantage—you may have less competition and greater demand simply because other gardeners did not have room to devote to pumpkins.

Cauliflower requires careful attention and a fair amount of work. It is a favorite of the cabbage worm and is rather temperamental to raise, requiring proper soil, moisture and temperature conditions in order to develop a nice marketable head. Perhaps because of these requirements, many home gardeners would prefer to let someone else raise their cauliflower. That is fine with us. A nice-looking green jacket cauliflower still wet with dew has good demand and a good price. A fall crop of cauliflower matures at a time when early crops are beginning to lose their demand. That is a good time for a real appealing crop to come along. One of the nicest features about cauliflower is that it is not sensitive to frost, resisting damage at 25°F (-4°C).

Green beans are very easy to raise but time-consuming to harvest. When the weather is hot green beans can go from too small to too large in just a few days. That means they must be carefully attended to and picked when ready. Once picked they must be sold or properly cared for or they will wilt. A crisp green bean will sell, but wilted ones are hard to move.

If the season is short, many of the largest and best varieties of watermelon may not have time to develop, and some of the smaller, early maturing varieties lack the flavor and sales appeal necessary for success. And, as everyone knows, the time to sell watermelons is when the weather is hot. Consequently, the marketing season is virtually over by the time the northern-grown watermelons begin to ripen.

We have tried several crops that weren't worth the trouble. One of those that has disappointed us is cabbage. We thought initially that everyone would buy freshly cut heads of cabbage, but customers showed little interest. Beside the relatively poor demand and poor price, cabbage requires a lot of work to raise, especially in controlling the cabbage worm. Added to this is the fact that a head of cabbage must be harvested when it is ready. Harvested too soon, the head is not yet firm; too late and the head will have split open. On occasions we have planted a few hundred heads just to add a little variety to the display, but we are getting away from even that.

Carrots are another less-than-profitable crop for our family. The demand is only fair. It improves when the carrots are washed up, but that is just another job that must be added to this already time-consuming crop. The real work we encounter with carrot production is weeding. One year we missed our guess on a field, thinking it was quite free of weed seeds, and as nearly everyone knows, unless your soil is nearly weed free, raising carrots the organic way is going to entail a great deal of hand weeding. The question of whether the field was worth the trouble was decided with a watch and a little calculation.

We weeded furiously for five minutes. When the time was up I paced out the distance covered, estimated the retail value of the carrots in that stretch, figured our return per man-hour and decided it was a losing proposition. I told my weeders to forget it, and then turned the crop back into the soil.

What about potatoes? Although many market growers have them, I feel the small operator who has very little equipment for planting and harvesting potatoes may be able to spend his time better elsewhere. There is a fairly good demand for new potatoes each summer but I find the job of harvesting them is simply too great to be profitable. Even with single-row planter and digger we are just not able to compete with the highly mechanized potato industry. However, growers in other areas find potatoes quite popular and worth growing.

We have tried peas, lettuce, dill, beets, and eggplant without success, yet others we know have found some of these items very profitable. This simply points out the need to experiment with different crops on a small scale and find out for yourself which ones have the most potential in your locality.""

20: Sweet corn

"AS MENTIONED BEFORE, sweet corn is our big crop. For us, the season opens with sweet corn. I like to hit the early market with a flood of top quality early roasting ears. The money is good; with decent fields we expect to see $2,000 to $3,000 worth of sales the first week from a single sales location. The second week will drop slightly and the third week is a strong 50 percent of the first week's sales. The remaining three or four weeks of sweet corn production (we go until frost) level off around $500 to $750 a week with a substantial burst just before the season comes to an end.

If there is no irrigation involved, a single person with a small row crop tractor and cultivator can easily tend this much sweet corn up to the time of harvest. Take away 50 percent of total sales for overhead and in a good year you're left with a very nice $4,000 profit. A moderate 400 to 500 hours time is invested in this scale of corn production. This means that every time you climb up on the tractor to prepare your corn fields in the spring, plant them, or cultivate the young plants, you are earning $8 to $10 an hour, which isn't bad, especially when you love your work, can be home for lunch, and maybe bring your young son or daughter back to the field with you in the afternoon to keep you company on the tractor. It sounds easy.

It looks easy, too. Many of our customers are convinced that market gardening is a cinch. Every morning the truck pulls in with a mountain of fresh sweet corn. The people crowd around. The pile goes down. The truck returns home with only a small pile of trash to be thrown out onto the field.

As in every business, however, only those involved truly know that success does not come as easily as it might appear. Just because the beginning grower may have a reputation for raising some pretty tasty corn does not mean that his first commercial year will net him $4,000.

Sitting around the kitchen table in the middle of winter, plans for spring and a successful sweet corn business come easy. But with warmer weather, matters take on urgency. Just for starters, have you settled upon a good early variety or two for the early market? What about your main-season varieties? Have you a schedule for planting to assure a continuous harvest up to frost? If you have chosen to raise corn organically, are you prepared to handle the weed problem on the scale you are thinking about? How far apart are your rows going to be? Have you figured out how to get three tons of roasting ears per acre out of the field and into the hands of your customers without killing yourself? These questions confront every beginning commercial corn grower. The following section looks at sweet corn production from the small garden patch up to an operation of 30 acres or so, keeping the retail market in mind. Needless to say, every experienced commercial sweet corn grower could contribute to this section. Whenever possible, consult other growers in your area.

Commercial corn by hand.

You don't need a tractor to start a commercial sweet corn operation. You don't even need a garden tractor. If you have an acre of land and can get someone to work your soil for you in the fall and then again in the spring, you can do the rest with hand tools and make money at it. This is not to say that raising an acre or two of sweet corn by hand is the recommended course. Nevertheless, it can be done.

There is an advantage to the hand operation, however, that the more mechanized operation does not have—the crop can be babied with more care and attention, meaning it is possible to recover more marketable corn from an acre than would otherwise be possible.

Theoretically you should be able to harvest 1,600 dozen ears of corn per acre. That is the number you would get if your corn stood nine inches apart in 36-inch rows and every stalk produced a marketable ear. In practice, however, things seldom work out this way. Sometimes germination is a little spotty. Blackbirds, gophers and crows may destroy young plants. Ears fall prey to blackbirds and to raccoons. Others are just a little slow in maturing and are either left in the field or picked when still too immature to be marketable. And the list could go on. Considering these adverse factors, we feel we have done very well if our return per acre is just half of the theoretical potential. However, the hand operator, with just a little extra care and attention, can recover 75 percent of the ideal figure or even more.

If you decide to raise an acre of corn by hand, aim for the early market with its high market value and then plan to be done with your harvest in two weeks or less. This means selecting one or two early varieties of sweet corn and planting half your field one week and the remaining half the following week. If it is not convenient to split your field and work each half separately, then plant the entire field at one time.

Back when I started raising corn for market, the first planting was always made extremely early, hoping that by doing so mine would be the first corn on the market. It usually was, but losses to weather-related problems were too costly and frequent. As the years have gone by I have come to delay the first planting a week or two until the weather is more moderate. This means giving up only one or two days on harvest dates and often spares the grief of poor germination due to the cold soil. In addition, by delaying the planting and preparation for two weeks, I give the first weed seeds of the season an opportunity to germinate. Then when the field is prepared for planting, the first crop of weeds is destroyed. Thus our soil preparation becomes our first cultivation as well.

When is the proper time to plant the first field of corn? Calendar dates are too relative. They vary from year to year and from one location to another. We look at the flower buds on the apple trees. Just before they open up and burst into bloom would probably be a good time to get the first early sweet corn planted.

One of your first hand tool investments should be a hand seeder such as the Precision Garden Seeder, listed in many seed catalogs for around $38. This is an all-around seeder that you'll probably use for other garden seeds as well. If your soil has been prepared so that it is loose, soft, and free of large clods, a good hand seeder can be used to plant a lot of corn without a great deal of work. Even a seeder is not necessary if you intend to put in just a few rows; just drop four to six seeds into a small hole every three feet in rows about three feet apart. The seed must reach moist soil when it is planted and ideally is not more than two or three inches deep after a light step of the foot has gently packed the soil over it. The extra-early "gamblers corn" will probably have to be planted even shallower to avoid burying the seed in the cold soil underneath. Using a seeder, drop the seed relatively thick (four to five inches apart). It will cost you an extra $10 to $20 per acre for the additional seed, and if the seed germinates well you will need to go through the field with a hand hoe and thin out the young plants. If poor germination occurs, however, the thick planting may just give you a satisfactory stand after all. This is important because you don't want to call upon your neighbor a second time to prepare your field, and more important you don't want to be starting out two weeks later on a second attempt with that first field of sweet corn.

Sometime before the leaves begin to overlap from one plant to another, thin the plants out so that the largest and healthiest plants average nine or ten inches apart. If you've planted the corn in hills, leave only three plants to a hill. This is the time to be ruthless with your cornfield. If plants are left too close together, your harvest will be set back several days. The cornfield may also be more susceptible to worm damage. Furthermore, some plants won't set any ears and those plants which do may yield only stunted ones. It is better to allow too much space between corn plants than not enough. Plants themselves will tend to compensate for too much space, sometimes yielding two marketable ears instead of just one.

Spacing between rows is determined in part by the type of cultivation that will be employed. If you intend to use a hand tiller for cultivation, space your rows out so that at least six inches is allowed on each side of the tiller and the row of corn. Thirty-two or 34 inches should be maintained as a minimum row width. In the event that you have no tiller and no tractor cultivator, space rows approximately 34 inches apart and use a wheel hoe with a large wheel. Instead of using the cultivator prongs that come with most such wheel hoes, bring the tool to a local blacksmith's shop and ask him to fix you up with a 15- to 18-inch blade. It will slice through the ground just underneath the surface of the soil and cut off all the weeds at their roots. A thin, highly tempered blade no wider than 1½ inches will do an excellent job. The strike strip on a reel-type push lawnmower will serve; it will take designing and maybe a little adapting, but once you get this wheel hoe fixed up you have a tool that will allow you to keep as many as three acres clean by hand. (I cultivated three acres one summer with a wheel hoe of this design, working only after-hours and Saturdays.)

The one important thing to remember about wheel hoe cultivation is that you must get out there in the field when the weeds have just begun to emerge. You might even go through the field before the corn has come up in what is called "blind" cultivation, using the planter marks to guide you down the rows. Allow yourself four days or so to make your first trip through the field. You may wish to break each day's allotment into two- or three-bite sizes. Set up a schedule for yourself and don't get behind.

More than likely it will be necessary to go through your field at least once with a hoe to clean away the weeds around each little plant. Again, the best time to do this is when the weeds are still small, providing of course that your corn plants are large enough to be easily seen and easily worked around. This is where you will see the advantage of the delayed first planting. When the soil is warm, corn will start coming up within one or two weeks of planting, about the time the weeds appear. If your corn takes three or four weeks to appear (as it may if you get it into the ground too early), you will find that many cold weather weeds will have germinated and be on their way. It is very disheartening to try to hoe through a field in this situation. In our experience, the wisest course is to till the field and plant again.

If you want to make time with a hand hoe in a cornfield, bury as many weeds as possible. Instead of stooping down and trying to clean around each individual corn plant, draw a quick hoeful of dirt up against the base of the plant and cover the weeds. For most weeds that sprout from seed in the spring of the year, this technique is as effective as chopping them off. Furthermore, the soil is not disturbed around the base of the corn plant.

An important consideration for the commercial grower, especially if much work is done by hand, is deciding just how clean the cornfield has to be to get a good harvest. The answer is not pat. We have seen some exceptional harvests from very weedy fields, and on occasions we have lost fields to weeds which did not look any worse than normal. The key is moisture. To be on the safe side, one should plan for three cultivations and (unless you can throw the dirt up around the plants with a cultivator) at least one or maybe two trips through with a hoe. Make final cultivation when the corn plants stand almost waist high; at this stage of their development they are tall enough to shade the rows.

Ten to 12 days from the time the tassels begin to show, the silk will start to appear. Twenty days later it is blackbird time. Don't be caught off guard; early sweet corn often matures before the nearby fields of small grain, meaning that your corn just might be the first taste of fresh farm produce for the neighborhood blackbirds. To aggravate the situation, the summer's first hatch of blackbirds has already learned to fly, and the birds are out in families. The most effective control that we have found for blackbirds is the shotgun with cheap target-load shells. Once the blackbirds have discovered your sweet corn to be out of this world for flavor, they will be very difficult to keep out. Even just a little negligence then may cost you the better part of your harvest, and you simply can't afford that after all the work you have put into your crop. I've found that it's best to take a daily swing through the field beginning a week or so before the ears are ready to pick, blasting away at the occasional blackbird perched on the tassels; this generally frightens the blackbird population away from the field before the birds have found any real reason to be there in the first place.

If raccoons and skunks become more than a nuisance, you might try tying your dog out in the corn patch during the night. Some people report success with a couple strands of electric wire strung around the perimeter of the field approximately 7 and 12 inches off the ground. An additional thing to remember is that the young tender roasting ears are not quite as appealing to the raccoon as the more mature ears. This being the case, move as much of the crop as you can before it gets big and full. The longer marketable corn stands out in the field, the more likely raccoons are to help themselves.

Sweet corn with a tractor.

A small wide-front-end tractor, with an old-time single-row horse-drawn cultivator, is a welcome substitute for the wheel hoe. Many acres can be cultivated with very little effort. One person rides the horse-drawn cultivator and steers it with his feet, and a second drives the tractor. We used this relatively inexpensive combination for several years before investing in a row crop tractor with a two-row cultivator. One valuable contribution of the tractor-powered cultivator is that, when the cultivator shoes are set at the proper angle, not only will the cultivator remove the weeds between the rows but they also will throw a small ridge of dirt up against the row of corn plants. This ridge of dirt comes at the base of the young corn stalks from both sides and buries small weeds that otherwise could be destroyed only with a hand hoe. If a horse-drawn cultivator is employed you will probably find it necessary to space your rows out to 38 or 40 inches. If you invest in a two-row tractor-mounted cultivator you will also need to pick up a two-row planter.

One other piece of equipment should be acquired if you have a farm tractor. That is a drag, preferably a vibrashank drag or mulcher. We have found this tool to be invaluable to our weed control program. Just before the corn emerges in the spring I go through the field with the drag. Virtually all of the stout corn shoots lying just below the surface will remain unharmed, but the many tiny weeds just beginning to send down their white, hairlike roots will be disturbed and either buried or jerked loose. Leave a small corner of the field untouched, and you'll see the difference this practice can make.

Later, when the corn plants stand six to eight inches tall, the drag can be used again. This time the young corn plants are large enough to deflect the vibrashank teeth and avoid damage. Those that lie in the path of the tractor tires will look pretty sad for a day or two, but even they will usually come back and become normal, healthy corn plants. It's best to choose a warm day to make this second trip because corn plants are more flexible and less fragile when the weather is warm. However, the drag must not be used when the corn plants are small enough to be buried by the moving dirt. Once a clod of dirt rolls over the tender leaves and covers them, the plant will never recover by itself.

Corn harvest.

Tomorrow is the big day. You have been eating selected ears of corn for three or four days now, and the last kettleful was perfect—no "blistering" white ears, no dark yellow ears. If everything went well during the growing season you may have 800 or 1,200 dozen ears or more out in the field. That's 200 sacks worth. It's one thing to go out and pick a few ears for supper; it is something else to go out into the field at sunrise and have 30 or 40 sacks picked and loaded by 9 A.M.

Presumably you have at least an idea of how you hope to move your crop. If you plan to wholesale it you will no doubt be delivering your corn in gunny sacks with a 60 count in each. When we sold this way, we entered the field with four or five empty sacks hanging at our sides from corn hooks on our belts. Each person would snap two rows at a time. When the first sack reached 60 ears it was quickly unhooked and made to stand up in the "pick-up" row. The pick-up row is a pair of corn rows selected as the ones to drive down with the truck or tractor. Needless to say, they are harvested before being driven on. Without pick-up rows to drive down, the sacks of corn would all have to be carried to the edge of the field, creating a great deal of extra work, especially if the field is large. When it becomes necessary to pick up another supply of empty sacks or to deposit a full one at the pick-up row, take your foot and break down a few of the last stalks which were picked. This marks where you left off and saves time relocating your place.

How do you decide if an ear of corn is ready to pick? You can always strip back an inch or two of husk and look inside. But, besides making for very slow picking, this method gives the harvested corn a slightly ragged appearance on the counter, as if inspected and rejected by an earlier customer. Furthermore, opened immature ears left on the stalk often fall prey to bugs or blackbirds. The best way of course is to snap the ears without peeking into them. I instruct most beginning pickers to go by feel. Grab each ear so that the hand closes over the end with the silk. The idea is to pick the ears which feel firm and have a blunt, plump end. These are the ones which are ready to go. Those that taper off gradually and have somewhat of a spongy feeling are still too immature to pick. Since each variety has its own distinct feeling, even pickers with experience will probably need to open a few each morning to develop a good touch. If the field contains a fair amount of questionable ears, it isn't a bad idea to open one now and then to make sure that your standard hasn't changed.

An experienced picker in a good stand of corn can pick 150 dozen ears of corn in an hour or so. Picking speed suffers greatly if the stand is a little light or if the corn is not uniform, thereby requiring greater selectivity on the part of the picker. Efficiency also depends upon your system of carrying the corn to the tractor—how quickly can you get back to your row?

Retail operators can use a labor-saving variation on the gunny sack method—one that requires no sacks, no loading of sacks, and no unloading of sacks. The corn is simply dumped loose into the vehicle that the customers will gather around a few hours later. A gunny sack apron is made by opening up a 100-pound potato sack so that it becomes a rectangular sheet of burlap. Two of the corners (two adjacent wide corners) are tied together with a tight, small square knot. The other two wide corners are fastened to the belt, one on each side of the waist, with stout wire hooks. When the square knot is held out in front a heavy-duty apron pouch is formed that will hold five to seven dozen ears of corn at a time.

Instead of picking into sacks that hang alongside of the waist, the picker snaps the ears off and drops them into this apron. When the apron is full the picker steps over to the pick-up row, quickly unhooks one or both sides of the apron from his belt, and dumps the ears into the low-sided trailer or truck.

One advantage of this system is that the weight is distributed more evenly around the waist than if a sack hangs from one side only; after a couple hours of picking, this feature is very welcome. Another important advantage with this apron method is that the corn is kept perfectly clean, whereas a full sack dragging on a wet or dew-covered cornfield quickly becomes muddy. A final advantage is that once you get the corn into the trailer or truck there is virtually no need to handle it again.

The initial obstacle to establishing a successful retail market is consumer buying habits. People are not accustomed to buying from you yet. Both you and your product are unknown to them. Why should they venture into the unknown when the familiar has handily supplied them in the past?

Once people discover you and your tasty corn, your marketing problem is half over. Just keep up the quality and people will be back for more. Believe it or not, you and your corn will become tabletime topics. Over the phone and at the shop or office, people will comment about the terrific corn they had the other night. When people start selling for you, your business is over the hump. But how do you get to this point?

Probably the best and fastest way to break into the retail market is to go where the people are. You can set up at your fields and spend time and money trying to get people to drive out to your stand. This has worked for many and might work for you as well. But chances are it won't move the thousand dozen that need to be harvested by the end of the week. It would take a lot of television commercials and radio spots to get a thousand people to change their buying habits in one week. The most effective way to get people to do something they haven't done before is to show up with your product and display it right before their eyes. Locate a strategic corner in town where a lot of people walk or drive by each day. Ask the owners of the location for permission to set up an experimental shop for a few days. (Check into city ordinances to see if this is allowed.) Put 20, 30, or 75 dozen on the line some morning and see if they sell. If they don't, you've lost a little corn. If they do, you will have broken into the retail market.

Selling tips.

Keep your corn fresh and looking fresh. Try to keep it out of direct sunlight, especially on a warm summer day. If the ears begin to look a little dry, stir up the pile and place fresh-looking ears on top. As time permits pick out inferior ears that have been opened and rejected and put them into a separate pile. Later in the day you may need to draw upon this pile of culls, selling them at a discount, but while you have good corn in the load keep it looking good. It is very important to keep your display looking fresh.

Never carry sweet corn over from one day to the next without refrigeration. If on occasions you do feel it necessary to carry over, make sure you inform your customers so they are not unaware of the situation when they make their purchase. Keep your customers' confidence in the quality of your produce.

If at the end of the day it looks like you will be a little long on corn, try this: rather than take it home and dump it back on the field, start tossing an extra ear or two into each sack. Or, after customers have picked up their corn and are paying for it, invite them to pick up a couple more ears. If the pile is obviously picked over and a lot of scrubs remain, keep looking for the good ears yourself—you know what a good ear feels like. Help locate them for customers who may be having a hard time finding real nice ones.

To compensate for the growing percentage of scrubs late in the day, offer more ears for the same amount of money. If you started the day selling a dozen ears for a dollar, offer 14 for a dollar or 15 or 18. Don't drop the price per dozen. If you do, people will usually settle for the dozen at the reduced price and you end up with less money in the pocket and more corn in the trailer. Keep your price up there and simply increase the size of your "dozen." People will be happy because they are getting a good bargain.

For a little fun with your customers when the corn is really picked over and a lot of small immature ears remain, tell them they can have all they can get into a good-sized bag for a dollar or $1.50 or 75 cents, whatever makes a good bargain for them. When it comes to this time of the day and you are left with poor-quality corn, be sure to level with your customers. Let them know that the quality is down from the morning; you might even suggest that if they can wait they should come around in the morning for better quality.

When you tell customers your price—13 ears for $1.25 or whatever it is—urge them to peel the husks down and look at each ear they select to make sure it is a good one and at just the right stage of development for their taste. I am convinced that this policy is a great help in establishing a sweet corn business. People are accustomed to buying corn in plastic bags. Consequently, they don't know what they have bought until they get home with it. And even if the stores carry it loose, no one there is likely to urge them to look into each ear.

Isn't a lot of the corn actually spoiled by allowing the customers to pick through it and peel it down? Not really. Most customers are not so picky that they would discard decent ears. Of course, there are a few who will open three dozen ears before they settle on a dozen to their liking, but try not to let any impatience show. These people, if treated in the right way, will become some of your most valuable customers. Note the kind of cars these people drive. More often than not these people have been just as selective in the new car showroom as they are at the stand. Be assured that if they eventually do get a dozen ears picked out they will be back for more. One choosy customer exclaimed to me, "I don't care what the price is. I'll pay $100 a dozen if that's what it takes to get good corn."

Then there are customers who have never had a garden of their own—have never learned how to tell when a melon is ripe, when a baking squash is ready to pick, or what to look for in an ear of corn. All their lives they have brought home plastic-wrapped packages from the produce counter in the supermarket. They would almost rather you didn't urge them to peel down the ears of corn because they don't know what to look for. Assist these customers whenever you can, and while you are picking out some of the finest roasting ears for them, give a few pointers. Tell them to get the corn home and in the kettle or refrigerator as soon as possible. Show them an immature ear if you can, or one that may be too mature so they know what it is you're trying to avoid.

As you get into the corn business, you'll discover that it is very difficult to guess just when and how much of each variety should be planted so as to assure yourself of a continuous supply throughout the sweet corn season with neither too much nor too little for any given day. The best that you can hope for is to get close and then learn how to stretch a lean week out until the field comes in, or on the other hand, how to push a surplus through the stand leaving as little remaining in the field as possible. This calls for careful planning and marketing. This week may see an abundance. But the following planting for next week didn't germinate as well. Will some of this week's corn still be marketable if harvest is delayed until the early part of next week? That would take the pressure off of the poor field. Or, it may be that the unseasonably warm weather is pushing the fields through faster than anticipated. Next week's field is ready to go and the present field has only just been entered. What can one do to catch up without actually losing the better part of a good field?

Consider yourself fortunate if the problem is that your supply does not match the demand. Whenever the demand exceeds the supply you are in the driver's seat, and within reason you can set your own price and at the same time get rid of almost every ear you bring in. Those who are reluctant to pay your price will readily understand when you explain the shortage. Your job will primarily involve budgeting your fields so that you have at least some corn to bring in each day. That way you can always tell your late-in-the-day customers that you are very sorry to have run out already but if they can manage to get to the stand at an early hour tomorrow morning they should find some good corn. If you budgeted your fields successfully you will always have some corn for those who make that special trip to the stand early in the day just for sweet corn.

If, on the other hand, you find yourself looking at more corn than you can normally get rid of, here are a few methods that may help to profitably move above average quantities.

First of all, decide upon a good quantity price. If, for instance, you normally sell your sweet corn at 13 ears for a dollar you may wish to offer three dozen ears for $2 and five dozen for $3. Post your quantity prices in a conspicuous spot. As your customers stop, point out the special bargain. Explain that you have a surplus for a few days and that now would be a very good time to pick up some good sweet corn for freezing. In addition to a very conspicuous sign next to or on top of the pile of corn, be sure to post two or three signs around the stand with the special buy lettered on them. You might also take advantage of some radio time. If you have another vehicle and another sales location available, you could try at least one day's worth of selling at a second location. This may turn out to be your most expedient answer even if it does cost you an extra $40 a day for an additional worker, vehicle and sales location.

Another option we have used profitably is to invite people over the radio to come out to the field and pick their own sweet corn for so much a gunny sack full. This requires an attendant at the field to assist those who show up, but his time can be spent weeding or hoeing when he is not busy with customers.

As mentioned earlier, avoid the mistake of lowering the price of individual dozens. It may seem reasonable that people would buy more corn if it were offered a little cheaper, but in practice most people have stopped to buy a dozen whether the price is 85 cents or $1. Dropping the price on an individual dozen seldom sells more corn; it usually just means less total sales for the day. Furthermore, you will find it difficult to put your price back up where you want it once the surplus is gone.**"**

21: Tomatoes: a tricky but profitable commodity

"WHAT IS WORTH two-thirds the price of ground beef one week, and two weeks later is cheaper than potatoes?

Tomatoes. If the market gardener is consistently two weeks ahead of everyone else with his tomato harvest, he can make money. If he misses, he may have trouble giving them away. The reason for this interesting phenomenon is not hard to find. By spring, after a winter of pink, waxy approximations of the fruit, almost everyone is desperate for a vine-ripened garden tomato. But the tomato also happens to be one of the easiest vegetables to raise in a backyard garden, and almost everyone sets out at least a couple of plants. Trays and trays of tomato plants are carried out of every greenhouse in the spring. And being one of the most productive of all garden plants, it is only a matter of time until the thousands and thousands of tomato plants in the area are loaded with tons of green fruit. If your tomatoes ripen before the others you will have a great market. If your tomatoes don't you face a struggle.

The first challenge for the commercial tomato grower, then, is to be ahead of everyone else. This involves an early variety that is started early in the greenhouse and then set out early in light, fertile soil with adequate moisture.

David offers deals for customers willing to buy in quantity

A second challenge is maintaining sales during the peak of the tomato season. The most important key to selling tomatoes when the country is flooded with them is quality. Customers stopping for melons or sweet corn should be made aware of a conspicuous display of attractive tomatoes, right alongside of the scale or wherever you do most of your business.

Whereas timing is the key to selling your first tomatoes, later tomatoes will sell by virtue of their quality. And all the care in the world will not give you a quality tomato unless there is something in the plant to start with. So begin with a good market variety. Try to find a tomato that is slow to split in wet weather, seldom develops any vertical cracks or lateral cracks around the stem, has no green shoulders, and is super tasty. Many home garden varieties are just fine for eating but don't measure up as market tomatoes. A veteran market gardener from another part of the state recommended Earlibird for an early tomato and Early Red Chief for a quality tomato. These became our standard varieties for several years, with generally good success. Later, another market gardener told us we should try a variety called Avalanche, and this tomato has now replaced Early Red Chief as a main-season quality tomato. And a year or two from now, who knows? New varieties are being developed all the time. Compare notes with other growers. Experiment with some that have proven successful for others.

Tending your tomatoes.

After choosing your varieties you must give them the proper care, or all your selectiveness will be for nothing. The basic care of tomatoes involves two parts: greenhouse culture followed by care in the field.

We give our market plants an eight- to ten-week start in the greenhouse. The normal practice is to scatter the seeds into a flat of moist peat moss, vermiculite and soil. Sprinkle a little soil on top and cover with newspaper. Keep the flat warm. After the seeds have germinated, remove the paper and leave the flat in a warm sunny room, or starter greenhouse. When the little plants are an inch or two in height, pot them into their greenhouse packs. For ease of transplanting into the field we prefer packs with individual cells. A single tomato plant is potted into each cell. When they are ready to be transplanted out into the field, it is only a matter of popping each plant out and dropping it into the furrow—far easier than ripping and tearing the roots of a dozen plants all growing in one large tray.

Forty-eight individual cells in a 10-by-20-inch flat are probably the very maximum one would wish to go, especially if they are to grow ten weeks before being set out. The tomatoes would actually fare better in larger cells with fewer plants per flat and fewer plants in the greenhouse. Whatever the arrangement, fill the flats with either a fertile commercial preparation or a nutrient-laden, half-rotted barnyard manure. Regardless of what you choose for potting soil, the plants will almost certainly need one, two or more feedings before they are set out. We have used manure tea with good success.

When the plants are small and rapid growth is desirable, keep the soil warm and moist but not soaking wet. Later on, as the tomatoes reach planting size, be a little stingy with the water so that the root systems are encouraged to develop. You might even let plants wilt down just a little before watering.

When the plants branch out and are crowding each other, spread the flats to leave several inches of space on all sides. The outer plants will quickly lean out, giving the inside plants more room. This is a very important time for your young plants. Unless they are fed they will lose their robust green and turn lighter in color. Growth will slow down and even come to a halt. The forward momentum you had going for you will be lost, and it may take some time for the tomatoes to turn around and recover.

One week before setting the plants out into the field, carry them all outdoors for hardening. Give them time to adjust to the wind and direct sunlight before introducing them to strange soil. Watch carefully that they don't dry out for want of frequent watering.

The second stage of tomato culture begins with the job of transplanting, which for early-harvest tomatoes should immediately follow the last killing frost of the spring and not a night earlier. This is a highly speculative matter, however, and keeps us guessing each spring. One veteran grower told me to watch the apple trees. It is usually safe to set out tomatoes, he said, when the apple blossoms start to drop. We have followed his advice for a number of years without losing any plants. Still, to be on the safe side we usually set out only half of our plants at one time. The second half follows about a week later.

Allow plenty of space between plants (especially for indeterminate varieties). We plant the sprawling indeterminate varieties six feet apart in six-foot rows and still sometimes find it hard to get in and around the vines during harvest. However, placing them three feet apart in four-foot rows should be adequate for most tomato varieties in most soils. Remember that methods of cultivation will help determine spacing; six-foot rows work out well for our three-point hitch-mounted cultivator; spacing them six feet apart both ways enables us to cross cultivate.

Keep the roots fairly shallow when setting out young plants; at this time of the year, deep soil is often quite cold and only the surface soil warms up. In one movement scrape out a shallow depression in the soil, place the plant in with the other hand, pull a little dirt back over the roots, and punch down firmly. If the flats were soaked down thoroughly before bringing them out to the field the young tomato plants will have enough water in their little ball of roots to last them several hours and perhaps all day, especially if the soil they are going into is moist and the weather not too hot. We usually set out a thousand plants or so in a couple of hours and then go back with barrels and buckets and give each one a drink.

We have been quite pleased with the way eight- to ten-week-old tomato plants hold their own against cutworms. This is very important to the organic grower. More than once we have discovered that although the tender little plants were sitting in a virtual hotbed of cutworms, only a small percentage were actually cut off and destroyed. This is not always true of other vegetable crops sharing the tomato field. One spring, cutworms were so thick and hungry that 100 percent of the cucumbers on one side of the tomato field were destroyed, and a substantial number of our squash and pumpkin seedlings on the other side were cut off. Furthermore, within the tomato patch a strip of green peppers suffered a severe setback. It was not uncommon to find, by the light of a flashlight, half a dozen cutworms eating the foliage of a single pepper plant while another three or four cutworms ate below ground at the base of the stem. Luckily, an eight-inch tomato plant has a stem that's sturdy enough to discourage the hungry horde, for although cutworms could be found in and around the tomato plants and even up on the foliage, damage was limited and in just a few days the young plants had outgrown the danger entirely.

Some commercial growers tie up and prune their tomato plants in order to harvest a higher percentage of large blemish-free tomatoes. Some even feel that this practice results in an earlier harvest. We tried tying ours up but have come back to the practice of letting the vines sprawl. Some fruit is lost to mice and some from lodging in the dirt. Some fruit is lacking in size and uniformity. But in the end we save a lot of time by not tying and pruning. We also save time by not messing with poles and wires after the season is over. Our greater production gives us more fruit to select from, which tends to compensate for the higher percentage of poor-quality fruits. Another benefit is that a sprawling vine hides more fruit with its leaves than a pruned and tied vine, and while this may delay their ripening it also gives a little better frost protection in the fall.

The first ripe tomatoes sell out quickly. Every day sees a little larger volume as the vines pick up momentum. Eventually the growing supply matches and then surpasses what has become a diminishing demand. This is when your selling abilities face their toughest test. One suggestion is to forget about selling tomatoes by the pound. Sell them instead by the three pounds or four pounds, by the bagful, or by a fixed price such as $1.25. When customers ask how much your tomatoes cost, don't say, "31 cents a pound": to some this will sound expensive for tomatoes and many customers will ask for only a couple pounds, leaving you with 62 cents worth of tomatoes sold and perhaps 20 crates to go. Instead, tell customers that they can pick up a four-pound bagful for $1.25, selecting their own tomatoes. For fancy, vine-ripened, selected tomatoes that's a bargain in anyone's book. Give customers a sack and instruct them to put it on the scale when they think they are close to the mark. When the needle finally comes to rest right on four pounds, pick out a nice tomato yourself and toss it in free as a little bonus. You get $1.25 instead of 62 cents and customers will be delighted with a good buy. Only if the four-pound offer is more than a customer wants should you give your individual-pound price. (Of course, make sure the price for a single pound is slightly higher per pound than the quantity price.)

Keep culling out your poorer tomatoes throughout the day. Always make sure that you have at least one box of super-perfect tomatoes for your customers to select from. Sell your culls by the crate for canning and juicing. If you detect that a customer probably needs a bargain rather than your most expensive number-one tomatoes, show your crates of culls. Many large families are delighted with the chance to get a whole box for just a couple dollars. In this way you pick up $2 or

$2.50, instead of $1.25; you get rid of tomatoes that might otherwise remain unsold; and a big family goes home with a lot of good food for a very reasonable price.

As the season progresses and the tomato field produces far more than you can sell, you may wish to open it up for people to pick their own for canning. Don't feel badly if some of your tomatoes go to waste. If you planted so as not to waste any of your later tomatoes you would have very few, indeed, to sell when the market is at its best. **" "**

22: There's money in muskmelons

" M Y FAVORITE CROP is the muskmelon. Whether a fragile seedling or a sprawling fruit-laden vine, this crop is thoroughly enjoyable. Perhaps the challenge and risk involved in raising muskmelons in the cold country adds spice.

Harvesting muskmelons is full-fledged work. The back aches. Fingertips wear thin from handling sandpaperlike skins. Arms get tired. And after a couple of hours of stooping and straightening, you're ready for a rest. The melons, still oozing sticky syrup from the stem end, fill the air with a special, vine-ripened muskmelon fragrance.

Watermelon sales drop when the sun goes behind a cloud, but muskmelons seem to be in constant demand. The gardener who can produce a good melon is going to build up a business. Perhaps this is more true on the fringes of muskmelon territory where the muskmelon is not as abundant and available as elsewhere. At any rate, I have found that muskmelons run a close second to sweet corn for drawing customers and for building up sales.

In central Minnesota the melon season is usually short and hectic. We hope to pick our first melons around the first week in August (though they have been as early as the middle of July). About a week from the time the first one ripens, we are moving small quantities each day at the market, and two weeks from the first melon we expect to be in full production. By September, we are in a race with fall and the first killing frost. Sometimes the harvest is virtually over before it comes. Other years we have been caught with a field of frosted plants. The regular melon harvest will continue as usual that day, the next, and perhaps for a whole week before the quality begins to go down. Then we drop our price and give notice that the melons are no longer top grade. The season has truly ended when the melons cease walking out of the field during the night.

For me, the muskmelon season begins in the greenhouse. I have been successful in the past by seeding directly into the fields but, with a shift toward some of the hybrid varieties with their $120-a-pound seed, I have turned more and more to starting them indoors. Besides making every expensive seed count, the greenhouse gives me a good week or two on the short growing season. In addition, I am granted an extra two weeks in the spring to work the field before setting out the little muskmelon plants. This offers a substantial advantage in weed control, especially when the young plants start covering the ground with their runners.

I fill three-inch-square pots with half-rotted barnyard manure, punch in two or three seeds to a depth of one-half inch, sprinkle very lightly with water, and cover with newspaper. It is especially important to keep the seeds and soil toasty warm at least during the germination period.

The first melon seeds go into pots around the last week in April. By spreading the seeding out over a two-week period you're not only likely to hit some excellent days for germination, but also the harvest is spread out over a longer period of time.

I used to raise the Iroquois variety with good success and good acceptance by the public. This variety being open-pollinated, seed was not too expensive and we could afford to seed it directly into the field. I have experimented with a number of varieties over the years which did not measure up to Iroquois. There were a couple hybrids, however, that eventually captured our order. Though I continue to try different varieties, Harris' Gold Star Hybrid and Burpee Hybrid still hold their own. Markets, soils, and weather all differ with locality, and every gardener will have to do his own experimenting.

If the seedlings grow well, four weeks in the greenhouse brings them to a point where they are crowding each other in their three-inch pots. So, figuring backwards four weeks from the time you normally set out your tomato plants, you should arrive at a pretty good date to plant melon seeds in the greenhouse. (If you choose to direct-seed melons, do it when you plant your cucumbers and squash.) Potting soil should be kept warm and not too moist. Be careful not to overwater the small plants. The top of the soil may look dry but still be very wet underneath. A small plant does not draw much water, and the roots may eventually damp-off, killing the plant. Keep a close check on the moisture level inside the pots by gently inverting a few pots and examining the ball of soil and roots that comes out into your hand. You may not need to do any watering at all on a cool cloudy day. Even on a sunny day small plants often need only a light mist to freshen up the top of the pot. As the plant grows, however, you will need to water more frequently. Once the plants come outdoors for hardening they may require a thorough soaking every few hours.

A good way of assuring rapid growth and vigorous plants at the time of transplanting is to feed them with manure tea (see Chapter 31, "Under glass"). The mess and bother of a feeding or two will be more than repaid by an earlier and more prolific harvest.

One of the important projects during the summer is preparing the following year's melon field. We did not always do this, but the result was that we fought a continual battle with weeds, sometimes with only moderate success and always with a big investment in labor. Now we do our weeding a year ahead, keeping the upcoming melon field black for the entire summer in advance of planting. Summer fallowing eliminates most of the hand work the following year and also contributes to a better crop.

To compensate for the lack of vegetation on a summer-fallowed melon field, I try to cover it with manure. I also usually delay the first annual working of the field until the initial crop of weeds has reached a fairly good size. Then, just before the weeds go to seed, I work them into the soil. Later in the summer a cover such as buckwheat could be planted; rye would serve in early fall. To build up moisture supply I choose to keep the field black all summer. Since melons are one of the last crops to go in each year, the delayed spring planting once again gives a chance for the weed seeds to germinate; so just before seeding or transplanting work, I till the field one last time. Then it's time to determine row spacing and plant the field.

Muskmelon is often planted in 6-foot rows placed no closer than 3 feet apart within the row. However, spacing must be in part determined by your cultivating equipment. What row spacing works out the best for your machinery? In some situations a 10- or 12-foot row might actually be the best choice. My own cultivator is a three-point-hitch field cultivator mounted on a wide-front-end tractor, which does a good job on 6-foot rows. On a large patch be sure to allow room for roadways. Our field is broken into sections of six rows, divided by roadways 10 to 12 feet wide.

If you use an open pollinated seed that is not too costly and you choose to seed directly into the field, then plant a seed every few inches. With perfect germination, no cucumber beetle trouble, no cutworm trouble, and few other problems, you will eventually need to thin your rows out; if conditions are not ideal, however, you should have enough plants to sustain a modest loss. Nothing is more frustrating, however, than to eventually end up with ten-foot gaps between plants. If time were not such a factor in muskmelon culture, poor germination could be remedied by digging up the field and planting it over. But by the time you finally realize that things did not work out well, two or three weeks have slipped by and that is likely too much time for most northern gardeners to recover. So if the cost of seed is not a factor, plant your seed every few inches apart. Let your plants grow until the last possible minute as insurance against misfortunes, and then, before the young vines start to compete with one another, ruthlessly hoe out all but the choicest ones so that you end up with two or three feet between plants.

If you have taken the greenhouse approach, soak them down thoroughly with water just before setting them out. Or better yet, soak with manure tea. Transport the still-dripping flats to the field and begin transplanting. You may wish to walk along the rows and gently lay the pots on the ground, a pace apart. After you have emptied the flat, retrace your steps, transplanting the seedlings as you go. If you choose to raise your plants in peat pots or peat pellets, simply scrape a shallow depression in the carefully prepared soil, insert the plant, pot and all, pull a little dirt back over, and pack firmly. Plastic containers must be inverted; carefully shake the ball of soil and roots into your free hand and then plant the vine. If you watered the plants well before transplanting you won't be in any rush to water them again. You might let them go until the next day in hopes that it will rain. If your soil is moist and the weather is not too hot, you may not need to water your plants at all; otherwise, plan on giving each transplant a good pint or two of water.

Transplanting can become a very long and tedious project. The easiest way to go about the job is with a transplanter. A little homemade system has worked out very well for us. I attached a platform to a single-blade subsoiler. Also attached is a kneeling bench that straddles the furrow. While one person drives the tractor, a second person plops the melon transplants behind the subsoiler blade, giving each one a good firm punch to pack it. The contoured subsoil furrows not only offer the young plants loose soil to as deep as 18 to 20 inches, but serve also to trap rainwater.

The important thing in putting young melons into the ground is that the plants be strong and healthy when they come from the greenhouse and that they lose none of their momentum after transplanting. This appears to be an important key in overcoming some of the enemies that threaten young melons. Plants that look poorest in the greenhouse become, as a general rule, more vulnerable to cutworms and striped cucumber beetles than those that are strong and healthy. So too, those planted on soil without a fresh application of manure seem to fall prey to enemies more often than those set out on land with a fresh covering of manure. There may be more than one way of explaining this phenomenon, but it is obvious that a strong plant can recover from damage faster than one that starts out in a weakened condition. If the field is infested with cutworms, almost every plant will receive some damage. Usually the stem of a four- or five-week old melon plant is already a pretty big mouthful for a cutworm.

Cutworms work on a plant night after night, on one leaf and then another. A plant that starts out strong and is transplanted into soil with peak fertility can withstand the loss of a few leaves much more easily than a weak plant on poor soil. If the nightly destruction is greater than the daily growth, the plant becomes rapidly weaker until all reserve is gone and it stands helpless. On the other hand if the daily growth keeps up with the nightly destruction, in just a few days the plant is running away from the cutworms and striped cucumber beetles. This is not to say that strong plants on fertile soil will withstand the attacks of all predators; but they probably stand a better chance of surviving. In addition to faring better against predators, a strong, healthy seedling tends to become a strong, healthy vine loaded with large quantities of early maturing fruit.

Soil and weather conditions play a big role in muskmelons. The best and largest melons are produced by heavy soil, though they tend to mature later in the season. Vines on heavy soil can take dry weather for a longer period of time than those on light soil but are more vulnerable to damage from an extended period of damp, cloudy weather. Wherever possible, try to set out melons on both heavy soil and on light soil, so that there will be melons for all conditions and for both the early and later markets.

Irrigation may prove to be a lifesaver during dry years, but those who have no irrigation system should not be disheartened. A couple of years ago we went through an extremely dry season. The hot dry wind blew day after day. As a rule the crops that we were unable to irrigate did poorly. There was a world of difference, for instance, between the irrigated tomatoes and those without irrigation. And without irrigation, the potatoes, cabbage, and broccoli all did very poorly, as did almost everything else—*except for the muskmelons*. The unirrigated muskmelons did surprisingly well. After this enlightening experience, I shifted emphasis away from irrigation to better weed control and better moisture conservation through a summer fallow program.

I usually cultivate the melon field two or three times. The larger the vines become the more teeth are removed from the center of the three-point-hitch field cultivator. The final cultivation of the season is made just before the vines close the rows off entirely. All but the outside teeth are then removed from the cultivator: the vines just barely fit between the wide front tires of the tractor, and some are actually driven over. In a week or two, the vines converge to form a solid mat that will hold down weed growth. This final cultivation is a very important one. I am always impressed by how quickly a clean field will turn green with weeds. On occasions I have let this last cultivation slide by, thinking that the field was clean enough, and almost invariably I have come to regret it.

By the time the last cultivation is made, the field is yellow with blossoms and perhaps even small fruits. With each day the field turns greener and greener. At first, from a distance, the field looks black with narrow green ribbons to show that any vegetation at all is growing in it. But once the row reaches a width of three or four feet, a week of warm weather can suddenly turn the field into a green carpet with a mass of advancing ends, all poised and alert. Tiny marble-sized fruit grow to baseball size in just a few days, then to the size of softballs or bigger, with lines of netting etching themselves across the glossy green skins.

With plant and fruit growth accelerating so rapidly at this stage, one would think that fruit would ripen up any day. But such is not the case. Almost as if it were deliberately bent on straining a person's patience, the muskmelon vine holds its full-grown, heavily netted fruit for what seems like weeks before allowing them to show even a trace of yellow on the crowns of their ribbing. It is during this time that the muskmelon plant is bringing its seeds to maturity. Once the first fruits ripen up, however, it won't be long before the field is in full produc-tion. When a melon has turned from its dark green color to a light shade of yellow, give it a gentle twist. If the stem releases without a struggle, the fruit is ready; if the stem doesn't let go, leave the fruit for another day or two and try again. Usually there are a few vines that wilt and die. Their fruit will turn yellow and release from the vine but will not have the full flavor. Some of these are the first to ripen and can be a bit of a disappointment. Don't worry, though, as the rest will be along shortly.

Learn to judge your own variety for maturity. During warm weather, it may take only four days from the time the fruits are yet too crisp until they have already passed their prime and become mushy. Most customers prefer the firm melon that can be eaten right down to the rind. Once into the harvest routine, we pick through the field every two days. If the weather cools off we may go through the field every three days.

As for sweet corn, we use burlap picking aprons fastened to the belt with stout wire hooks. Care must be taken not to load them too full, or the bottom melons may bruise. Melons are deposited along the edge of the roadways from where they can be loaded onto the trucks or trailers. Unlike sweet corn harvesting in which we harvest virtually every decent ear, this melon harvest is quite selective. The rationale be-hind this is that it is more difficult for customers to pick out a good melon than a dozen good ears of corn. Consequently, when there is an abundance of truly superb melons I leave behind the questionable ones, such as those getting too ripe or those that have ripened on dying vines. Small underdeveloped melons may never make it out of the field, either.

Marketing melons.

Selling muskmelons can be enjoyable, especially when you know that your melons are prime and that customers will be delighted.

Offering a free sample is a very important part of my muskmelon marketing. The melons look good and smell better, but it is the taste or the memory of a taste that sells them week after week.

Over the years a consistently good melon gains a reputation. People will look for your melons and talk about them. You will get your price especially when people are seldom disappointed by a bad melon and when they learn they can get a free replacement without even showing the poor melon.

A good display is essential to moving muskmelons. We have found that the more produce you set out on display the more you move; in other words, the appearance of volume creates volume. Hired hands are reminded to unload the melons and get them piled up on the ground. If the melons are at their peak and each day presents a challenge to move as many as possible, then be sure to get them off the truck and out on the ground. Stack a dozen or two out by your roadside signs. Make mountains of them around your stand so that shopping means navigating around piles of melons. Open up a dozen melons or more and ring your display with the halves. (Use your culls for this purpose; we save melons that have been sampled by mice, or that have cracked open, or that have started to ferment around the stem, because once open the melon's blemishes can be hidden. No one samples these opened display melons for flavor so you are safe with whatever you use.) Then, as the day progresses, keep your display neat. Freshen up your open halves by shaving off the cut surfaces so that they will appear moist and orange. Round up the stray fruit that has rolled away from the piles as people work the melons over. As the day wears on and the big melons become harder and harder to find, sort through the remaining ones yourself and put the big ones in a very conspicuous place.

For your own reputation it is a good policy to send home with your customers the big melons that have been favored by the vine. As a rule they are the tastiest. So, if you are selling melons by the pound it is especially important for you that at the close of the day you end up with melons that sell for an average of 35 cents each instead of 85 cents each.

If it looks like you will run out of melons before the day is over, you need not bother about selling more than one melon per customer. In fact, so as not to be sold out when a devoted customer stops later in the day, it might even be wise to steer away from the muskmelon department and talk about sweet corn or tomatoes or whatever you happen to have in abundance.

If, after giving samples and tending to your display you are still having difficulty moving your harvest, try giving a little volume discount. This can be done in several ways. If it looks like you will end the day with only a few left over, get rid of your prime melons first and then put out a 5 P.M. special. Mention to your customers that you would like to sell out and go home, and offer, say, four melons for $1.25. Or you can offer a fourth one free if they purchase three. If it is a slow Tuesday and you have more melons than you think you could possibly get rid of in eight hours of selling, start your offer first thing in the morning. Go four for the price of three. If the customer selects three jumbos, make the free one another jumbo. A community can absorb a lot of melons at the right price.''

23: Cauliflower: a good fall crop

''WHAT CAN A market grower sell when the normal growing season is over? After sweet corn and tomatoes comes melons. But what is there to sell when the melon season is past?

In the North Country, we have but seven or eight weeks from the time the first field of sweet corn is ready for market until killing frost.

Those are good and profitable weeks, but make up but a fraction of the year. For the market grower who is depending upon these brief weeks for much of his yearly income, the period is all too short. Even another four weeks of profitable selling would make a big difference, and many growers take full advantage of such season-extenders as baking squash, pumpkins, ornamental corn, gourds, onions, and cauliflower. Not a single one of these items moves for us like sweet corn or melons, but the combined daily sales are usually quite good. One of the best items on this list is cauliflower. While we absolutely cannot sell cabbage, large white heads of cauliflower sell rather well—fortunately, because the plant is hardy and the best heads form after the summer heat is over, as the cool fall weather moves in. The cauliflower plant is not hurt by normal fall frosts. In fact, we have picked them as late as November, even digging around in the snow to find them.

Perhaps one of the reasons cauliflower sells so well is that it is not often raised in the home garden. People who would never stop for your corn and tomatoes because those crops are growing in their backyards will pick up your cauliflower. Growing cauliflower is a little tricky, as evidenced by the number of people who try it once or twice and then give up. Unless carefully tended it will be eaten up by cabbage worms. Also, at a certain stage of development it needs to be tied up, and this is a bother. Finally, cauliflower needs proper soil and adequate moisture. All these things tend to discourage the home gardener.

To be honest, though we have raised it for both the retail market and the wholesale market, selling it by the truckload, cauliflower is not one of our more spectacular success stories. We have seen thousands of young plants bolt. Thousands have been destroyed by cutworms. And thousands of promising plants have failed to reach maturity before the weather turned cold. We have worked till late at night trying to meet market deadlines. During warm weather we have had entire shipments go bad. Sometimes we have been so discouraged with the cauliflower market that we have resolved to drop it entirely. Yet we return to this vegetable each year and can even recommend it for others. Here are some of our thoughts.

After three years of wholesale marketing, my conclusion is that good-quality green-jacket cauliflower in uniform containers is in demand and will sell, but that the wholesale price is poor reward for all the labor and hassle in raising, packaging, and hauling it to market.

Now obviously, some growers feel differently, as there is always cauliflower for sale in the supermarkets. You may be one who can do it. However, for the average family-sized, organic truck farm, the best market for limited quantities of cauliflower is retail. There are no deadlines to meet. And there is no packaging to be done. Although you spend your day selling, which you wouldn't need to do if you simply delivered your load to a warehouse, you come home in the evening with a retail price for each head you sell. Besides, it is a lot more fun standing beside your truck, trimming out the cauliflower with a machete and handing them to delighted customers.

Start the season off with a good variety. My own story would probably be different if my first attempt had been made with some of the unsuccessful varieties I have since tried out. As it was, I scored a success the very first time. There was nothing to it. Starting from seed, I had giant heads by the end of August.

Other varieties have bolted—that is, formed premature half-dollar-sized heads in the hot summer weather. One variety failed to reach maturity before the short Minnesota growing season was over. Some varieties had a rather high percentage of poor-quality heads.

If you choose to raise cauliflower from seed, be sure to start with a relatively weed-free field of rich, heavy, black soil. Plant seed a half-inch to an inch deep every few inches apart. Allow at least 30 inches between rows and more if your cultivation equipment so requires. When your plants stand six inches high, thin them out so that the nicest plants are spaced about 30 inches apart. I have successfully experimented with 18- and 24-inch spacing but recommend extra distance for the biggest and nicest heads.

To avoid the extra weeding created by seeding cauliflower directly into the field, the organic grower may find it more economical to start the plants in the greenhouse. When it does come time to cultivate, the plants are already standing six to eight inches high. This allows for close cultivation without burying any plants.

We raise plants in eight-celled plastic packs, with eight packs in a 10-by-20-inch flat (in other words, 64 plants to a 10-by-20-inch greenhouse flat). Fill your flats with the empty plastic packs and then scoop in the potting soil. With a clothespin or finger, make a half-inch depression in each cell. Drop two or three seeds into each depression, and level off the soil, adding just a little more if needed to fill the packs up nicely. When your quota for the day is reached, sprinkle the flats lightly with water and cover with newspaper. Moisten the newspaper once or twice a day, and remove after the plants have sprouted. While the seedlings are still very small, pull all but the best seedling in each cell.

Planting dates are important with cauliflower. We don't want to see any mature heads until after Labor Day. Any earlier and the weather is too warm; plants don't make the beautiful heads that they do later in the season, and it is too hard to retail them because they wilt so quickly. For us this means seeding the crop into the greenhouse from the middle to the end of April and transplanting them into the field from the first week in June to the middle of June. (We have harvested cauliflower that was set out as late as the first week in July.) A six-week-old cauliflower seedling is a nice size for transplanting. It is big enough to grab by its stem and jerk out of the greenhouse pack, and it stands tall enough so that it can be quickly popped into the ground without burying any leaves. If younger than six weeks, the plants are too small to handle and transplant with ease. If much older than six weeks, they may become stunted and tend to bolt. As long as they remain in the greenhouse flats, keep them looking green and healthy with occasional feedings (greenhouses are covered in Chapter 31).

Yellow lower leaves are a sign of stress. The longer the plants remain in this stress condition, the worse they will become. Remove the cauliflower plants from the greenhouse at least a week before you anticipate setting them outdoors to harden them to cooler temperatures, wind and sunshine. Transplant cauliflower as you would tomatoes or peppers. Leave approximately 30 inches between plants. This may look a little far apart, but under good conditions a healthy cauliflower plant will eventually take up all that space and more, standing 30 to 36 inches tall. A plant this large will often conceal a forming head without being tied up until the head is of marketable size. If tied up, the head will remain firm until it reaches the size of a dinner plate and a weight up to six or eight pounds. As a rule it is easier to sell one of these jumbo heads for $1.25 than it is to sell a smaller one for 75 cents.

Controlling cabbage worms is very important to successful cauliflower production. For poison-free biological control we use the bacterium *Bacillus thuringiensis,* sold as Dipel and other tradenames. While very effective for the cabbage worms, it is harmless to birds, fish, and humans. You can purchase the dry powder and mix it with water as needed. For a simple, inexpensive spray unit we use a common household spray bottle that sends out a fine mist. A pint or quart bottle holds enough solution for many, many plants. In order to spray with the bottle in an inverted position, the little tube that reaches down to the bottom of the bottle must be pulled out. A single person taking two rows at a time can move right down the field at a slow walk. When the plants are small the entire plant can be covered with a single squirt or two. As the plants get bigger, poke the nozzle right into the very heart of the leaves and give the core of the plant two or three squirts.

As the field begins to approach maturity and occasional heads start to show deep down in the center of the plants, it's time to wrap up the cauliflower. Tie a carpenter's apron around your waist and fill it with number-32 rubber bands. When you find a head that is starting to show through the leaves, spray the head and center leaves thoroughly. Then slip a rubber band over the thumb and fingers of one hand, gather as many leaves possible with the other, and slip the rubber band over the plant so as to tie the entire plant up into a bundle. Give the leaves a firm squeeze to seat the rubber band securely. For ease of identification, use different color bands for different trips through the field.

Harvest heads when they are large and yet very firm and tight. If you wait too long they will become coarse underneath and some of the leaves around the base of the head may turn brown. If you cut the head too early it will be good and tasty but smaller and less valuable on the market than if you had waited just another few days. When just a week can make the difference between a 50-cent head and a $1 head, you might as well wait.

Harvest your cauliflower in the cool morning hours while they still retain the dew and cold of the night. Keep the leaves around the heads for protection and place them in the shade. On warm windy days you may wish to cover harvested heads with a tarp to hold evaporation down to a minimum.

The more cauliflower heads you can display at your stand, the more you will sell. By the same token, the more heads you open up for display, the more will wilt down and become unacceptable to your customers. If the day is warm, open up two or three of the very choicest-looking heads for display. Then to make up for lack of display, talk cauliflower.

Always sell the biggest and best heads first unless a customer specifically asks for a small one. Offer to trim each head that you sell. As long as the freshly trimmed leaves look crisp and green, you may wish to let them accumulate in a pile beside the truck or scale as a sign that you have already had a number of cauliflower customers.

Your cauliflower sales will probably never match those of sweet corn or melon. But in the late fall, this crop should keep your stand busy." "

24: Weed control

"COMMERCIAL GROWERS TYPICALLY handle weeds with herbicides, used either alone or in combination with cultivation. It's probably safe to say that most of the fruits and vegetables displayed on our grocery counters have been exposed to these chemicals. Many producers and consumers alike would prefer to get away from chemical herbicides. Is there any economically feasible way to work a truck garden without herbicides?

The organic movement in our country until now has been primarily associated with home gardens, and with great success. But a commercial garden presents different problems. Not only will inefficiency and poor gardening practices show up more quickly than in the smaller home garden, but success is also measured in entirely different terms. The home garden is successful if it bears a reasonable harvest. A truck garden is successful only if it makes money. The question is: Can a truck garden make money using only mechanical measures to control weeds? To put it another way: Can mechanical weed control match chemical weed control in a business venture, in terms of time and money?

I feel the answer at this time is no. Many USDA and extension people are sympathetic toward the organic movement as far as home or hobby gardens are concerned. But when it comes to commercial-scale operations the prevalent feeling is that organic agriculture is not profitable or even possible. Time, of course, will prove which type of agriculture is actually best and more than a yearly balance sheet will enter the picture. But for now, no amount of wishful thinking or sincere conviction on the part of the organic market grower will change the fact that he is in the very competitive business arena with all other commercial gardeners. To stay alive financially he must come up with a product that is either no more costly to produce than with the chemical approach, or else he must locate customers who will pay a premium for organic produce. It's as simple as that.

Organic truck gardening is still in its infancy. But I can say from experience that our family-sized operation, with its selection of vegetables, its climate, its location, and its retail market, is proving successful with the organic approach. There is a challenge to it. We entered the competition with certain built-in handicaps, but also enjoy certain advantages.

Organic weed control is more involved than aerial spraying, incorporating such practices as summer fallowing, delayed plantings, crop selection, cross cultivation, dragging, and prompt tilling after harvest is removed. But based upon my experience, I feel that through diligence and care an organic grower can indeed compete with chemical agriculture.

Summer fallowing.

Summer fallowing is the practice of keeping a field tilled up and black throughout the summer without planting it. There are pros and cons to this practice. One disadvantage is that valuable land is kept out of production for a year. It also costs money to run a tiller or field cultivator periodically through the field during the growing season. A third disadvantage is that a black field is not raising any humus, while the existing humus is breaking down. Without an outside application of manure or humus of some sort, the net result is likely to be a decrease in total humus, resulting in poorer tilth or soil texture. On the positive side, summer fallowing encourages accumulation of moisture and destroys weeds and weed seed.

I have found a summer fallow program very profitable, especially in controlling weeds. Onions, for example, can be a hard crop to raise because of the need for hand weeding. Keeping the onion field fallow the season before planting saves a great deal of hand weeding. Occasionally we have mistakenly gotten outside of the area which was summer fallowed—the ends of the onion patch, for example, may have extended into land that was not kept black, or an outer row or two—and it does not take long for us to discover the mistake. In a couple of weeks the outline of the summer-fallowed field is evident. Any part of the onion field lying outside that outline is covered with a mat of green weeds, and the prepared patch is always noticeably cleaner.

Summer fallowing may prove to be the best approach to weed control for all small row crops. Otherwise, such crops as onions, lettuce, and spinach are apt to be plagued by weeds. I am also turning to the summer fallow approach for melon crops, finding that the savings in labor more than offsets the cost of land, fuel, and machinery wear required to keep land black for a season.

I do not normally use the summer fallow practice with sweet corn production because with my tractor-mounted cultivator and drag, weedy fields are little trouble. But for growers relying primarily on hand tools for raising corn, summer fallowing can practically eliminate the need for cultivating the field. Just plant the seed, perhaps run quickly through the field with the hoe or wheel hoe, and then wait for harvest. Of course this type of program requires an extra field each year, as one is not in production. It would also require the services of a tractor and digger or tractor and disk to periodically run through the field during the summer. You may be able to find a farmer who does custom work for others.

Where yearly rainfall allows, a cover crop can be grown and then turned into the earth to build up humus. This cover can even be the first crop of weeds that springs up early in the season. The important thing, of course, is to turn your cover crop into the soil before any of your weeds go to seed. If other humus is available, such as barnyard manure or old haystacks, the fallow period is a good time to spread it over the field. In this way humus can be maintained even though nothing is growing.

Where rainfall is limited, it may be wise to keep the field entirely black throughout the summer in order to accumulate as much moisture as possible for the coming year. In this case it might be best to plant some contoured erosion strips to hold the soil during heavy rains and strong winter winds.

Delayed plantings.

Delayed crop plantings are sometimes employed as a modified form of summer fallowing. Early plantings are more apt to run into stiff competition with weeds than late plantings, since early spring is the time of the year when weed seeds germinate fastest and most prolifically. In the early garden both radishes and weeds come up together. Carrots and weeds come up together. Beans and weeds come up together. For backyard hobby gardeners this presents no problem; they have been waiting to get into the garden all winter, and the weeds are often little more than a weekend diversion. But a commercial operation is different. Every weed that sprouts in the truck patch cuts into your potential profit. Enough weeds in your carrots for instance, and the labor needed to weed the crop will be so great that no one will be able to afford them. Either that or your time spent raising them will be worth very little after you finish selling your carrots at the market price.

For a certain few cases, however, a modified summer fallow practice will also work out quite well. You simply wait with your plantings until most of the weed seeds have already germinated, then till your soil and plant. The late tilling destroys those very weeds you would otherwise have had to pull by hand. The longer you wait before planting your crop, the more the weed seeds are allowed to sprout and the more you will destroy by tilling. Obviously this practice lends itself to only certain items. You cannot hit the early sweet corn market, for instance, if you wait to plant until the weeds have sprouted. Cool-weather crops such as potatoes, peas, lettuce, and radishes can't wait until the weeds have sprouted either, as the weather might become too warm. Other items need all the growing season just to reach maturity by the time the first frost comes in the fall. To delay their planting would be unwise.

What crops remain then? For us, late plantings of sweet corn work out well. We try to plan our season so that the weediest fields are reserved for the latest plantings of sweet corn. Our last planting of sweet corn goes in around the final week of June. That gives us two months of prime weed time to keep those weedy fields black. In central Minnesota, a fall crop of cauliflower planted around the middle of June also works out well. Even a delay of ten days or two weeks is helpful. Melons could be set in the field sometime around the middle of May, but by starting the plants indoors and then transplanting fairly large seedlings into the field around the first of June, we get a small jump on the short Minnesota summer and can keep the melon field black just a little longer. Those extra two weeks mean a lot when it comes to weeds.

Plant your squash and pumpkins in the weeds.

Both pumpkins and the vining squash varieties offer the organic gardener an excellent opportunity to beat the weeds. Again, success depends on a modified summer fallow program. Plant pumpkins and squash when the soil and weather are warm. This means that by the time the squash field is ready to plant, the weed seeds have already had several weeks in which to germinate. This is good, as the sprouted weeds will be destroyed as the seed bed is prepared. Then plant your squash or pumpkin seeds. The key to using these vigorous vining plants to control weeds lies first of all in the fact that relatively few seeds are required to plant a large field. Whereas onions may be planted, for instance, every 4 inches in 34-inch rows (actually onion rows need be only half this far apart) with a total of some 40,000 plants per acre, squash and pumpkins can be planted every 3 or 4 feet in 12-foot rows with a total of only 1,000 plants per acre. Just having 39,000 fewer plants per acre to weed is in itself a big help. Second, and more important, those 8- to 12-foot rows are easily kept black by tiller or tractor for some time after the seeds have been planted. Then just before the young vines choke up the rows with their sprawling runners, make a final pass through with your field cultivator or digger. A few runners will be cut off but in a week or so the vines will converge over the wide weed-free rows, and weeds won't have much of a chance. This method not only gives the organic grower a way to use fields that are full of weed seed, but if done properly will also provide a relatively clean field for the following year.

Cross cultivation.

One of the old-standby methods of weed control is cross cultivation, which can be used with such crops as tomatoes, peppers and muskmelons, all of which are set out by hand as little seedlings. It is difficult to line up the rows for cross cultivation using a transplanter, but plants set out by hand are no problem at all.

In order to transplant seedlings by hand it is necessary to mark out the rows beforehand to assure proper spacing. With but a little extra work the row marker can be drawn through the field a second time at right angles to the first marking. Where the lines intersect, down goes a little plant. All those weeds that would otherwise be left in the line of the row itself can now be whisked out with a pass of the cultivator.

For cross cultivating such things as melons and tomatoes, I use a three-point-hitch cultivator outfitted with overlapping sweeps. The single row passes under the middle of the tractor. For small melon plants, a set of rolling shields (discussed later in this chapter) is attached to the cultivator to defend the fragile plants from tumbling dirt clods. The nice thing about this particular style of cultivator is that, as the vines extend themselves and take up more room in the row, the cultivator sweeps can be removed one or two at a time until eventually vines four or five feet wide are passing between the remaining sweeps.

Dragging weeds out.

Spring's first crop of weeds is the most difficult to contend with, as they are abundant and aggressive at a time when the garden plants are still very small. Later in the season your plants will have grown larger, making it easier to cultivate them or to work around them with hand tools. They are then large enough to start giving the weeds a little competition of their own. Besides, later in the season the crop has been cultivated once or twice already, and though the weeds never cease coming up, their numbers are now greatly reduced. But what method can be used on that first set of weeds when the garden plants are still very small?

Dragging can be an answer for certain crops. Take sweet corn for example. Sometimes in order to hit the early market, commercial growers push the season just a little by planting seed when the weather is still a little too chilly. The result is that germination may take two or three weeks instead of just one week, while hardy weeds thrive. They spring right up and will quickly crowd out the emerging young corn plants if given the chance. This is where the drag comes in. Just before your little corn shoots begin poking their way up through the soil, go over the field once or twice with the drag. As you do this you will notice the countless white, hairlike roots lying disturbed on the surface. In another week these tiny weeds would have become firmly established, but at this stage, they are not securely fastened and any stirring around in the soil easily dislodges them. The corn lies just below the surface and suffers very little damage. It will emerge in a day or two into a relatively clean field.

By the time you are presented with a second crop of weeds, your young corn plants will already be several inches tall, and well enough established for either their first cultivation or a second trip through with the drag. As explained in the chapter (20) on sweet corn production, it is very important that you only drag your field of sweet corn before the plants come through the ground and again when they reach six inches in height. (At other times, tiny seedlings will be buried, or tall plants will be broken off.)

This method of dragging out weeds also works for both peas and potatoes, providing the plants are still underground. And you may find that there are other large, deep-rooted vegetable plants that lend themselves to this practice. Of course, there are some such vegetables that do not. Squash, melons and beans do not fare as well, being rather fragile and having large folded leaves. Still, even with these crops you may find it expedient to simply plant more seed than normally required and then use the drag anyway. Although a large percentage of plants will be destroyed, the extra-thick planting should compensate for the loss and ensure a good stand in spite of the dragging. The money spent for extra seed may be more than repaid by the savings in labor gained by not weeding. The dragging method is obviously limited to those crops which have large, deep-rooted seedlings. Small plants such as carrots, beets, onions, and spinach would, of course, fare no better than the weeds.

Burying weeds.

Mechanical weed control typically involves pulling the weeds out of the ground or chopping them off at the roots. A tool goes into the ground and the weeds are either dislodged or severed. It is hard for some people to think of any other type of weed control.

With a tractor and a cultivator, however, one can also bury weeds under a layer of dirt. This is done in the course of regular cultivation. The cultivator shovels go into the ground and dislodge or sever the weeds between the rows and at the same time the shovels next to the row, being set just right, actually toss the dirt up against the young garden plants. Viewed from the tractor, an inch or two of dirt actually seems to flow around the plants, completely covering all but the tallest weeds. Providing the weeds are small, the garden plants are at least five or six inches tall, and the soil is loose, this type of cultivation can be used to great advantage. A field that is beginning to turn green with small weeds can be quickly and easily taken care of both between the rows and in the row itself with a single pass of the cultivator at the strategic time.

This method works for sweet corn, tomatoes, green peppers, cole crops, potatoes, and erect squash plants. Almost any crop that grows tall enough and stout enough to withstand the movement of dirt around it can be cultivated in this way. Needless to say, there is a stage for every crop at which the plants are too small for this kind of treatment. Experience will teach which crops can have dirt thrown around them and when.

What about mulching?

In recent years organic gardeners have popularized the use of mulch in controlling weeds. Mulching can be done with barnyard manure, compost, leaves, grass clippings, old hay or straw, sawdust or wood shavings, and a number of other organic products and by-products. Properly applied, mulch will effectively eliminate weeds. When the plants are up and large enough to be clearly visible, mulch is laid down between the rows to form a three- or four-inch-thick blanket. This blanket covers and kills existing weeds and at the same time prevents the germination and growth of new ones. No hoeing and very little hand weeding will be required through the entire season. The catch for the large-scale gardener is, where does one get sufficient organic material to mulch even half an acre, not to mention many acres? Seven hundred fifty cubic yards (a large dump truck holds 12 to 15 cubic yards), on a 16-acre field, for instance, would only make a layer one-third inch deep.

Even if an abundance of mulch material is readily available, you still would have to use it with care. Sawdust, wood shavings, and other slowly decomposing organic matter may monopolize the available nitrogen in the soil for a time before they are ready to release it themselves. Don't be hurt by the nitrogen cycle! Furthermore, just as mulch may give the hot-climate gardener a chance to raise crops that would otherwise demand cooler weather, so hot-weather plants requiring all the warmth a northern summer can muster may be jeopardized by this insulating cover of humus. Tomatoes appear late and melons may not come in at all. Even if large quantities of mulch material are available, use a great deal of caution in applying it extensively for weed control.

Don't raise weeds after the harvest is over.

After you have taken your harvest off, be quick to turn your stubble and weeds back into the ground. This is especially important with vegetable crops that mature early such as peas or early sweet corn. Very likely your peas, for instance, will finish bearing before most varieties of weeds have been able to produce viable seeds. By turning in your pea field immediately after harvest you actually have a chance to sneak a harvest out of a field that is essentially kept fallow all summer. Later maturing crops do not offer the same opportunity as peas but the principle remains the same—turn your weeds in as soon as possible after harvest is over and you will fight fewer weeds the following year.

Tools and equipment for weed control.

For small commercial gardens of an acre or two, a good hand tiller will handle both tilling and cultivation. Be sure that you plant your rows at least 12 inches wider than the width of your tiller; if your tiller will make a 24-inch cut, plant 36-inch rows. This may sound like an unnecessary amount to allow for cultivation, but to leave less is to invite trouble, unless you are familiar with the best row width for your tiller.

There is a way to cultivate an acre or two without an expensive hand tiller. A wheel hoe is an exceptional tool for keeping a big garden clean. They are available new or can often be picked up very reasonably with the help of a little ad in the newspaper. Rather than using the familiar cultivating attachment that scratches the ground with its five or six fingerlike shanks, as most of these wheel hoes come equipped, you may wish to improvise a knifelike cultivator that slices through the ground just under the surface, cutting off weeds at the roots.

Cultivation must be done while the weeds are small, especially if hand tools are used. If the weeds are small and grow in loose soil, the wheel hoe can actually be rather fun to operate. Using a wheel hoe with a thin, well-tempered blade, measuring 15 to 18 inches wide, you can cultivate a garden almost as fast as you can mow the lawn with a manual lawnmower. Of course, if you wait until the weeds are several inches high you will fight with cultivation just as you would fight to mow six-inch grass.

As the market garden grows in size, growers consider small farm tractors and attachments. For help in selecting equipment, consult university extension services, government bulletins and other truck gardeners, as well as equipment dealers. But most beginning commercial gardeners can't afford to go out and buy the complete set of tailored farm equipment. More than likely you will end up purchasing a used row-crop tractor at a farm auction with a plow, disk, and two-row cultivator. Then, like many others, you will simply learn to make do with what you have. With a narrow-front-end tractor and a mounted two-row cultivator, you should be able to cultivate all of your 36- to 40-inch rows including tomatoes, peppers, and cabbage—providing you transplant these items at precisely the right distance apart so that you don't dig up one row while cultivating the other. A two-row transplanter adjusted to match the width of the cultivator will solve the problem of spacing. If you have a matching two-row corn planter and cultivator you can use your two-row corn planter to mark the field. Your little plants are then transplanted down the impressions left by the packer wheels of the corn planter. This way you are assured that they will line up well with the corn cultivator.

To accommodate the two-row corn cultivator, some crops should be planted wider than normally required. Onions, carrots, beets, and peas do not need 36-inch rows. But here it may be cheaper to plant your crops to match the available cultivation equipment than to buy the proper equipment for properly spaced rows.

A cultivator accessory that is very useful when the plants are small is the rolling shield. A two-row cultivator would use two pairs of rolling shields. An implement dealer or blacksmith can provide you with a set to match your equipment. Both the straight floating shields and the round rolling shields are intended to guard small plants from the dirt tossed up by the cultivator shovels. Either style is better than none, but the rolling shield is best.

A row-crop tractor with a mounted two-row cultivator is an ideal tool for cultivating small acreages of sweet corn as well as other row crops having similar spacing between rows. But it may lack versatility needed for other types of cultivation and field work. I have found a more versatile tractor for the small commercial operation is one with a wide front end and a three-point-hitch hydraulic lift. In combination with a small three-point-hitch field cultivator, this tractor can cultivate two rows of corn, beans, onions, and other crops (though perhaps not quite so perfectly as the mounted two-row cultivator). With a small adjustment of the sweeps, it can be converted into a single-row cultivator for bushy crops such as tomatoes and sprawling crops such as melons and squash. In addition, by simply inserting sweeps or chisels to fill up the entire width of the cultivator, this combination can be used for seedbed preparation and summer fallow work. The more versatile any single piece of equipment is, the less you need to invest in additional equipment. This being the case, the wide-front-end tractor and three-point-hitch field cultivator may prove to be the best buy all around.**

SPECIALTIES

A closer look at what it takes
to grow or process for market.

Four

25: Growing herbs for market

T HE INCREASING INTEREST and popularity of herbs in recent years suggests growing these plants for income, either part-time or full-time. A large-scale business can be planned with sufficient capital or financial backing, but for those with limited funds or experience in business, it is wiser to start out on a small scale. The operation can always be expanded as business develops and experience increases.

Before launching on any business enterprise, suggests herb grower Marion Wilbur, time would be well spent in a thorough self-analysis. First, you should be a self-starter; some people are happier when another makes the decisions and takes the responsibility. Also, commercial herb growers should be able to plan and schedule operations and then follow through on the schedule; a great deal of repeat business will depend on your ability to make delivery when promised. Are you willing to put in long hours, with little return, until the business becomes established and produces a fairly dependable income? Or would this place an undue burden on the needs of the family? Do family members share your interest and enthusiasm? If so, then you could occasionally take off on a business day instead of keeping shop.

Get all the necessary information first.

Become informed of the local, county, state, and federal regulations governing the type of business you are planning. Check out the zoning regulations. Most cities and counties require a business license, usually involving an annual fee. To grow or sell plants, you probably should have a license from the state agriculture department; you'll also be subject to regular inspections by this department to assure that stock sold is free of diseases and pests. The fees will vary with location and type of business; a temporary permit to sell at a fair or show may cost as little as $5, while the annual fee for a nursery may be based on annual sales.

149

In states with a sales tax, a tax permit is required for all retail sales and this will often require a deposit of funds with the state. If herbs are prepared and packaged to be sold as herb teas, you may face health department regulations governing the handling and packaging of these items.

If your plans include hiring outside help, you will have to consider labor laws, social security, unemployment insurance, and workmen's compensation. Some states regulate the hours and wages of juvenile help, and require work permits as well.

The Small Business Administration has area representatives to assist people planning to start their own business, and sponsors courses at some city and community colleges. The SBA also can assist in obtaining financing.

The extension service of your state department of agriculture is a good source of information on subjects relating to soils, crops for commercial growing, greenhouse operations, and plans for building greenhouses. Pamphlets are available, usually at no charge.

Another informative publication *The Small Business Reporter* is available free of charge at any Bank of America community office. Some pertinent issues include: "Advertising," Vol. 9, No. 1; "Financing Small Business," Vol. 8, No. 5; "Opening Your Own Business: A Personal Appraisal," Vol. 7, No. 7; "Retail Financial Records," Vol. 10, No. 4; and "Steps to Starting a Business," Vol. 10, No. 10. To request copies by mail, write Bank of America, Dept. 3120, P.O. Box 37000, San Francisco, California 94137. There is a postage and handling charge.

Where to start.

The best place to start is right where you are. Let's assume that you live in a town or city and have a large backyard area that can be devoted to increasing the family income. Should you check the city zoning department and find that your area is zoned for residential *only*, this usually disallows selling, signs and advertising. However, you aren't restricted from having a hobby greenhouse or gardens, and selling whatever you grow elsewhere, perhaps at a farmers' market or flea market. By using one or more of these outlets regularly, you can develop your own repeat

Marion Wilbur

customers who know they can depend on you to be there at a specific time. Since these events are usually well advertised, you are spared this expense.

The local health food store may wish to carry a line of potted herbs from your backyard garden. In this case, you are getting a wholesale price—less than if you take the plants to the market or swap meets and sell them yourself.

Your little backyard venture may generate all the business that you want to handle, and satisfy you completely. Or, you could consider opening a nursery garden shop. The variety of herbs offered for sale can be greatly expanded. In addition the garden shop can offer for sale a variety of pots, hangers, hand tools, growing mixes, organic fertilizers, and so on. Packaged seeds and a good selection of books on growing would also be suitable.

Another direction for expansion might be an herb–gift shop, with an assortment of plants, pretty pots and planters, and perhaps hand-thrown pottery by local craftsmen taken on consignment, gift packs of herb teas, china or ceramic tea pots, cups and strainers, hanging baskets of herbs, potpourri jars, sachets, herbal pillows, fancy herbal soaps, perfumes and oils, herbal jellies in pretty jars, spice jars with home-grown herbs and spices, books, herbal note paper, and dried arrangements. Herb teas and home-baked goods might be served in a small adjoining room.

Selling at home.

If your property is near an urban area, you may have the ideal location for both growing and selling your wares. With good management, even a few acres can produce a vast number of plants for sale. Location on a through highway or main road would be an advantage, but not a necessity. Once you have established a good business reputation, people don't mind going out of their way for something special they want, and the best advertising is always satisfied customers.

A display garden of herbs, in which the plants can be seen growing in their natural environment, is an effective marketing aid. Plants should be marked with legible tags.

The grower–wholesaler.

Suppose you are located out in the boondocks on a dead-end private road with no traffic other than an occasional neighbor. You might consider becoming a grower–wholesaler growing herbs to supply nurseries and retail outlets in nearby towns and cities. Farm co-ops, grange co-ops, plant shops, and garden shops are all prospects, and prefer locally grown plants to those shipped in with the additional freight charges. You'll need a greenhouse, pots, markers, and flats. Most nurseries sell herbs in three- or four-inch pots. For delivery, a van can be equipped with a rack to hold trays or flats of plants.

Contract growing.

Producers of herbal teas (there are new ones appearing on the market all the time) contract with growers for the herbs they need. To sell by contract, you would need irrigation equipment, a tractor, and equipment for drying, chopping or cutting. Of course you also must have sufficient acreage to work at this scale.

These same companies that market teas are also in need of growers for seed. Herb tea crops are harvested just before the plant goes to bloom, so a separate crop is needed to produce seeds for the next season's planting.

Growing a crop for extracted oil.

This type of operation takes a considerable amount of capital to get started. Marian Wilbur says that growing for the production of oil would require a minimum of 50 or 60 acres for a profitable operation. The investment in equipment, even if some of it were purchased used, would likely be in the neighborhood of $120,000, which would include two large tractors, trucks, pressure tub wagons, choppers, windrower, and the biggest expense—a still. Currently, yields per acre are approximately $950. Expenses per acre are about $600, leaving a profit per acre of $350. This of course varies from year to year, depending on usual farming conditions: weather, amount of moisture, and so on. Normally, good yields can be expected by the third year and thereafter. An additional source of income here would be compost made from the residue after oil is extracted. The local agriculture department agent would be the best source of information for this type of operation.

Mail order.

If yours is a good growing area that is not situated for retail sales, consider mail order. Also, mail order could be a secondary outlet for any of the other retail or wholesale herb-growing businesses already mentioned.

Apparently, it isn't even necessary to have any land at all to be in the herb business. Marian knows of an enterprising young man who has built a very nice business selling seed by mail. He collects seed of native wild herbs, and also collects seed in gardens of friends and acquaintances and packages these for sale.

The beauty of a mail order business is that it can be conducted wherever mail service is available—the residential area in town, or the rural farm that isn't suited for retail trade. It can be maintained as a small family operation or balloon into big business.

One way to contact prospective buyers is by placing ads in local or national publications. Farm and garden publications are the most logical of these. Women's magazines that have a gardening section would also be suitable. Rates are available from the individual publications, and many of them list their classified rates in that section. Cost of an ad may range from several dollars in the classified section to a thousand dollars or more for a full page. Frequency discounts are usually allowed if ads will be continued for several consecutive issues. Ads can be worded to invite inquiry only:

> Jones Organic Herb Farm, large variety culinary herbs, send for catalog (free, SASE, or price). Address.

The wording can also be directed toward a sale:

> Spring special: One each of rosemary, lavender, lemon balm, $X.98 postpaid. Name and address.

In either case, the returns from the ad are the beginning of your customer or mailing list.

Whichever method of advertising you use, keep an accurate record of the response received from different wording, various publications, or lists used so that you can determine which is the most productive for the cost involved. Once you are underway in the mail order undertaking, the best advertising is satisfied customers. Not only do they tell their friends and relatives, but you will also find that some of them will write to the garden section of their local papers or club publications and recommend you as a good source. Because there are always a few unreliable or dishonest people in any type of business, including mail order, some people are hesitant to order by mail from a company unless they have some personal recommendation.

Price lists and catalogs may be no more than a typed list of what you have to offer with prices, rather than a brochure or elaborate illustrated catalog. There is a wide range of prices for printing, depending on method used, paper, and how it is done. A large firm specializing in letterhead and envelope printing may be set up for this type of production and would therefore charge less than the local printer. Also, in most areas there are print shops that put out the advertising papers, which will offer a speed print service. You bring in your camera-ready copy. This can be your typed catalog list, possibly with pasted-on illustrations. The printing costs are quite reasonable, currently about $12 to $15 per thousand for one side printed.

If the time is not overly important, you may decide it is more economical and convenient to prepare your own catalog, order blanks and other literature. A spirit duplicator is adequate for about 200 to 300 copies. A mimeograph will make several thousand copies from one stencil; a hand-operated mimeograph machine can be purchased for about $150, while electric machines will range from about $400 up to $1,000 or more. Most business machine companies allow you to lease the machine of your choice for a monthly fee, which will be applied to the purchase price if you decide to buy it. Paper is cheaper if bought in case lots (ten reams, or 5,000 sheets).

As your business increases and the mailing list grows, you may find that it takes more time than you care to spend to prepare and mail your advertising and plant lists. Some direct mail advertising companies will assist you in planning, preparation, and layout work, and then do the printing, addressing, and mailing for you. They will maintain your mailing lists, keeping them up to date from information you supply. They can do any part, or the whole operation, and if your business is a large one, it may be the best way to go.

Postage rates have been steadily increasing and will probably continue to do so. To keep costs at a minimum, you should closely watch the weight of items shipped. Ship plants in lightweight plastic pots or containers, suggests Marion. Use vermiculite or perlite instead of sand in the mix. If plants are dug from beds and wrapped for shipping, remove as much of the soil as possible without disturbing the root ball, and replace with peat moss.

A quantity of literature or catalogs can be mailed out cheaper by bulk, although service is slower. Apply for a bulk mailing permit at your local post office; at present the cost is $45 for the first year and $40 for the following years. A minimum of 200 pieces of identical mail must be sent out at one time to be eligible for the bulk rate, which is currently 7½ cents per piece of third- or fourth-class mail. The mail will have to be pre-sorted according to zip codes. Your local postmaster can furnish you with all the necessary information.

Planning the first crop.

Having determined what marketing avenues are available, the next step is to start growing the plants. If you have never grown herbs before, then by all means start by raising an assortment of the better-known culinary herbs, both annual and perennial types. During the early spring months, before outdoor work can be tackled, small flats of seeds can be started indoors in a sunny window. A starting selection should include basil, borage, parsley, savory (both summer and winter), horehound, marjoram, catnip, oregano, lavender, chamomile, sage, mints, thymes, and rosemary. Become familiar with all of them, their needs and growth habits. Are they evergreen, or do they go dormant in the winter? Are they annuals or perennials? This will of course mean a whole growing season, spring through winter. Do they need full sun, or will they thrive in partial shade? These are some of the questions buyers will be asking of you.

The perennials you grow will provide you with stock plants from which to take cuttings or divisions for plants to sell. Save seed from the annuals for next season's crop. Start a record book, using a separate page for each variety you plant. Put down the name of herb, source of seed, date of sowing, germination date, and date of transplanting into the growing flat. Also note any special cultural requirements, either from other sources or from your own experience. Make a note of the date plants have developed into a size that would make a saleable herb in a three- or four-inch pot. This information will be valuable when you want to get plants ready for market by a specific date. If the danger of frost is about over by the middle of April, then this would be the date to have saleable plants ready for market. By checking your notebook, you can tell when to sow seeds of the various herbs to have them ready by April 15. You will find that some take a much longer time than others.

Starting seed.

Soil for seed flats should be finely screened and pasteurized. Small amounts can be handled in the kitchen oven. Put about three inches of moist soil in the bottom of a deep pan and cover with heavy aluminum foil or a large-size roasting bag. A meat or candy thermometer may be poked through the foil to about one-half the depth of the soil. Set the oven to 180°F (82°C) and let the soil remain in the oven for 30 minutes after that temperature has been reached. (Higher temperatures will destroy soil structure.) You can use a potato instead of a thermometer; when the potato is done, so is the soil.

Later on, when you really get into growing, you may want the convenience of an electric soil sterilizer. These come in several sizes, with soil capacity ranging from an eighth cubic yard up to a half yard or even larger. They are equipped with a thermostat and automatically shut off when the desired temperature of soil is reached. Prices start at about $300.

As soon as the ground can be worked, start preparing the beds. Most herbs prefer full sun but a few, such as the mint family, will take partial shade as well. Most herbs are not too critical in their soil requirements and an area suitable for a vegetable garden will do well for herbs. Level beds are easier to maintain, but even a hillside can be terraced for herb beds. Almost all of the perennial culinary herbs are winter hardy and can be grown in any part of the country, but there are advantages to the longer growing seasons found in milder climates.

Soil for the beds should be well worked. If needed, work in compost, well-rotted manure, bone meal, rock phosphate, and limestone. Beds for perennials should be worked especially deep. Add enough organic materials, leaf mold, peat moss, decomposed sawdust or shavings so the soil will be loose, mellow, and won't pack hard. This last quality is important: cuttings and divisions are made from stock plants in these beds, and it is much easier to remove side shoots and rooted branches when the soil is loose.

When seedlings have developed the first pair of true leaves, transplant into growing flats. Gradually expose the plants to more sun and air. Cooler temperatures encourage sturdier plants.

Allow plants to harden off before setting into outdoor beds. This is done by setting them outdoors into full sun, at first for an hour or two and gradually increasing the time until they have become well adjusted to the outdoors. They are then ready to set into outdoor beds. Keep each variety separate, and mark the bed. Use waterproof ink, or a nursery marking pen for this. You may remember where each variety is planted now, but by next month you may have forgotten. Water as needed and watch them grow. Note any special characteristics in your notebook. If one crop is not faring well, do some research and find out what it needs.

Use your herbs in the kitchen for seasoning and as teas. Learn as much about each one as you can. These first plants provide a learning experience.

Annuals supply you with seed for next year's crop. Perennials will be your stock plants from which to take cuttings and divisions. When fall and winter come to the garden, make notes of which perennials are evergreen and which ones die back in your area. Make notes of height and size of full-grown plants. Your customers will question you about these characteristics.

As your herb garden grows through the spring and summer months, survey your situation and consider growing on a larger scale to produce enough plants for your anticipated markets. To have plants ready for early spring sales, some type of greenhouse will be needed to start seeds and seedlings while the weather is still cold. A structure adjoining the house or garage may be an economic solution. Heat from the house can be channelled into the greenhouse. No matter what size you decide on, a greenhouse never seems to be large enough. If possible try to lay it out in such a way that additions can be made later on.

A southern or southeastern exposure is best, but not essential; a northern exposure would be poor since herbs should have a maximum of sun during the cold winter and early spring months. For general information on growing under glass, see Chapter 31.

Place greenhouse benches to make the most economic use of available space. Wide spacious walkways may be desirable in a display greenhouse, but cut down on growing space, while costing money to heat and maintain.

If you plan to grow plants directly on the bench, you will need a well-supported and heavily braced bench with sideboards approximately six inches high for holding soil. A bench should be redwood, cedar, cypress, or a wood treated with non-toxic preservatives (avoid creosote or pentachlorophenol). A satisfactory bench for holding pots and flats can be made either of slatted boards, or heavy hardware cloth stapled securely to a sturdy frame; this is preferable to a solid wood platform as it will be a deterrent to slugs and snails. Expect a great variance in lumber prices, according to the area and time of year. Check local prices for estimated costs.

You may wish to consider supplemental lighting for use during the short days of winter, and for overcast periods. A four-foot fixture with reflector and two fluorescent grow-light tubes can currently be purchased for about $24. A timer to turn lights on and off automatically at pre-set intervals now costs roughly $5.

A watering system might be an expensive setup complete with fully automatic drip waterers and misting system; or, a simple hose and sprayer for hand watering can be adequate for a small greenhouse. However it is accomplished, watering is one of the most important greenhouse operations. Water only when the plants need it. Frequency depends on the type of plants, as well as the kind of pots and soil mix used. Clay pots lose moisture through their porous surface, while plastic pots hold moisture longer. Soil additives (such as perlite and vermiculite) retain water longer. During hot sunny days, it would be difficult to overwater, but in winter plants will suffer more from too much water than not enough. In any case, water sufficiently to wet soil thoroughly to pot bottom and allow it to dry out somewhat before watering again. It's best to water early in the day, as plants that don't have time to dry off somewhat before night may be plagued by damping-off. Humidifiers are available, but aren't likely necessary; instead, wet the aisles or floor and use shallow pans filled with water to increase humidity.

You can prepare your own potting soil from compost, well-rotted manure, peat moss, sand, and vermiculite or perlite. It should be pasteurized and screened. Of course, prepared sterile mixes can be purchased to save work and time, but they add to the expense.

Other supplies needed include seed-starting trays or flats, carrying flats, pots, and labels. Bedding trays measuring four-by-eight inches can be used for seed starting in a small operation; in most cases the seed would be sown at intervals of two to three weeks, rather than all at once, to provide a continuing supply of plants. Trays can be purchased either in plastic or fiber material. Plastic trays can be sterilized and used again several times; fiber ones are used once only. The cost for either is approximately $25 to $35 per thousand. Growing flats measuring 12-by-18-inches can be used for seeding in larger amounts, and are convenient for the first transplanting. The cost of these is about $25 per hundred. If you have the material and time, you might build redwood or cedar trays at home. These are much more durable. You would use three-inch pots of peat, fiber, or plastic at about $45 per thousand. Lightweight plastic flats, about 16 inches square, are convenient for holding or transporting pots and bedding trays. They will hold either eight bedding trays or 36 of the three-inch pots and are priced at about $45 per hundred.

Plastic labels may be printed or plain. There are very few pre-printed herb labels available; and if you want to order printed labels with plant variety and your name and address, they must be ordered in very large quantities to be reasonably cheap. To start with, use plain labels and mark the name or variety with a permanent marking pen. These labels cost from $8 to $10 per thousand.

Prices on all supplies vary with area and fluctuate from week to week. Many suppliers do not show prices in the catalog for this reason, but will quote when you are ready to order. Check your phone directory under nursery supplies, wholesale, for sources nearest you. You can also check with nurseries in your area to see where they order supplies.

Harvesting and drying.

For teas, most herbs are cut just before blooming; the oil content is highest at this time and herbs are at their most flavorful and aromatic. An exception to this is chamomile, from which only the flowers are used.

Herbs to be dried should be sprayed with water early in the day to remove dust. When they have dried off, they are ready to cut. Small operations can incorporate the same type of equipment used to dehydrate foods. In order to retain their color and flavor, herbs must be dried in the dark, away from sun and light. A cabinet-type egg incubator can serve as a drier if the temperature is adjusted. Drying temperatures range from 100 to 120°F (38 to 49°C).

For a larger tea-producing operation, a drying room would be more adequate. Drying trays are arranged on racks, and warm, dry air is circulated around and through them.

Herbs being dried for dyeing can be tied in bundles and suspended upside down from rafters in a dry attic or garage. This method is not recommended for herbs to be consumed, for sanitary reasons.

After herbs are dried crisp, strip the leaves from the stems and store in airtight containers, away from light. The package can be no more than a small paper bag with a neat label showing contents and weight; or you may wish to design your own package and have it custom-made for you by one of the container companies.

26: Berry-and-honey money

BERRIES AND HONEY are two popular crops for the part-time grower. They seem suited for generating extra income, as not much land is required, and there is little trouble in selling them. The time was never more favorable to plan for part of your livelihood by the sale of berries and honey—alone or in combination. Your crops, experience and income will grow together along with the increasing demand for natural quality foods. Before starting, consider these general remarks on selling by Charlotte Waldron, a grower from Henderson, North Carolina.

- Assess yourself, your interests and backgrounds which will influence your method of operating, your location, your markets, assured and potential, your income goal from your produce, and any labor sources other than yourself.

- Start small. Unless you already have a toe in the door for a large operation, or can foresee some special favorable circumstance, go easy at first.

Her own honey sales the first year were a modest $64. They grew until she was selling, mostly from the house, between 1½ and 2 tons of honey yearly.

You and your location will determine the type of selling best for you. If you like dealing with an amazing assortment of customers (and non-customers), and if you live on a well-traveled or easy-access road not too far from a population center, then you're set for optimum retailing from the house or from a roadside stand.

If you are already selling other produce from a stand, your customers will welcome the addition of berries and honey. But if you are specializing in berries or honey alone, and want to try it, a small stand that's close to the house is advisable.

In the beginning, at least, sales may not be numerous enough to justify the time and expense of a larger stand even if you do have a traffic-stopper like strawberries or raspberries to sell alone or with your honey. Charlotte tried a small stand, but disliked it because it gave her too much time for darning socks.

If you prefer a minimum of human contact, look for outlets where you can deliver, collect your price, and depart, returning or telephoning at intervals for re-orders. Between honey deliveries it's a good idea to stop by for the purpose of exchanging smeary or label-less jars for fresh ones, and to replace leaky honeycombs—damaged ones are the buyer's responsibility, or should be. Comb honey, being very perishable at the hands of questing little ones, should be displayed up out of their reach. Charlotte never tries to sell large quantities of comb honey, because even if kept properly warm over a long period of time, it may leak if not wrapped airtight, or crystallize and lose its waxen beauty, though not its flavor.

The same is true of chunk honey, so popular in the South where the cut comb speeds the granulation or "sugaring" of the liquid honey surrounding it. It's better to pack as needed, and your retailer will appreciate your concern for his sales.

If your retailer is unfamiliar with selling honey, impress upon him the importance of bagging the jars. Charlotte remembers a sweet old lady who firmly refused an offer to put her five-pound jar into a paper bag. Next morning she was back for another jar, the first having slipped from her grasp while she was hunting for her door key. This time a bag was not declined.

Also, it's advisable to pack your honey in screw-top jars only. Snap-top lids are not reliable, and can be treacherous. Customers bringing such jars to be filled should be warned of possible leakage. If they decline a screw-top substitute, you might place plastic wrap tightly around the top of their own, and secure with a rubber band. An unsuitable container drooling honey over one's car seat is *not* recommended as a booster of honey sales.

If yours is a location unfavorable for drive-in customers, your best bet is to sell wholesale to the best-paying outlets nearest you, such as quality established health food or other retail stores, the busiest roadside markets, or reliable middlemen who will pick up your production.

Selling on consignment is often risky, and payment too long in forthcoming. With perishables like berries, which demand almost daily picking, it's time-expensive to be much on the road, unless another family member can do the delivery. Berries are the most urgent of all produce except sweet corn.

Charlotte has sold honey and berries in a number of ways. The owner of one health food store took delivery once a week at his home. In a nearby suburb another health food store took any berries that didn't go to her private customers. During fall and winter she combined personal trips with deliveries of honey to several stalls in a farmers' market, to a large department store, to a woman's exchange (which usually sold on commission only, but was induced, by charming little eight-ounce jars of honey and honey jellies, to shell out on delivery), and to a hospital gift shop. Besides these outlets, two dealers stopped by, each on his scheduled day.

Another possibility in berry and honey sales is to take orders from co-workers in your factory, office or shop. Charlotte knew of one part-time beekeeper who had a lively trade from his car at the steel mill where he worked; many of the workers were of Slavic origin, known to be honey lovers, and when he arrived at the end of their shift they cleaned him out.

If a local farmers' market is reasonably near, consider renting a table outdoors. You may do well enough—especially with berries—to be able to rent a more expensive location inside the usual adjoining building, free of weather hazards. Each market has its own day or days, and some marketers have regular routes, setting up at each location in turn.

Selling direct from the home has many advantages. With no middleman, you receive full value for your crop. Over the years you can build up a predictable clientele, a reputation for a good product, and a dependable, increasing cash income.

Charlotte pays out five cents when customers provide or return containers. Many have long-saved collections of canning jars which they are happy to sell very cheaply or even give away. The empty screw-top jars are thankfully received, washed, sterilized in the oven, and stored for future use. These cut down very noticeably on the Waldron's glass purchases. It also gives them the advantage of selling by volume rather than by weight. For resale, weights should be stated on the label, but a pint is a pint, whether the honey weighs 22 or 24 ounces. Honey weighs about 1½ times as much as water, varying with climate and weather conditions—honeys from arid regions are lower in moisture content and heavier—but as long as a quart jar is filled to the proper level, no weights-and-measures official can embarrass your resale outlets.

Other advantages of selling from the home are the saving of delivery costs and labels, the convenience and ease for yourself, and the strictly cash nature of the business. All you need is a neat room or screened porch, a display table well stocked, and plenty of change, bags and cartons.

In these days of scant storage space, the Waldrons sell many eight-ounce jars. Small sizes are more costly and time-consuming to handle, but they are a convenience to customers and their lower price spares a tight budget. Charlotte buys new lids for all used jars—12-ounce, pints, two pounds, five pounds, and half and whole gallons. She always overfills a little.

Honey production brings bonuses—you can sell honey cappings for hay fever and sinus troubles. "Many people who had read Dr. Jarvis's *Folk Medicine* come for cappings," says Charlotte. "I would insist on giving a sample before selling a jar, for if the allergy is not caused by pollen, the cappings may not give relief. It is wonderful to see a child chew at first reluctantly, then more vigorously, and in a few minutes turn to his parent and say, wonderingly, 'I can breathe better.'"

Comb honey and cappings.

The most saleable forms of comb honey are individual selections, as cut comb honey, and chunk honey, especially popular in the South, but better known now in other parts of the country than formerly.

The individual section is the fanciest form, and takes the most skill to produce well. Sections are framed in basswood squares or oblongs, based on delicate, almost transparent wax foundation which the bees hopefully will draw out, fill with honey, and seal with a snowy wax coating. Honey in this form commands the highest price, but its production is *not* recommended for the inexperienced beekeeper.

Cut comb is much easier. Standard shallow frames are filled with the same expensive type of wax foundation, but without the supporting wires used in extracted-honey frames. A good honey flow will fill these cut-comb frames with the same honey that would go into sections, but much faster and more abundantly, for bees dislike working in those little partitioned boxes. When filled and capped by wax, the frames are taken from the hive, placed on a cutting board, divided usually into four pieces, allowed to drain a few hours through a level wire sieve (which can be homemade), and then wrapped in the special transparent sheets sold by bee-ware suppliers. As this type of honeycomb is very fragile, it's best to place it in the same standard cardboard cartons that most section combs are sold in. Cut comb is just as delicious, but much messier and time-consuming to prepare for packaging, whereas the section comb, except for a little scraping of any wax or bee glue on the basswood, is ready for wrapping and/or boxing with a minimum of labor.

Beekeeping equipment suppliers sell comb honey wrappers and containers. Dadant's of Hamilton, Illinois, and A. I. Root, Medina, Ohio, have attractive window cartons. The combs or sections really need the protection of double-wrapping, first in transparent sheets sealed with gum arabic dissolved in a little water, and then in the cartons.

The chunk honey pack uses cut comb, but it's cut to sizes most suitable for insertion in a jar, preferably wide-mouthed and squat.

The pieces of comb are arranged so that the largest, most perfect surfaces are visible, packed in snugly, and then surrounded by slightly warmed extracted honey, preferably light enough to display the comb's beauty. If the comb isn't likely to win a beauty prize, use a darker pleasant-tasting honey. This can be a tricky, sticky operation, but it results in luscious eating.

Incidentally, no type of comb honey should be left long on the hive after it's sealed, because the bees' little feet tramping over the snowy surface may darken the wax a bit.

The wax that caps the combs may be white and the honey beneath dark; or light honey may lie below dark-looking unattractive wax. If the bees cap the honey and leave a little air-space between it and the wax, the comb will be much lighter than if they had placed the wax right on the honey. This seems to be a characteristic of some strains of bees; it seems the meaner dispositions usually go with the most attractive work.

Professor Edwin J. Anderson of Pennsylvania State University discovered an ability in certain colonies not only to cap with the airspace, but also to make an exquisite little design, like a tiny star, on each cell. This beautiful finish adds greatly to the comb's appearance—it looks as though fairies had been knitting a popcorn stitch on a waxen coverlet. The problem is to find queens which can transmit this unusual ability, and once Charlotte Waldron was shown a sample, she was on the lookout for it.

"All our 60 colonies were among the great ungifted majority; but visiting an old Quaker orchardist with a few hives, I noticed the pattern on one of his honeycombs, was told which colony had produced it, and received permission to inform Professor Anderson that he could take the queen for breeding purposes.

"Professor Anderson was unexcelled in bare-handed, bare-armed bee-handling expertise, and could locate a queen with unerring speed. We arrived at the orchard, I with a pair of elbow-length gloves that proclaimed my inexperience. I offered them to him, but he declined, rolled up his sleeves, and got to work. In a few minutes he rolled down his sleeves and accepted the gloves. After a twenty-minute battle in vain search for her majesty, Professor Anderson concluded that a queen which handed down that intolerably vicious temper to her offspring was not fit subject for breeding, wax star or no wax star. However, if you ever come across this waxen lace in a decently dispositioned hive, you might try a spot of queen-rearing."

Honey cappings are the cut-off wax which the honey-knife slices from the combs when you prepare to extract. The uncapping is best done over a tub or metal-lined box with a wire sieve supported halfway down and an outlet at the bottom, so that the honey which clings to the wax particles may drain for later skimming or straining.

Beekeepers who know the value of beeswax save these cappings, melt them, and sell or swap them for foundation; but since Dr. Jarvis wrote *Vermont Folk Medicine,* people have learned that chewing these cappings can relieve allergic conditions such as hay fever. Locally produced cappings, moistened with local honey, may contain pollen allergens. Chewing the wax as long as it can be kept in the mouth acts beneficially upon the suffering mucous membranes. Some mean beekeepers put more honey than cappings in their jars, but this is unfair, especially as cappings sell for more than extracted honey.

Beekeepers sell beeswax for candles, for salve, and for dyeing batiks. Hardware stores carry wax for carpenters to ease the starting of nails and screws, and to lubricate sticking drawers and window frames. Tiny molded shapes can be sold for waxing sewing thread to prevent knotting. One day a Pepperidge Farm Bakery employee ordered 20 pounds from Charlotte for their endless-belt cookie ovens. Wax leaves no greasy stain as other lubricants do.

Charlotte suggests keeping plastic spoons on hand to let customers sample different honeys; it's good business to educate their tastes and acquire a name among honey gourmets. To insure having a variety, she takes care when extracting to separate as much as possible the different kinds: bitter-sweet dandelion, peach, apple, locust, tulip poplar, clovers, goldenrod, and fall aster.

"In starting with honey production," Charlotte cautions, "first make sure that no one in your family is allergic to bee stings or to pollen. After reading Dr. Bodog F. Beck's book on the use of bee venom for arthritis by using living bees to sting patients, I went to his New York apartment from which his bees sailed from their hives through special window exits to Long Island and Central Park, and watched him treat a patient. Returning home, I plucked a bee from a flowering clematis vine and induced her to sting my arthritic hip joint. Within minutes my eyelids and lips began to swell and I broke out in great red welts. I phoned the local hospital, and was told to have someone drive me over unless cold water applications would reduce the swellings within 20 minutes. Luckily, they did. Since stings never bothered me much, I guess it was the clematis pollen that caused the reaction—a guess which Dr. Beck confirmed, along with an indignant scolding. He always applied bees *before* they went out on their collecting trips. One sting can prove fatal to allergic subjects."

It is important to place your colonies where they won't cause harm or damage to customers, neighbors or passers-by. Charlotte tells of a doctor she knows who kept his hives out of sight on a garage roof, keeping the line of flight high enough to avoid collisions with humans. A location behind a screen of tall bushes or fence would also insure protection. Where winters are cold enough to keep bees from frequent flights to relieve themselves, a mild winter day may bring relief to them, but not to you. Their droppings on drying laundry or parked cars will win you no popularity contests. Lawsuits have been filed against beekeepers "for harboring a nuisance." If the objections are not too serious, the beekeeper often receives legal help from the local or state beekeepers association, and legal precedents often protect him. But it's best to place hives where the bees will cause no trouble.

Start with two or three colonies bought or acquired from a reliable source, and line up possible customers among neighbors and acquaintances. Your county agent can find out for you the average honey yield in your state. This figure is usually low, and you should be able at least to double it. In southeastern Pennsylvania, for example, when the average state yield was under 45 pounds, good beekeepers were getting 75 and more per colony. In a good season, a production-bred strain of bees gave the Waldrons over 200 pounds. In favorable parts of the nation, yields of hundreds of pounds per hive are not uncommon.

Once started, your operation will be a magnet for bees and equipment. You will be called for removal of stray swarms; your attention will be called to ads offering bees and all that goes with them. If you can go on a tour in your area with the state bee inspector, you will find all sorts of beeware discarded by aged, or departed, or discouraged owners. Never buy uninspected colonies, however, and sterilize all used equipment; one disease-carrying cell can wipe out your entire investment unless you have help, or enough experience, to take prompt and sometimes drastic action.

The cost of setting up a couple of hives.

The ideal way, of course, is to begin with brand new equipment from first-class sources such as Dadant, A. I. Root, or Walter Kelley in Kentucky. It is shipped knocked down for the beginner to put together, and the packaged bees, with queen, are shipped from the South at the proper season, when fruit bloom is starting. Equipment from mail-order houses seems of lesser quality. Prices have risen to the point that a new hive with bees, smoker, veil, and hive tool (a stout screwdriver will answer) will now cost from $75 to $100 each.

But it's possible to start with a much smaller outlay of cash, even for barter, depending on luck and exploring talent. The price is often nominal if you can find used equipment with bees (checked by your state inspector for disease—never buy without such inspection) or used empty equipment which should be sterilized.

If you check classified ads in the *American Bee Journal*, (by Dadant), or in *Gleanings in Bee Culture* (by Root) you may find what you want much reduced. Equipment and bees may pop up in unexpected places; the county agent may know of a source. Ads in a North Carolina farmers' service sheet offer hives, some with bees and (alleged) honey for $35 each. Many would-be beekeepers buy the best equipment, fail dismally their first year, and give up for lack of a little preparation and help. A classified want ad may flush out one or more of these in-and-outers.

It's best to take an experienced beekeeper along to look over the offerings before you buy, and be sure to find out if the bees have been inspected, and when. Some states issue an inspection certificate as proof hives have been checked.

After a year or two with bees, you will know which nectar-bearing sources yield good, poor, or uncertain crops. Keep a diary of blooming dates by noticing what flowers bees are working. By checking the contents of your hives, you will learn if they are gathering a surplus or suffering from lack of food. If you have a good location, don't boast of it. Too often a greedy bee-man will move his hives into an area that can support only a limited number of colonies.

To begin with, count on about twice the average state yield. Your increasing experience and discovery of nectar-lavish outyards will increase your crop.

The Waldrons keep some 60 colonies, and rent to orchards—peach, apple, cherry, and holly—for pollination, another source of income in early spring, when farm incomes are low. Moving bees for pollination usually cuts a yield, but some orchardists are happy to allow a permanent, more productive location in addition to paying for your service.

If honey is cleanly handled, it needs no filtering or straining. The Waldrons extract their honey as quickly as possible after taking it off the hives, placing it into wide-mouthed gallon jars, preferably glass, to stand overnight. In the morning, wax, bee glue, and other flotsam are skimmed off. Unheated honey, quickly sealed, is so much more delicious and healthful that customers taste the difference with pleased surprise, and many will serve as walking advertisements for you.

You can reap free publicity and boost sales by cooperating in swarm removal with your local police department. Offer to speak to school classes in connection with their nature study or biology courses. Take along a glass-walled observation hive, and a supply of small jars of honey for classroom sales, and have the teachers provide disposable spoons for sampling from a large container of your honey—many children have never tasted it. If your bees are gentle, invite visits to your apiary for a demonstration of bee-handling. You might notify your local paper's photographer in advance. Take small jars of honey with you if you give talks on bees or organic gardening to clubs or church groups. They invariably sell.

The number of colonies you plan for will depend on your region. Overstocking your location will result in lowered yields and weak colonies. It's usually impractical to try to supply bee-pasture by plantings, except for pussy willows or filberts to serve as hedges and to supply the early pollen which stimulates and heartens the bees. Figure the poundage you must sell to reach your money goal, calculate your own average yields, and you will succeed to the extent your area permits. Many beekeepers supplement their own crops with purchases from other beekeepers or honey dealers. If you do, buy only honey which meets your own high standards, and don't pass it off as your own.

If your trade requests it, stock special honeys. For instance, around Easter customers of Italian background may want a very light, mild honey for cakes; buckwheat honey is often sought by Jewish customers for Purim baking; Christmas honey-cakes (lebkuchen) are a German specialty.

Berries and honey do together in marketing as well as they do as a dessert, each glorifying the other. From a labor standpoint, the ideal crop combinations with honey are raspberries or blackberries. For largest sales and profit, strawberries and honey rank first in Charlotte's experience; but they compete for labor at the busiest season—the strawberry crop comes in May and June, just when bees demand the utmost attention to prevent swarming and insure a good harvest. This is why you should start on a small scale with these two best sellers, or you'll bitterly regret that you were not born twins.

For a specialty crop that practically sells itself, strawberries stand alone. Of all the berries they require the most labor, so don't decide on the size of your planting without budgeting your available working hours and then testing your estimate with a small planting intensively cultivated and thoroughly harvested. With full-time labor it is possible to produce 10,000 quarts per acre, but for a specialty, a quarter-acre is more than ample. Narrow rows with spacings so as to obtain as many outside plants as possible—that is, bordering the 3½- to 4-foot "middles" or spaces between the rows—yield the greatest number of the fancy berries that bring you top prices.

Strawberries.

Before investing, check the berries offered by nearby growers for earliness and quality. Your county agent can recommend the most suitable kinds. The earliest strawberries command the highest prices, even though they lack the sweetness and size of later bearers. However, you should make your main and later crops equally irresistible and urge your earliest customers to return for the greater delights in store. Charlotte says, "For the utmost in flavor, I have never yet met a strawberry which can approach Fairfax, an old 'non-commercial' variety. It is not recommended for North Carolina, yet 25 trial plants made themselves at home and produced the most abundant crop in my experience; so it's worth testing a variety which has recommended itself to you, whether or not it is supposed to flourish in your locale."

The earliest modern berry, Earlidawn, is certainly worth trying for that early dollar, says Charlotte, even though one catalog mentions "tart" in its description of the variety. "My all-time favorite is Fairfax, incomparable for sweetness, flavor, and, if well-grown, size.

How quickly can you expand a field by dividing plants? An acre with plants spaced two feet apart in the row, with rows four feet apart, takes 5,445 plants; if spaced three feet in row, rows four feet apart, the number of plants is 3,640. A beginner starting with 100 plants in good soil, allowing six of the earliest, strongest runners per plant, and limiting each primary runner to one good secondary runner, would have: 1,200 runners, to plant a bit under a quarter acre with 2-by-4-foot spacing, or almost one-third acre with the 3-by-4-foot spacing.

Using these well-rooted runners from the 100 mother plants, set, say, in 1979, would keep the original 100 in the hill system, which would yield larger, but fewer berries, in 1980. The runners, late-summer planted in 1979 into the larger area, would yield a moderate crop in 1980. By 1980 both plantings, having set runners in 1980, would be in full production. Using 200 original plants, these areas would be doubled.

Of course, some varieties make more runners than others. "In 1975 I planted 25 Fairfax," recalls Charlotte, "described in one catalog as 'a good but not excessive plant-maker,' and not recommended for this north-central North Carolina area. But they simply went wild in the compost-rich soil and after a bumper crop in 1976, shot runners after runners from the original parents and grandparents into an almost solid carpet. After digging up hundreds of the largest runners to give to neighbors whose plants were either damaged or entirely wiped out by the 1976–77 winter, and ripping out baskets of smaller runners stunted by crowding, I say—if there is any more excessive plant-maker, I don't want to meet it."

Some customers new to Fairfax may be put off by the darkening of its red color as it ripens. Just give them a dark-red sample, and objections are forgotten immediately.

Strawberry boxes have become expensive. Veneer (thin wood) quarts are currently quoted at $10 per hundred, and plastic quarts at $7. Plastic boxes are hard on strawberries—the thin edges of their lattices often mar or cut the ripe flesh, but this is unlikely if the tougher commercial varieties are grown. Train your customers to return your boxes and donate store-supplied ones. In a pick-your-own operation, the customer supplies containers or pays extra for yours.

Everbearing strawberries are not a good choice for the market grower. They come in at a time of season when they must compete with cherries and raspberries, and later with blueberries and blackberries, early apples, peaches, pears, and grapes. Another strike against them is that their first-year crop, such as it is, is their best, while main crop strawberries should be good for at least two years. Under skilled care, a third smaller crop can be coaxed out of them.

Everbearers need irrigation in dry weather to produce decent fruit. They need more care; blossoms must be picked off during the first months after planting until mid-June, if off-season bearing is wanted. One plant grower suggests that if they are suffering from drought you should continue to pick off flowers until better weather arrives—if you have that much time to spare and can delay your income. In order to bear, the plants must make enough growth to sustain the demand on their strength. If they don't, you are advised to remove the runners and grow them in the hill system—all this for an uncertain crop of out-of-season berries! The Pacific Coast, though, with its more moderate climate, may find them suitable and profitable.

Strawberries are best picked in early morning, while they are cool. A little dew does no harm, but heavy moisture should be allowed to evaporate in order to prevent heaped berries from growing disastrous beards of mold. If they must be picked wet, place them in containers as shallow as you can provide and store in a cool, airy place until they are fit to go into conventional baskets. This preference for early picking is the only break you'll get if your bee work is heavy in May or June— bees are best worked between the hours of 10 A.M. and 4 P.M., on clear days—standard time, please. Strawberries have no objection to being picked toward sunset, but bees do, and will let you know it.

In a favorable season, strawberries require daily picking. Ideally, you may have someone at home who can take care of selling what you have picked. If you have solicited orders, to be called for at specified hours, your picking times can be tailored to their arrival. Be sure to pick clean, even if you have to freeze or use the surplus; leaving ripe fruit on the plant to mold will endanger the developing berries.

If you aspire to a large enough planting for a pick-your-own (PYO) operation, start classified or display ads before the berries are ripe so that you can space the arrivals. Charlotte suggests you make it an unbreakable rule to bar small children from your fields. "If a customer must bring them, you'll do well to set up a pleasant shaded enclosure with a few large unbreakable and unswallowable toys with a responsible person to take charge while the mother picks. This no-kids rule should be understood before the customer visits your place, or you may have both trampled plants and a resentful parent when you try to protect your property. In fact, you should be on hand to observe and demonstrate technique to inexperienced pickers, both teen and adult, until you see that they can safely be left alone."

There is something about a patch or field of large, ripe berries which arouses passion in the amateur picker, observes Charlotte. Expect to tolerate a certain hand-to-mouth consumption, even a bit of gobbling, also the tendency to fill a quart container to overflowing and then expect to be charged for a normal quart. To nip this inevitable practice, arrange for a single exit from your field, distinct from the entrance, and set up a table or counter with an accurate scale, several of your own containers each with its empty weight marked conspicuously on the side, and a prominent sign pronouncing "Sold by weight." As a picker leaves, his or her collection of berries is carefully transferred from their containers to yours, weighed, and charged for, and replaced in the buyer's baskets or bowls.

If customers appear without containers, have quart baskets in homemade carriers available, and charge for the baskets—they're not cheap nowadays. If you have shallow cartons stocked in readiness, the baskets can travel safely and reach the customer's home in proper condition. Don't split hairs on the weights, but don't cheat yourself. As the season ends, you will probably be deluged with returned baskets, besides donations of all sorts, plastic as well as veneer, and sizes. Sort and store them for your own future use.

Many PYO growers harvest the earliest berries of each planting, skimming the biggest, handsomest ones for their own private sales to high-paying individuals or retailers, and letting in the paying pickers to the later berries in these rows. It's essential that you have your varieties separate or clearly marked with numbered stakes or placards so that you can assign pickers to specified rows. Otherwise they may wander hither and yon, grazing at their own sweet will.

In charging, guide yourself by comparing prevalent prices and by the scarcity or overabundance of the crop. If you have brought your crop through when others have failed from frost, drought, or excessive rain, you can charge almost as much as retail store prices. But remember your poorer customers, and prune the prices to them on the smaller, season's-end berries.

If you begin your strawberry venture with a small pilot planting, you will have the opportunity to take samples of fruit around to prospective outlets (though preferably not on busy weekends). It will give you a chance to explain your plans and standards, and to find out what amount of business they may be interested in doing with you. A complimentary quart of big sweet berries, perhaps sampled during your conversation, may be the clincher for future sales.

When you do sell, retail or wholesale, fill the quarts and pints above the marking line—not quite heaped, but generously convex. "I've seen one storekeeper bring out an empty quart box and fill it from the excess in the ones I had just delivered," says Charlotte. "He was pleased at the little extra profit."

In small country or suburban communities, some churches put on a traditional strawberry festival. Berries may appear on shortcakes, as sauces, sweetened for spooning over ice cream, or whole, having lain in their sugared juice overnight to be served with cream. Sometimes boxes of fruit are displayed for sale, and the greater the eye-appeal, the better the sales for the church's benefit.

Interest in homemade wines is so keen that you might ask permission to post a small sign in a nearby wine-making supplies shop to help sell a large supply of season's-end berries. Here again a gift of a pint or quart to the proprietor helps out; he may even suggest customers to you, knowing that his own business will be stimulated thereby.

Raspberries and blackberries.

These crops both are less labor-demanding than strawberries. If you keep bees, the pruning work is over before the season is advanced enough for nectar flows, and the fruits are ready for picking after the most critical and heavy bee-yard work has subsided. Bees or no bees, if your bushes are properly staked or supported, picking is easy compared to the stooping, squatting, or bending among the strawberries.

But in spite of these advantages, raspberries, unless frozen, are rarely seen in markets—partly because they are more delicate and perishable than their earlier and later cousins, partly because of labor scarcity and cost, and partly because they tend to be a locally favored fruit. They are typically confined to genuine farmers' markets and roadside stands in raspberry-growing areas. Southern New Jersey is still such a region, and Michigan, with its thousands of acres of cut-over forest, was once nationally famous for red and black raspberries and for raspberry honey.

This very scarcity makes raspberries an ideal crop for the organic gardener in a receptive area. If black raspberries are the favorite, there will be no trouble in selling to their eager fanciers at top prices. And black raspberry jelly is as expensive as it is rare in the shops.

The same outlets that buy fancy strawberries will buy your other berries, and again, classified ads will bring PYO customers. European-background buyers, especially Scandinavian, prefer the red raspberries, which are combined with red currants to make a delicious ethnic dessert.

Health food stores with well-managed produce departments would be Charlotte's choice for the most favorable retail outlet; their customers appreciate the fact that these berries are free from chemical sprays. But being a comparatively rare treat, they are easily sold.

To reach the jelly-and-preserve-making elite, check on any county fairs within easy reach. Look at the displays of these delicacies, note the names of the prize-winners, or inquire at the grange or farm bureau booths which are usually present at such affairs for information.

If you are not too far from a real luxury market, or a high-priced farmers' market catering to wealthy suburbanites, plant some everbearing red raspberries and prune for a fall crop in September and October, when they ripen their largest, sturdiest, highest-flavored fruit. Market them as a strictly gourmet out-of-season crop in little cardboard "boats" holding six to eight ounces. Then, if you're disappointed in their sale, next year let them bear their summer crop when the demand peaks around July 4.

For PYO plantings, allow for plenty of space between bushes and between rows so that a thorough job of harvesting is possible. The same applies to blackberries, the thornless varieties being ideal if they have proved themselves in your area.

Before going in for blackberries, inquire of your county agent and the extension home economics department how much demand there is for them. They are such rampant growers and require so much labor to control that you want to be assured of adequate payment for growing them.

In selling to outside markets, be sure to pick the fruit of any berries before they are fully ripe—a piece of advice that goes against the grain, but a practical one. They continue to ripen, or to overripen, in the containers, forcing the buyer to discard much. The result is a loss to the buyer of time, labor, temper, and sales; to you it's a loss of a customer and a reputation. Refrigeration may help for a time, but the beauty and luster of these most beautiful of all crops is gone.

Currants and gooseberries.

Years ago, when the Geneva, New York, Fruit Testing Cooperative was offering Red Lake currants, Charlotte planted some, and was charmed with "the little bushes with their graceful pendants of brilliant translucent fruit-rubies." A bit tart for much out-of-hand eating, they make fine jellies, sauces, and fruit-soups. A PYO operation is best, as the ripe berries burst under slight pressure and it takes time to fill a quart, or even a pint, unless you're a skillful harvester. Before you plant any currants, make sure that the local department of agriculture does not ban them, especially if white pines grow in the area.

It's a pity that black currants are not easily available for home use, because their flavor surpasses that of the refreshing reds, and their vitamin C content can reach over 200 milligrams per 100 grams (about 3½ ounces). The native Missouri black currant yields less fruit than the European varieties, but in spring bears tubular yellow flowers as deliciously scented as spicy carnations.

As for gooseberries, unless you dote on them or can locate eager customers, better ignore them or keep only a few bushes for home use. The variety Pixwell is one of the best, and the fruit makes good preserves. Their bushes specialize in small sharp spines, and when you gather the ripe gooseberries on a hot summer day, the plants can deliver their own version of prickly heat.

27:   Quality eggs for coddled customers

O NCE A PERSON samples the flavor of a home-grown egg, perhaps reawakening memories of long-ago, you've got a regular customer. Like other crops, eggs do go through a seasonal drop in production, when amid cries of protest and disappointment you announce reduced quotas and ration the precious objects.

Color preference is regional. New England, home of the great Rhode Island and New Hampshire Reds and Plymouth Rocks, favors brown eggs from these breeds and their modern crosses. In other areas, white (usually Leghorn) eggs command a premium price, with browns bringing two cents less per dozen. The pro-browns claim greater richness for their choice, sneering at the tombstone-pallid shells. But scientists have been unable to find any difference in food value—or taste—between the two. There is, however, a big difference between store-bought and homestead eggs. Charlotte Waldron relates: "My Pennsylvania doctor, passing the farm one day with a rare moment of leisure, stopped in while I was weighing and boxing eggs. Charmed with their impressive size and shells of rosy tan, subtle browns, and deep ivory, he bought four dozen for his numerous children's breakfasts. Next morning the phone rang. Did I have white eggs? The doctor's children couldn't eat the brown ones: they were too rich, he complained, and what's more, they tasted strange."

Charlotte can sympathize with the children. Raised on a standardized product from commercially fed hens, they were used to lemon-yellow yolks and bland taste. Such customers should be prepared for meaty eggs, orange red yolks and firm whites from your hens. Explain that these characteristics derive from a chicken whose daily life includes contact with the earth, sun, comfrey and other greens, and yellow corn in their specially mixed laying mash. It's not the breed, but the feed and management that makes the difference. The children

Charlotte Waldron

had learned to prefer the inferior product, just like those who would rather start their day with Tang than with fresh orange juice.

Your egg customers will fall mainly into two groups: those seeking organically grown food, and connoisseurs of fine food—egg experts with high standards. If you can satisfy and even surpass those standards, you'll be praised, thanked, and fairly paid. Trouble is, production may well fall off so that you can't meet the demand. In hot weather, when the more portly brown-egg layers reduce their output, you may wish you had chosen slimmer Leghorn types which are more wilt-resistant. In winter, unless your laying house is heated, the

Leghorn contingent huddles depressedly and their production sinks lower and lower, while the rugged New Englanders go out to take the air even with snow on the ground.

To insure at least a minimum lay, the Waldrons turn on lights at 6 A.M. on winter mornings to coax the hens to their feed and warmed water, and again before the short day darkens into night. Warmed water is helpful, and a head of cabbage suspended just above their heads will induce a little healthy exercise. Charlotte once made a hot mash spiked with red pepper for the chickens' breakfast. This apparently set up an inner glow in a score of chickens, for even in the New York farm's unheated henhouse they kept the Waldrons in eggs from late January on.

Today when cage-factory hens are bred to average 250 eggs annually in the brutal cage-factories, an organic household should be able to achieve at least 150 to 200 per hen per year. To become acquainted with the various modern breeds, consult your county agent, cultivate any neighbors and old-timers who keep, or have kept, hens humanely, visit the big county or state fairs, and talk to sellers of poultry feed who know the local scene intimately. Back issues of *Organic Gardening and Farming* offer many excellent accounts of personal experiences with poultry. You might either hunt up some of the older, pre-cage era books on the subject now gathering dust in the stacks, or consult *Chickens in your Backyard* by Rick and Gail Luttmann (Rodale Press, 1976).

If you live in the southern or milder western states, you might want to try the lightweight white egg breeds. Despite her pleasant acquaintance with those Empire State birds, Charlotte prefers the brown egg breeds and crosses. "The chicken is not noted for its I.Q., and Leghorns least of all," she says. They are "a nervous, hysterical lot under slight stress; a loud auto horn blast or other sudden noise can send them into anything from a lively dither to full-fledged panic, resulting possibly in broken eggs and other calamities. None but the owners and accustomed tenders should ever be allowed in a chicken house; but let even the daily attendant appear in a different costume— skirt instead of slacks, for instance, or even a noticeably different hat-style—and uproar ensues. Furthermore, when the time comes to dispose of them, Leghorns must be used, or sold very cheaply, for soup, since they dress out from 3 to 3½ pounds, and rarely more."

Rhode Island and New Hampshire Reds, and the Plymouth Rocks, and their crosses have been bred for egg production comparable to the Leghorns. Their temperaments are calmer, and when their egg-laying days are over, they dress out from 3½ to 5½ or even 6 pounds, and make flavorful stewers, fricassees, and salad. The Waldrons never have any trouble selling all their surplus. They use sex-linked crosses between Rhode Island Reds and Barred Plymouth Rocks. Lighter-colored hens from these crosses dress out more attractively because any pinfeathers left after plucking are inconspicuous. Black-feathered birds are less acceptable to most buyers.

Before deciding on any particular breed, you might want to write the Agricultural Research Service, USDA, for the latest report of Random Sample Egg Production Tests for the United States and Canada. It's a very detailed, rather technical study, and lists the names and addresses of breeders whose birds were entered in the two-year tests.

Before starting your egg sales, you can save your egg carton costs by asking friends and acquaintances to save their store-bought empties for you. If you operate on a large enough scale, however, you may be required to give your name, address, and egg classification (pullet, small, medium, large) on the boxes. Consult your county agent. The Waldrons bypass this grading technicality by marking all cartons "un-classified," although the eggs are mostly larger sizes. If hens are kept into the second year, you may find yourself gathering occasional dou-ble-yolkers—enormous eggs, which don't fit in regulation cartons without being squashed. Keep them for family use or for an impressive gift.

Despite plentiful nesting material, eggs may come from the henhouse less than perfectly clean. Instead of dipping them into de-tergent solution, which destroys the natural protective coating pro-vided by the hen, lightly use emery paper or a wire brush, or scrape very warily with a sharp knife. Some farm suppliers market an inexpen-sive soft plastic brush with replaceable sandpaper bands; if your birds are properly fed and gritted, the shells will be strong enough for a treatment.

Many states have regulations regarding the sale of eggs, so it's best to acquaint yourself with them, and if you sell in any quantity, be prepared to receive visits from some type of inspector on a checking-up tour. Some avoid this kind of visitor by selling only to private customers, and by omitting mention of eggs on the farm sign offering honey, berries, and other red-tape-free produce.

Supplying a good egg.

A bloodspot is apt to spoil an egg in the eyes of many customers. So, before you buy your laying stock, be sure to find out if the particular strain you want is likely to carry this undesirable characteristic. Bloodspots may result from injury to hens under the stress of heavy lay. This tendency is hereditary. Charlotte always asks customers to report any imperfect egg for replacement. Most people who chance to find a blood spot simply remove the speck with knife-tip or spoon; but a customer should receive a replacement if you aim for perfect service and its accompanying goodwill.

Less appealing is a bloody yolk, especially when that yolk has followed several flawless ones into the mixing bowl. This defect may reveal a temporary derangement of the hen's laying apparatus, perhaps never to appear again. If the problem continues, the hen must be identified and detoured kitchenward. Until she's found, especially if you're selling to a store or roadside stand, let that little candler throw its beam and prevent trouble.

In gathering any quantity of eggs, it's safest to use a strong basket or pail lined with something soft and disposable, or a plastic-coated wire basket, which allows more ventilation. Charlotte always visits the houses several times a day, especially in warm weather, to insure optimum freshness, and to avoid the results of hen half-wittedness. "Even though you provide enough nice dark nests, generously lined with fresh straw, pine needles, or shavings, for all your layers—invariably certain nests will be more alluring than others. There will be not only a waiting line for those nests, but the most aggressive cluckers will try and often succeed in forcing their way into the already occupied cubicle. Often I've had to dispose of one or even two intruders who have squeezed in beside the prior tenant, removing each to an equally attractive (to me) nest next to the desired one, which they abandon the moment one's back is turned, and return to the siege. In frustration, they may fight, and broken eggs result."

Charlotte has found that hens enjoy sitting on a number of eggs—

perhaps they get a pleasant massage from those warm rounded surfaces. So when you reach in to withdraw any accumulated eggs, beware of a swift peck that could draw blood from the back of your hand. A peck may even make you drop the henfruit before reaching the safety of your basket.

It's best to place newly laid eggs into the refrigerator, with the box open, in order to draw out the body heat as quickly as possible. A warm egg in a closed container loses its freshness faster than a chilled one.

Pricing.

Charlotte checked what the highest-priced or fanciest farm markets were charging, and added five cents per dozen for each size. Converts to organic food will more than likely be eager for them, and you may have to decide how to meet the demand without getting into more work and building outlay than you wish.

Feeding suggestions.

To lessen the expense of feed, perhaps you can buy shelled corn, or wheat off the combine at harvest time, and then carry this grain to the feed store for use in your mix.

One of the easiest ways to insure deep orange yolks is to plant comfrey, kale, or any winter greens all around the sunny sides of the pens, protecting them with boards against the cage wire until the plants are well started. If the greens are planted just far enough from the wire, they won't be destroyed since enough leaves will be left on the outer side to sustain the plants. If the birds clean off the inner side of the clump to the ground, replace the boards until the new leaves emerge from the crowns. Meanwhile, you can pull some of the outer leaves for the expectant fowls. If you can provide alternate pens in which to start grains or rape or mustard, and switch hens back and forth, you'll have the best setup short of free range.

If you keep bees, and cut out or damage drone cells—a help in swarm control—place a board before the hive entrances, on the ground. The bees will carry out the fat white larvae within a day or

two, and you can pick up the board after the bees have retired and toss
its contents into the runs. Also, a donation of dug-out ants' nests is always enthusiastically received by the flock.

Hens make wonderful compost in their runs if you give them
sods, weeds, *short,* fresh grass clippings (long old ones congest their
crops), wormy fruit, or chopped borer-infested cornstalks. In a few
months the resulting manure-enriched mixture is ready for your
garden, and the birds will have lots of exercise.

For the fun of it you might buy a few Araucanas. Their eggs range
from blue green to khaki (miscalled gold), pink, and plain white. The
Waldrons kept several as a curiosity and sold the small eggs at Easter
for a dollar a dozen, or ten cents each, "but they are not a money
project unless you go in for the sale of breeding stock. If your time and
labor must be budgeted, there are more profitable ways of spending
your hours and money."

For commercial programs, layers are usually replaced yearly.
Those held over lay fewer but larger eggs. Organically treated hens last
much longer than these wretched forced creatures, Charlotte finds.

28: What's a tofu?

" "T OFU?" WHAT'S A tofu?" Many people have yet to make the acquaintance of soybean curd, or tofu. But not for long.

Tofu, a staple in the diet of millions of people in the Orient for
over a thousand years, is an ethnic food that seems destined to dupli-
cate the pizza boom in America after World War II. While the sale of
health foods is expected to double by 1980, the consumption of soy
protein in the United States is predicted to increase 12 times in the
same interval. If recent years are any index, tofu will be one of the chief
foods responsible for that increase.

When *The Book of Tofu* (Autumn Press) was published in 1975,
there were 65 tofu shops in the United States, all Oriental-owned.

This chapter originally appeared as an article by Ellin Stein in *Whole Foods* magazine.

Now there are over 100, most of the new ones started by non-Asians. Since their book appeared, authors William Shurtleff and Akiko Aoyagi have received hundreds of letters asking for more information on setting up tofu shops. Perhaps this growth is partly due to an increased awareness that soy products are the most economically efficient source of protein. And the introduction of tofu into the mainstream American diet may be aided by its diversity: you can chill it, freeze it, grill it, deep-fry it, powder it, crumble it, spread it, and—counting its by-products—drink it.

In the Orient, the production of tofu traditionally has been labor-intensive, employing only a minimal technology. This labor-intensive pattern has so far been repeated in the United States, where small-scale commercial tofu shops have tended to be collective operations in which the workers agree to pay themselves low wages, making tofu as a labor of love. Asian-American tofu firms show a reluctance to talk about their operations, apparently from a concern that a market which has been firmly in their grasp might be invaded by the occidental newcomers.

Larry Needleman, a former food consultant to the state of California, started Bean Machines, Inc., with Bill Shurtleff in order to distribute quality Japanese tofu-making equipment in the United States, and to develop American-made sources as well. Needleman estimates that tofu consumption by non-Orientals in this country has doubled every six months for the past two years. In his view, the few large tofu manufacturers cannot keep up with the growing demand, and there is plenty of room for the smaller tofu shops on everything from the community to the regional level. He suggests that the prospective community-level tofu producer first consider (1) production goals, (2) cost of raw materials, (3) the kind of equipment to be used, (4) the corresponding labor costs, (5) packaging expenses, (6) competition from established tofu firms, (7) the amount of capital investment, and (8) how to raise the capital.

Operators of the new tofu shops agree that it is best to start small, producing about 30 or 40 pounds per week. They advise learning how to make tofu at home to develop skills. Their experience confirms Needleman's statement that tofu shops "are an experimental business, and there is as yet no way to determine general costing for a tofu shop."

The size of the step from home-kitchen to commercial production varies. Steve Fiering of The Soy Plant, a small tofu collective in Ann Arbor, Michigan, suggests a minimum output of 100 pounds per day. The Farm, a large Bay Area collective, places the minimum at 250 pounds per day. A new tofu plant in Berkeley, California, produces up to 300 pounds daily, sells about 80 pounds through Berkeley Bowl, their market on the premises, and the rest to five other stores. The two Berkeley Bowl owners, working 14-hour days, find that the small scale of operations is not worth the effort, so they plan to expand.

A problem shared by many shop-owners was how to strike a balance between, on the one hand, investing too much in equipment which will not be operating at capacity for a long time and, on the other hand, investing too little with the result that workers must labor 60 hours each week just to fill the demand. All agreed to one thing: plan ahead carefully.

The successful tofu shop generally starts with traditional hand-labor equipment in a space large enough to accommodate expanded operations, and suitable for meeting health codes. As tofu-making skills are being perfected and money is set aside for new equipment, sales increase and the original equipment begins to operate near its full capacity. When the demand is greater than the shop's current output,

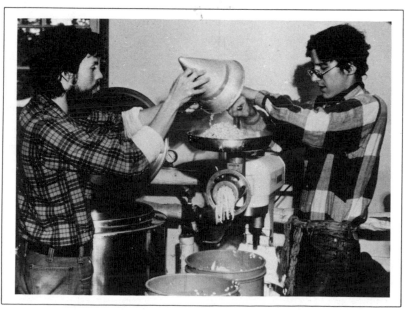

Paul Kagan

labor-saving machinery can be introduced. According to *The Book of Tofu, Volume II,* a manual for commercial production, the cost of starting a traditional tofu shop with a daily output of 330 pounds ranges from $2,500 to $7,500, with the equipment costing from $1,500 to $4,000.

Basic business skills predictably prove to be necessary for the success of tofu shops. Benjamin Hills at Surata Soyfoods in Eugene, Oregon, said that their growth sometimes outstripped their adminis-

Paul Kagan

trative abilities, and he recommended taking business courses such as bookkeeping. The owners of Laughing Grasshopper in Massachusetts credit their success partly to a good financial advisor, and suggest thorough research of the business aspects before starting a shop.

Tom Timmins at Laughing Grasshopper suggested "figuring out neat production systems," and mentioned Crystal Hill, a New Hampshire tofu shop that created a soybean grinder from an industrial garbage disposal unit. More usual is the Hobart Vertical Cutting Mixer.

Despite a concern for tofu-making as an ancient "art," the traditional Japanese settling boxes were universally condemned. Stainless steel cuts down considerably on clean-up time, which easily won first prize as the most tiresome part of the process.

Labor-saving plans and devices are welcome throughout this industry, both to cut costs for larger operations and to reduce the physical burden on the workers. "Tofu-makers must be in Olympic physical condition," Timmins remarks. Tofu-making equipment has not been manufactured in the United States, and the complexities of obtaining it from Japan are immense. Producers have their eye on Bean Machines, Inc., Larry Needleman's company, as a possible source of reasonably priced, good-quality equipment.

The problem of tofu's short shelf life appears to have been solved at Redwood Natural Foods in Santa Rosa, California. Redwood has begun marketing vacuum-packed, date-coded tofu with a shelf life of three to four weeks, a great improvement over the usual seven to ten days. An additional advantage of vacuum packing is a reduction of freight costs, due to a decreased bulk and weight. The standard tofu packaging method has included about one pound of water along with each one-pound carton of tofu.

Jim Yancey of the American Soybean Association—a lobbying group for soybean growers—described tofu as "too foreign," requiring a major change in American eating habits. He says it would probably be at least five years before a large corporation started marketing it.

The Food Protein Council commissioned a Gallup Poll, published in April 1977, that showed that 33 percent of the people polled believe that soybeans will be the most important source of protein in the future—ahead of fish at 24 percent and meat at 21 percent. Fifty-five percent said that soy products provide adequate or superior food value. Younger age groups living in large cities were the most favorable to soy protein, indicating that support for soy products is likely to grow in the future.

Whatever the corporation response or the polls might suggest, small-shop tofu production is on the increase, responding to a real demand, with a focus on offering a quality product. Producers often take an artisan's pride in their work, and aim to run profitable businesses without being overwhelmed by hard labor, and without exploiting the consumer. "Tofu-eaters have high food consciousness," Steve Fiering says. "A good product at a good price will withstand corporate competition."

Down on the Farm.

The Farm, a branch of Stephen Gaskin's Tennessee commune, opened a soy dairy in San Rafael, California, in the fall of 1976. For one year they sold their tempeh, soy-mayonnaise, "ice bean," soy milk, and tofu in their downtown Farm Food Company store.

Economically, things were fine. Individuals worked four hours per day—unpaid—to produce 250 pounds of tofu daily at a cost of 50 cents per pound. And they could not keep up with the demand.

Although most small tofu operations mention lack of space as a major problem, The Farm is probably the only successful one to shut down because of it. At this writing, The Farm was looking for an old milk dairy as an ideal site for a wholesale-scale soy dairy.

People at The Farm recommend starting small and graduating first to a semi-automatic batch method, and then to a vacuum-pressure method. They indicate that one important matter to consider when expanding to a major, commercial level is compliance with USDA and local inspection standards.

Rochester, New York.

In May 1977, the Rochester Tofu Shop started making 150 pounds of tofu per week. Now that upstate New York plant is producing 1,000 pounds per week, but reports discouragement about supporting the shop solely by the local market.

"We underestimated the costs and overestimated the market," according to Rochester Tofu partner Andy Schlechter. "The demand here is climbing steadily—but not rapidly." Oriental restaurants were seen as potential customers, but some continue to buy their tofu from a large manufacturer in New York City.

Compared to most shops its size, the Rochester plant began with a higher capital investment—$8,000—but fewer people. The two partners usually work a grueling 60-hour week, using a lever press and a steam cooker backed by a home boiler. But despite the investment of time, money and effort (and an unusually high yield of around 2.9 pounds of tofu per pound of soybeans), the cost analysis does not look good.

Of their 50-cent-per-pound wholesale price 10 cents is for materials, a high 40 cents is for overhead and packaging, and for labor—nothing. The discouraging truth has been fewer people working longer hours for less money.

They sell via twice-weekly distribution in four-gallon buckets to two dozen stores, one Oriental restaurant, two university dormitories and two natural foods restaurants. Still, income does not meet their costs. However, Schlechter hopes that the sales will double now that a natural foods distributor, Clear Eyes, has started handling their tofu on a trial basis.

A four-person operation.

When The Soy Plant started serving the Ann Arbor, Michigan, area in January 1977, it was producing 50 pounds of tofu per week. It now manufactures 1,000 pounds per week at a rate of 350 pounds per day. To maintain that output, four people work a 40-hour week, which includes about ten hours of clean-up. They have recently begun to pay themselves $2.25 per hour.

Initial capital at The Soy Plant was $2,500. That figure does not include their boiler and steam kettle, which they obtained free. Their main expense was a $1,200 soybean grinder from Japan.

The most troublesome piece of equipment has been their home-built press. Soy Plant worker Steve Fiering estimates that they could produce 500 pounds of tofu per day with a better press. In addition to this upcoming expense, they expect to spend $1,000 to install a new drain.

The Soy Plant produces 2.5 pounds of tofu for each pound of soybeans. Their wholesale price, 65 cents per pound, breaks down to 8 cents for supplies, 10 cents for overhead, 10 cents for packaging, 30 cents for labor, and 7 cents for capitalization. Retail prices range from 70 to 80 cents.

Their local distribution of 1-pound and 24-pound tubs includes two restaurants, the two co-ops, and eight other retail stores. Their market has doubled since fall 1977, when Midwest Natural Foods began distributing one-third of their output to shops in Pittsburgh, Milwaukee, and other cities. Fiering predicts that it will double again within a year.

A ten-person operation.

The Laughing Grasshopper, located at Miller's Falls in western Massachusetts, has been so busy meeting the existing demand for tofu that they have had no time to do any merchandising, except for giving out free samples. But there are no profits yet, because costs have kept pace with sales.

Their initial output of 1,000 pounds per week was a larger beginning than that of most new tofu shops, and it grew to 4,000 pounds during the summer and reached 6,000 pounds in the fall of 1977. The shop distributes to over 100 small shops, supermarkets and restaurants in Boston and the western end of the state.

Members of the Laughing Grasshopper collective bolstered the $8,000 investment of their own money with a $10,000 nine-month loan. Since their beginning, they have invested no more in the business, except for leasehold improvements such as sinks and drains.

Currently, ten people work 40 hours per week in crews of four, using one member of the crew just for clean-up. Most of their equipment was found locally. They use four cauldrons, but worker Tom Timmins estimates that the addition of a pressure cooker would more than double their production of tofu with no increase in labor. He stresses the importance of experimenting with production techniques in order to reduce the considerable physical labor.

The wholesale price of their tofu is 44 cents per pound—about 15 cents for production, 15 cents for labor, 7 cents for distribution, 5 cents for overhead, and 2 cents for supplies. Workers are paid $2.75 per hour.

Laughing Grasshopper tofu retails for 52 cents to 79 cents per pound, with one-fourth of the output marketed through a distributor. The tofu is sold in tubs of 50 eight-ounce pieces, or in recyclable five-gallon cans for which the customer pays a refundable deposit.

29: Dairy beef growers' co-op

A FEW YEARS BACK, a group of Bucks County, Pennsylvania, farmers became so disgusted with the giveaway prices they were getting for their livestock through conventional marketing channels that they took matters into their own hands. They decided to try selling the animals in the form of meat.

It's been a tough struggle. They've had to learn marketing methods as they went along. They've suffered from lack of development capital. They've battled bureaucratic red tape. They've been hard-pressed to find the extra hours needed to explore this new venture. And although the co-op still markets most of their livestock the old way, on the hoof, a number of market outlets for the meat have now been established.

"We're not out of the woods by any means, but we feel we are on the right track, that our basic idea is sound," says Terry Keim, sparkplug of the group.

The Bucks Meat Producers Cooperative, Inc. makes no attempt to sell through supermarkets. Instead, it has gone after selected markets—food cooperatives, farmer-operated roadside markets, restaurants, and ethnic groups. As Keim says, the co-op is "seeking groups of people who want good meat at reasonable prices and who are unhappy with the kind of stuff they find in the average supermarket."

The co-op stresses that its meat is free of hormones and antibiotics. Its processed meat contains no preservatives such as sodium nitrate, sodium nitrate, or BHT. Keim says this enlightened attitude has become a strong selling point. As a case in point, the Feingold Association of Philadelphia and Surrounding Counties, Inc., which operates a food program designed to eliminate unnecessary chemical additives from the diet of children, now carries their meat. Dr. Ben F. Feingold established that hyperactivity in some children is caused by sensitivity to food additives.

Twenty-three farmers currently make up the co-op and they represent a wide range of livestock enterprises: dairy cows, veal calves, beef steers, hogs, and sheep. Since most of the members are dairymen the major thrust is on dairy beef, something that has been winning attention ever since steer beef prices took to the rarified atmosphere. Dairy beef can be sold cheaper than steer beef.

At the outset, the co-op members felt they must find if consumers would buy their meat and come back for more. They set up stands at public farm markets and offered frozen ground beef, chip steak, ground veal, and veal cutlets. Several months of steady sales proved that consumers would buy their meat and would come back for more. But members couldn't afford to take the time to man such stands and didn't feel they could afford to pay people to do it for them. They approached farmer-operated roadside markets, food co-ops, and restaurants, offering to put the meat on trial with no obligation to the seller. It has been slow work, mainly because the members can devote so little time to making sales calls. Currently the co-op is selling through four farmer-operated markets, a food co-op storefront, individual buying clubs, and a restaurant. Individual sales are handled in minimum orders of 30 pounds.

Taste tests have shown that dairy beef can be highly acceptable. Such tests have been carried out by Rodale Press, the Pennsylvania Department of Agriculture, and others. Some of the tasters actually felt such beef was more flavorful than steer beef. It's also leaner, which appeals to many buyers, especially with steer beef prices so high. What about toughness? Steaks and roasts from good dairy cows not more than four years old can be quite tender.

But to insure tenderness the co-op puts them through a mechanical tenderizer—a machine that thrusts hundreds of closely spaced needles through the meat, breaking the tissues that cause toughness. This kind of tenderizing is widely used, especially for beef used by the fast food steak houses that offer steak, french fries, and tossed salad at such low prices. Unlike chemical tenderizers, the mechanical device does not affect meat texture or flavor.

There is no official grading of the co-op beef, but the co-op is fussy about the quality of cows it accepts from members and Keim says that many of the cows would probably grade out USDA "Choice."

Dairy beef long has been used for ground meat. But the co-op found it couldn't sell all its meat in this form and still come up with an acceptable price to the consumer—much to the chagrin of the members (and also to the chagrin of other farm groups that have tried grinding up whole cows for direct sale). At a time when the supermarkets are selling hamburger for 69 or 89 cents, the co-op had trouble coming up with a ground beef price under a dollar.

That's when the co-op learned one of the secrets of meat merchandizing: that supermarkets can feature hamburger at those low prices because the steaks and roasts are priced to balance out the overall gross profit. The co-op lost no time in developing the necessary product mix. First this amounted to adding steaks and roasts made from the loin. Later it found that, with the tenderizer, it could expand the mix to include a wider range of roasts and steaks. Only the filets (the tenderloins) are not tenderized.

Ground beef continues to be a major seller for the co-op. Dairy beef is leaner than the cuts off the steer beef used by the supermarkets. The dairy cow ground is tastier and doesn't shrink down to the size of a silver dollar when cooked. That's because the fat content of the co-op's ground is only 16 to 18 percent, compared with 30 percent for supermarket hamburger—the maximum allowed under federal law and the level most supermarkets shoot for. Supermarkets toss in additional fat to reach the allowed level. They can get a higher price for the fat that way than by selling it to a renderer.

Keim recently noted that a store-front co-op handling some of his group's steaks and roasts, but not its ground beef, was offering five-pound packs of ground meat from a commercial packer. The store manager said this was because commercial stuff was cheaper. Keim, fast becoming a knowledgeable meat merchandiser, suggested the store offer a "two for" price special—one pack of his ground and one package of the other at less than the price of the two purchased separately. This got the customers to try the co-op's ground and now, because of customer demand, that's the only ground the store offers.

Another popular seller for the co-op is the "family pack." This is made up of assorted cuts that represent one-eighth of a whole animal. The mix weighs 60 to 65 pounds and includes, on the average, 25 pounds of ground meat (in 2-pound packages), 12 pounds of steaks, 15 pounds of roasts, two pounds of cubes, 5 pounds of shin meat and short ribs, and a small bag of soup bones weighing 2 or 2½ pounds. These are sold on a pre-order basis. As this is written the co-op sells such a pack at $1.25 a pound, profit included. In a test with steer beef, Keim said the co-op found it couldn't duplicate the same pack for less than a break-even price of $1.43. Except for these family packs, none of the meat cuts sold by the co-op include any bones. All the steaks and roasts are of the boneless type (filets, strip steaks, sirloin tip steaks, round steak, bolar roasts, sirloin tip roasts, eye roasts, and sirloin roasts).

The co-op was able to sell Delmonico steak (rib steak with the bone removed) at $1.95 a pound at a time when the same steak was bringing anywhere from $2.49 to $2.90 at the supermarkets. What's more, customers have told Keim that they like the co-op Delmonicos a lot better.

Keim raises fancy veal, the kind that you seldom see in the supermarkets anymore. But the co-op manages to sell it. It has found a major outlet in a co-op food store located in a silk-stocking section of Philadelphia. The store sells both veal chops and cutlets, as well as veal patties. Pre-ordered family packs include 30 pounds of veal cutlets, tenders, chops, and a roast (breast of veal); veal connoisseurs who buy such packs do not want patties, Keim has found.

Bacon and sausage are the principal pork products sold by the co-op, but other pork items are available on special order. The co-op has not yet developed outlets for lamb.

For its beef processing, the co-op has arranged with a nearby slaughtering plant to do the killing and then deliver the quarters to the co-op butcher. The slaughterer keeps the offal and the hide. When these are bringing a good price he makes no cash charge. Otherwise, the fee is three dollars.

The co-op butcher removes the bones and then makes up the assortment of cuts required. He makes up the ground meat in two-pound packages or in patties. There is no additional cost to make the patties, but they bring a slightly higher price than the bulk ground. The butcher wraps and freezes all the meat and holds it in his freezer until it is picked up for delivery. Meat cuts for display in freezer cases are wrapped in clear plastic. The pre-ordered family packs are in white freezer paper.

Meeting the fussy federal requirements for labels for their meat has caused the co-op many months of anguish, but they finally got labels that won an okay. The co-op also had to make sure it was meeting all the government requirements for selling meat. Under federal law, meat that is to be sold must be killed in an approved slaughtering plant and okayed for wholesomeness by a federal inspector. Also, federal inspection is required for a butcher to prepare meat that is to be sold away from his premises. Meat at the various retail outlets is subject to state inspection.

As indicated earlier, the co-op doesn't accept just any cull cow from its members. According to Keim, only the best are used, such as those being disposed of for one of three reasons: a two-year-old heifer that has failed to breed successfully; a heifer that has developed birthing problems; and a three-year-old that is a low milk producer.

None of the cattle may be over four years old and they must be a type that would make official USDA "Cutter" grade or better.

The co-op pays its members on dressed weight (which, by experience with such animals, has proved to be about 50 percent of live weight) and uses the highest price reported by the Pennsylvania Department of Agriculture for such cows anywhere in the state for the week of purchase. This is a higher price than the member would get selling to an area packer—buyer or through an area auction. Dairying in the county has declined to the point where so few cows are offered at public sales that only a handful of buyers are attracted, thus holding down prices. Likewise, so few packer—buyers roam the area that there is little competition from this source.

So, the Bucks Meat Producers Co-operative is proving that direct marketing of meat by a mixed group of livestock producers is both possible and feasible. They've also shown that there is a demand for meat free of hormones, antibiotics, and preservatives.

30: From sheep to shirt

S PINNING AND WEAVING is a satisfying hobby for many, especially if
the wool comes from one's own sheep. The repetition of the hand
processes is relaxing. The product is finer than can be bought. And
articles of clothing fashioned from handspun wool are uniquely handsome.

Can this hobby, like gardening, be turned into a profitable cottage industry? Jennifer Hamburg of Los Osos, California, believes so.
Weaving proficiently on a fly-shuttle loom, you should be able to
average $3.50 an hour, she says. Constructing and tailoring clothes can
generate about the same.

This is not a top wage, by any means, and to do even this well requires experience and concern for efficiency. First, it isn't practical to
both tend sheep and make wool products for market. To make a decent
income, Jennifer has found you have to buy wool, preferably in the
greased roving state with the fibers already separated and ready to be
spun. This wool now costs roughly $2 a pound and up.

Christina and Isabel Smucker, sisters of West Liberty, Ohio, also
buy the wool that goes into the clothes, towels, and tapestries they
make. Like Jennifer, they spin wool in the grease before washing it. "If
you wash and card wool before you spin it," says Christina, "you lose a
lot of its quality. We wash the skeins of yarn afterward. But that means
of course that the raw wool must be clean. It is difficult to find sheep
raisers who will take care of sheep properly for our requirements. Wool
should be free of dirt, burrs, even chaff."

You should explore the types of yarns that you can produce on
your own spinning wheel, as yarn character is very important to producing weaving yarns suited for the finished product that you plan to
make. Yarns that will be used for garments require a softer twist than
yarns for rug weaving. Yarns can be spun in varying degrees of thickness: continuously thick tapestry yarns are used for large rugs; uniform,
thin yarns are used for handwoven yardage, blankets, and upholstery

fabric; and alternated thick and thin areas are used to produce a type of *slub* yarn, used for weft, or for filler threads when weaving pillows, blankets, and garment fabric of an interesting texture.

The direction of spin has a great deal to do with the type of yarn to be spun. There are two kinds of twists related to the rotational direction of the wheel when spinning. The clockwise direction of the wheel is known as a Z-twist; the counterclockwise direction is called an S-twist.

The variety possible through using different directions in twist becomes apparent when you begin *plying* the yarns. Plying can be easily accomplished by running two tightly Z-twisted single strands of handspun back through the spinning wheel while treadling counterclockwise (the opposite direction in which the singles were spun). This will create an even, two-ply yarn highly suitable for garments that require a great deal of strength and resiliency.

For unusual effects, you can ply two slubby spun singles, or a thick and a thin single, or singles of two different colors, direction of twist, or fiber type. There is room for endless variation in yarns. You might even try incorporating some commercially spun yarns with your handspun for color and texture.

Dyeing.

Traditionally, yarn has been dyed with flowers, leaves, bark, roots, berries, insects, and minerals. The shades available range from subtle earth tones to fiery, brilliant hues. Wool accepts dye more readily than any other natural fiber, and is a perfect material for natural dyeing.

The Smucker sisters dye their fabrics with materials gathered from their garden and nearby fields and woods, including goldenrod, walnut shell, elderberry, pokeberry, and butternut. "With natural dyes you can never be sure of the exact results," says Christina. "That's why dyeing is so interesting. The final color will be determined somewhat by the fabric, too, of course. In a silk and wool fabric, the white silk dictates the color; in a wool and camel's hair weave, the camel's hair." Dyeing is done in a copper boiler, with skeins of yarn immersed in simmering water. "It's like making tea and steeping the brew," says Christina. "You don't want to boil the dye materials too hard."

Dyeing is time-consuming, and Jennifer Hamburg prefers chemical dyes for this reason. She observes that handweavers have been getting away from natural dyes over the past few years, although customers are sometimes led to believe that chemically colored yarn has been lovingly steeped in a wild herb broth. She finds that most people can't tell how a piece was colored.

Dyes fall into one of three general categories: substantive, or direct dyes, adjective or mordant dyes, and vat dyes. The substantive dyes will take to the wool without a mordant, such as tumeric and staghorn moss, but the majority of natural dyes are of the adjective type, or those which require a mordant to fix the dye to the wool. A mordant is a chemical which reacts with the dye and the fiber to develop certain colors and makes the colors "fast" so that they won't fade or wash out of the yarn.

Some commonly used mordants are alum (potassium aluminum), chrome (potassium dichromate), copper sulfate (blue vitriol), cream of tartar, iron (ferrous sulfate), and tin (stannous chloride).

A third type, vat dyes, includes tyrian purple, the luscious color that is extracted from the glands of a Mediterranian snail. These dyes are rare in nature and have a complex breakdown process involving bacteria or chemicals to release the dye from the dyestuff. Vat dyes are the most color-fast and fade resistant.

Woven clothing.

Woven clothing can be as simple or complicated as your weaving skills permit. For a first project, it is always best to make something simple that you will be able to wear and enjoy. A Mexican rebozo or shawl woven to the desired width and length can be woven out of any type of yarn and is especially attractive if the fringed edges are finished off with a fine macrame border.

If a long poncho is desired, the width of the weaving should be increased to the measurement from wrist to wrist across the shoulders. The length of the finished weaving should measure twice the distance from shoulder to knees or mid-calf. Leave a slit in the direct center of your poncho (widthwise and lengthwise) for the head. Test out the length of neck slits on brown paper bags.

The threading of the loom and drafting of patterns are involved tasks, and should be studied at some length. There are many books on handweaving available at bookstores and libraries.

Marketing handspun yarns.

Handspun yarns are more than just a carry-over from a primitive craft technique. They make handwoven and handknit pieces truely unique. But handspun yarns must meet standard quality and uniformity if they are to be used instead of commercially spun yarns. The handspinner has greater control over the type of wool produced and therefore can create a wider range of thickness, twist, fiber counts, tensile strengths, and novelty effects.

Jennifer thinks of handspun yarn as a statement made by the handspinner to the purchaser or user of the yarn. The statement must be a fine quality product, available in enough quantity for a sweater or other project; the yarn should be clearly marked as to the specific kind of fiber and the yardage and weight of each skein.

The yardage of a skein can be easily calculated by winding the wool off the bobbin and onto a niddy-noddy or wrap reeler. These tools will allow the spinner to count off a skein in yards (two yards around an 18-inch niddy-noddy, and the measurement of the circumference on a wrap reeler).

The weight of each skein can be taken on a postal, food, or gram scale. A good-sized skein will weigh from 2½ to 4 ounces.

It is important to have the weight, yardage and fiber information recorded clearly on tags affixed to each skein. A tag will attract attention to the yarn if it displays a logo or symbol identifying the name of your business. However you design your tags, they should be legible, informative, and leave a name or impression by which people can identify your product. This is especially important when you are selling your handspun along with other artisans at craft fairs and next to commercially spun yarns in weaving and knitting shops.

It is also important to set a price for your handspinning that is reasonable and comparable to the current prices of both handspun and commercially spun yarns. There are two such ways to set a value to your work.

The first is to keep a log of the hours that you spend at the wheel.

Calculate the average time that it takes you to spin a skein of wool by clocking yourself. Include the time it takes you to wind off the skein. If you can estimate an hourly wage to your time (for example, $3 per hour) and it takes you one hour to spin a four-ounce skein, then you will be charging $12 per pound, or approximately 75 cents per ounce.

Another means of pricing your spinning time is to set a fixed spinning charge per pound of wool spun. You may decide to charge about $14 per pound spinning charge. The amount will have to be added to the value of your fiber. If the wool is more difficult or easier to spin, you may want to alter your price accordingly. Jennifer adds on 10 cents a skein for dyed yarn.

Both Jennifer and the Smuckers agree that simplicity in design is important if you hope to make a decent return from woolen items. The sisters plan on a minimal amount of cutting and no seam allowances to finish—in fact, few seams at all. Coats and tunics are easier to put together than, say, a blouse. Jennifer sells ponchos, tunics, and scarves—all on-loom projects—and dresses, which must be taken off the loom and cut and sewn.

The Smuckers sell their wares in a small barn near their house. The upstairs loft is the sales room, and the lower floor is used both for spinning and as a classroom and demonstration room for groups who come to learn fabric-making. Their capelike coats and tunics run to $90 and $150. Jennifer has sold through shops and mail order, aiming for an affluent clientele. The competition is tough in California, and the market is full of shoddy merchandise. It's hard for shoppers to know just what they're getting. "Homespun" does not mean an item is handcrafted. And "natural-type" colors aren't necessarily from natural dyes.

To think of yourself as successful in this business, says Christina Smucker, "You have to be content with what is considered a lower standard of living because you surely aren't going to get rich selling handmade clothes. You will always have more hours involved than you get paid for, like a good farmer. We have learned how to be happy without spending a lot of money, and so we do not have to make a lot of it either."

Says Jennifer, "It's the greatest feeling in the world" knowing that "someone has paid $30, $40, or $50 for something you have made."

31: Under glass

Growing plants for sale in the greenhouse.

Many direct marketers find that a greenhouse serves not only as a place to start their own plants, but also as a place to grow flowers, herbs and vegetables for sale. Each year sees more established direct marketers expanding into plants of various kinds. They typically start with bedding plants—both vegetable and flowering—and then progress to potted foliage and flowering houseplants.

Alvi Voigt of the Pennsylvania State University Extension Service reports that between 1970 and 1976 bedding plant sales in the United States more than doubled, judging from a survey of 80 growers whose annual sales ranged all the way from $400 to $1,400,000 for the year 1970. By 1976 these same growers showed a range from $800 to $2,250,000 each. Which means the little guys did just as well, relatively, as the big fellows.

The USDA Statistical Reporting Service is authority for figures that show wholesale sales of foliage plants leaped from a national total of $27.7 million for the period 1959-70 to $187.2 million in the single year of 1975. That's an increase of nearly seven times.

By far the best selling bedding plants in 1976 were petunias, according to the Bedding Plant Institute. Impatiens were in second place, closely followed by tomatoes. Other leading sellers included geraniums grown from cuttings, peppers, begonias, marigolds, geraniums grown from seed, and pansies. But the total list of saleable bedding plants is as long as your arm. The experts suggest you start out with the most popular and wait for customer demand before adding on.

Bedding plants showing the greatest rate of sales increase in 1976 were impatiens, begonias, vegetables, geraniums, petunias, and marigolds, according to the Bedding Plant Institute. These same six have been leading the field in rate of increase since 1970.

Bedding plant marketers tell us that vegetable plants have a shorter selling period than flower plants because of the need to get vegetables in the ground at the right time. Potted foliage plants can be sold the year around.

Many organic growers involved in direct marketing make good use of greenhouses. David Hull of Applewood Orchards, Warwick, New York, grows mums, herbs and vegetable bedding plants in his 14-by-28-foot unit built of fiberglass. He operates the greenhouse from March to November and helps heat it in the cold months with his own solar energy contraption. He uses propane gas as a backup.

The Coouse family of Brenham, Texas, operators of the Yankee Peddler Herb Farm, built three greenhouses covering 2,500 square feet

and are contemplating a fourth unit. Herb plants and seed for mail order sale are the main stock in trade of the Coouse family, but they also grow some vegetable bedding plants. Their greenhouses are home-built using wood and fiberglass. Because of the Texas climate, Judy Coouse says they need supplemental heat only at night, using liquid propane gas for the purpose.

Linda Wey of Dewitt, Michigan, grows herbs and potted plants in her 12-by-24-foot greenhouse. It was built of redwood and fiberglass, with advice on construction from the Michigan State University Extension Service.

Gilbert Calta, Valley City, Ohio, grows a wide range of organic bedding plants, houseplants and herbs in his 1,400-square foot greenhouse. These supply his roadside stand. Sales from greenhouse items alone totaled nearly $3,000 in 1976. He has a glass greenhouse built from old parts he picked up here and there. He heats with gas.

Besides ornamental plants, some commercial greenhouse operators also grow vegetables ready to eat—tomatoes, cucumbers, lettuce. These are popular with restaurants and hotel dining rooms, as well as with some supermarkets that try to supply quality produce during the off-season.

Boyd Mertz of Northumberland, Pennsylvania, is the third generation of a family greenhouse business that started in 1917. Tomatoes and looseleaf lettuce (Grand Rapids) are sold mostly to wholesale distributors, although he does have some direct sales to consumers and area stores. He got seven pounds of tomatoes per plant in 1976, which he considered a good yield. He charged 56.5 cents a pound wholesale in the fall and 62 cents a pound the following spring. He says he can make money on tomatoes, but may discontinue lettuce because increased energy costs have cut too deeply into the price he can get for the lettuce.

To help enlarge his gross income, Mertz produces bedding plants and has begun growing geraniums from both seeds and cuttings. He says geraniums grown from seed make a more compact plant than those from cuttings, a feature that pleases many customers. He has started growing poinsettias in hanging baskets in the same greenhouses with his tomatoes, thus saving on space and fuel. Boyd's older greenhouses are enclosed with glass, but he has found he can reduce fuel consumption about 50 percent by adding a layer of plastic over the glass and

blowing air between the two surfaces, thus providing insulation.

In Ringtown, Pennsylvania, the Yarnells grow vine-ripened tomatoes in their greenhouse of nearly 3,000 square feet. The setup holds 800 plants trained on overhead wires. The Yarnells sell about half the tomatoes direct to consumers who come to the farm. The balance goes to several area grocery stores. There are two selling seasons. One starts in early October and continues into early December. The other starts in May and is over by the middle of July, when local outdoor tomatoes become available.

The Yarnells try to hold their prices constant throughout the selling season. In 1976 they got $1.50 retail for a strawberry box holding five tomatoes, or about two pounds. They sell the same tomatoes at 60 cents a pound wholesale, delivered. The store owners who sell Yarnell's vine-ripened tomatoes have learned that customers will pay at least 20 cents a pound more for them than they will for tomatoes picked green and ripened later.

The Yarnells find that customers who come to the farm to buy are at first a bit skeptical of tomatoes grown in a greenhouse. So, they are invited to take a look into the greenhouse to see what goes on. This seems to convince them that all is on the up-and-up and they buy. From then on, say the Yarnells, customers are hooked, buying not only for themselves but for their friends and neighbors, even giving the tomatoes as gifts.

As with other greenhouse growers, the Yarnells are being hurt by increasing energy costs. They have found coal as costly as oil for heating, and much dirtier. Now they are trying to find various ways to cut operating costs in order to compensate for increasing charges for oil.

Few greenhouse growers in the northern half of the country make an attempt to operate all through the winter months. Bedding plant operations start early enough in the spring to have the plants ready at the time they can be safely set outdoors. As noted with the Yarnells, those who grow greenhouse tomatoes and lettuce, for instance, produce only spring and fall crops, hitting the market before and after the local outdoor supply is available. For most growers, it just doesn't make economic sense to grow all through the winter.

Several land grant colleges have set up research programs to find ways to cut greenhouse heating costs. Experiments explore various sources of energy, with solar heat getting a high priority. Also under study are new types of structures that will make more use of the sun's heat while suffering less heat loss.

Many growers are building their own greenhouses, whether they are small organic growers or big commercial growers. Few, when questioned, have a good idea what the actual building costs came to. The Yarnells estimate they spent $7,000 to build their house of about 3,000 feet. They figure they saved about a third of what it would have cost if professionals had done the building. Their $7,000 figure includes the cost of watering and heating equipment, beds, ventilators and blowers, and electrical work, as well as pipe for framing and a double plastic covering.

The Yarnell's figures check pretty closely with those put together by researchers at Rutgers University, New Jersey, who surveyed plastic greenhouse operations for growing tomatoes in that state. They found the most common size house was 96-by-30 (2,880 square feet), which can handle 720 plants. Such a greenhouse in 1974 would have cost about $7,600 if you supplied your own labor. This figure includes the structure and such equipment as blowers and ventilators. Investment in tools, miscellaneous equipment such as pollinators, and growing medium would add several hundred dollars. New Jersey's figures for a complete house, including labor and equipment and an allowance for investment in land, came to $9,546, or $3.31 per square foot.

Rutgers figured the total cost of producing one harvest of spring tomatoes in 1974 was $4,080, which included depreciation, interest and labor. Out-of-pocket production costs, not counting labor, came to $1,505.

Total labor requirements for a 21.5-week growing and harvesting season were estimated to total 433 hours, including everything from growing seedlings to harvesting. The survey indicated the commercial growers in that state were getting an average of 12 pounds of tomatoes per plant, or 8,500 pounds per 96-by-30-foot house.

Throwing in all possible charges, including depreciation and interest, Rutgers figured it cost 47.2 cents to produce a pound of spring greenhouse tomatoes under the type of setup described and at a yield of 12 pounds per plant. However, depreciation and interest accounted for about a third of the total cost, as did labor. So if you toss those out, you'd come up with a production cost of about 15 cents a pound. The going wholesale price at the time of the study was 50 cents a pound. You'd get a much higher price, of course, selling direct.

The Rutgers study indicated the break-even yield for spring tomatoes, under the New Jersey setup, was 11.33 pounds per plant. Most of the growers grow only the spring crop. But Rutgers said if they also grew a fall crop they could make a profit for that season on a yield of only 6 pounds per plant since most of the overhead costs, such as depreciation, would have been written off on the spring crop.

Rutgers also has done research on the costs of producing bedding plants in greenhouses. As with their work with tomatoes, the researchers found that plastic houses are the most economical to build and operate. For bedding plants, they deducted that a Quonset-type house measuring 30-by-96 feet could be completely set up and equipped for about $8,500 in 1974. Such a house would be capable of handling 2,571 flats of bedding plants. Each flat holds 72 plants. At an estimated 15 minutes per flat, a total of 643 man-hours would be required to handle the operation.

Rutgers figured six months of operation with two crops of plants. The analysis gets pretty involved, but it would appear actual out-of-pocket costs per flat would amount to about $1.55, not counting labor. The total cost per flat, taking into consideration depreciation, labor, management, taxes and the like, ran to $3.04.

Alvi Voigt of Penn State analyzed the costs of three bedding plant growers in various-sized communities and came up with figures not far out of line with the Rutgers findings. A grower in a large city next to a metropolitan area had cost figures showing $3.08 per flat. Identical figures of $2.27 per flat were shown for both a grower in a city of 150,000 and for a grower in a rural area.

All three growers checked by Voigt sold plants at retail, mostly from the middle of April to early or late August. One grower with 14,000 square feet of greenhouse sold $25,000 worth at retail. Interestingly, one grower grossed $3 per square foot of bed space; another $2.50; and the third, $1.50. The wide variation probably can be attributed largely to varying costs of materials and labor, and management and marketing conditions.

It would appear that bedding plants offer the most feasible starting point for the small operator, followed by potted plants of one kind or another. Greenhouse tomatoes, lettuce and cucumbers are further down the line.

Plans for do-it-yourself greenhouses are available from your state extension service. For example, a New York State extension bulletin offers 11 different greenhouse building plans, ranging in price from 50 cents to $2.

Prefabricated greenhouses are widely available, of course. You've likely seen all sorts of the small, non-commercial type advertised in gardening magazines and catalogs. Commercial types come both as pre-fabs you can erect yourself (except perhaps for the use of an electrician and a plumbing-and-heating man) and as turn-key structures, fully complete and on your site.

The cost of a commercial size house measuring 96-by-30 feet, fully equipped with heaters, ventilators, and related items, would run about $2.25 a square foot, FOB the factory, in the summer of 1977. This figure is from the Geiger Supply Corporation of Harleysville, Pennsylvania, for a double-wall poly house, not including erecting cost. The polyethylene sheet covering the house will last about two years, many growers find, even though the company gives its life as only one year.

A fiberglass house of the same dimensions and similarly equipped was priced at about $3 per square foot in the summer of 1977. With a special coating on the outside, the fiberglass is said to have a life of 20 years. However, the double poly house, with its insulation barrier of air moving between the plastic layers, is credited with 30 percent greater energy efficiency. Smaller size houses are slightly more costly per square foot, the price going up as the size goes down.

Getting a jump on the season.

With cold weather comes dreams of owning a greenhouse. The trip to the local nursery for tomato plants, cabbage and peppers is an annual reminder that you could be raising your own. A further enticement is that a small greenhouse can be put up very easily and inexpensively.

A greenhouse grants you the pleasure of starting your own favorite varieties, in your own special way, on your preferred planting date. But more important, working in soil and shirt sleeves two months before anyone else just makes good business sense. You would feel reluctant to turn important income crops over to a caretaker for six to eight weeks during the critical growing time in summer; why should those *first* weeks be an exception? Plants need just as much care and attention in the greenhouse as they do later on in the garden, and maybe more.

Minnesota grower David Schonberg struggled through his first years without a greenhouse, purchasing plants from local nurseries. In some cases it worked out quite well. But if there is even one spring in which the arrangement doesn't work out, you may be looking at a lean year. One year, David arranged to buy a couple thousand tomato plants from a wholesale greenhouse, requesting a certain planting date. A date was scheduled to pick them up. Two or three long-distance phone calls assured him that everything was looking good and growing nicely. But when he arrived to pick the plants up he discovered that they had not even been planted. David laments, "To be so completely dependent upon another business for very important plants in the spring of the year is like having someone else pack your own parachute—the job may be done well but you hate to take chances."

Having said this, David points out that first tries at greenhouse work may not be as successful as one would wish in spite of care and attention devoted to the job. Few of the skills involved in raising strong, healthy seedlings can be learned without mistakes, and on occasion you may still have to call upon your local greenhouse. Even with costly mistakes, however, in time a greenhouse investment should pay for itself and go on to become a real asset to the business. Some growers work into a successful retail business selling bedding plants.

There are scores of excellent greenhouse designs and packages. For a full-time year-around operation, it's likely best to invest in a well-tailored unit; for seasonal use, however, a very inexpensive design may work out quite nicely. One simple greenhouse is constructed from hoops of pipe fastened into the ground at three-foot intervals and covered with a double layer of polyethylene.

The poly is fastened down with strips of wood lath around the base and then inflated (between the two layers) with air. For David Schonberg, the cost of materials looked like this:

$60   1¼-inch thinwall pipe for hoops (picked up at an iron salvage company)

$50   rough-cut lumber for door frames and baseboard around the perimeter of the greenhouse.

$80   polyethylene (purchased new every year)

$50   Jungers oil heater

$10   stovepipe

$ 5   fan and motor

$255   TOTAL

Says David, "If you have priced some of the greenhouses advertised in gardening publications, you may be asking yourself what kind of a toy can this be? Well, our greenhouse measures 67 feet long and 16 feet wide, and holds approximately 6,000 three-inch pots for melons plus 2,000 individual tomato plants and several hundred plants each of cabbage, cauliflower, and green peppers."

To be sure, David did his own work and, as may be guessed from the prices, much of the material was picked up here and there very reasonably. The tubing was purchased by the pound from a scrap iron dealer and bent around a silo to shape it into hoops. The hoops were spliced to give them extra length. The fan came from a car heater, and was fitted to a 110-volt electric motor. The lumber was rough-sawed pine. The product, however, is as sound and operable as a much more expensive unit.

Maybe even $255 is more than you care to spend on a greenhouse, and 1,000 square feet could be more than you need. With a little improvising you can build a 12-by-18-foot greenhouse for $125. This one takes but seven hoops and less than one fourth of the plastic. It goes up quickly and will hold 75 flats (10-by-20-inch), which is enough to raise thousands of individual seedlings.

Select the size you want. For a 12-foot-wide greenhouse, 20-foot pipe is required; David used two 10-foot electrical conduits (¾-inch diameter) spliced together to make 20-foot hoops. A 16-foot-wide greenhouse requires 25-foot pipes, and a 20-foot-wide greenhouse would take 30-foot pipes. Hoops are fastened to the ground by means of short (18-inch) sections of pipe driven into the ground at three-foot intervals. The hoops must fit snugly into these sockets. Opposite the first row of sockets, a second row is driven into the ground, providing a place to anchor both ends of each hoop. Leave six inches of each socket above ground for fastening down the wooden baseboard.

It is important to avoid damaging the ends of the sockets when driving them into the ground. Insert a snug-fitting bolt into the end that is struck with the maul. Remove the bolt after the socket is in the ground. Failure to observe this precaution may result in bent pipe ends, making it difficult to insert the hoops.

Bolt for driving sockets

Hoops erected and ready for the plastic

Slip only one end of each hoop into position. The other end must be allowed to remain loose until the ridge pole is slipped over it. The ridgepole is a 2x4, 8 to 16 feet long, drilled every 3 feet with holes large enough for the hoops to slip into. If a single ridge pole is not long enough to span the entire length of the greenhouse then two or more 2x4s must be butted end to end. After all the sections of the ridgepole are in place at the top of the hoops, fasten the remaining end of each hoop down into the sockets and splice the sections of the ridgepole together. Wire or bolt a 2x6, 2x8, 2x10, or 2x12 to the outside of the sockets around the entire perimeter of the greenhouse. If bolts are used, drill completely through the wood, the socket, and the end of the hoop which is inserted into the socket. If wire is used, clench it down tightly. The wooden baseboard may tend to come up unless fastened securely. Frame in a door at both ends. For ease of construction you may wish to allow room for a stovepipe to go out above the door. This eliminates the need to cut into the plastic, and is worth keeping in mind when designing door frames.

A small electric motor with a squirrel cage fan must be installed at this point. For size and capacity a hair dryer will do the trick, but the rigors of continuous duty suggest selecting something with better bearings. The fan is mounted to a board, and then fan and board are fastened to the baseboard of the greenhouse at a point handy to an electrical outlet.

Pad all sharp corners and edges to avoid tearing and wearing of the plastic. This being done the greenhouse is ready for its skin. Unroll the clear polyethylene (four mil or six mil will do) down one whole side of the greenhouse. The polyethylene must be a foot or two wider than the length of the hoops to assure plenty of material for fastening down to the baseboard. It must also extend far enough beyond each end to reach to the door frame after being wrapped around the corner. Firmly cleat down one edge of the plastic sheet to the baseboard all along one side of the greenhouse, using wood lath or other strips of wood. If the wind is blowing at this point, weight down the unrolled but still folded sheet of poly and wait until the wind dies down in the evening or early morning. When everything is ready, assemble all available hands and start working the skin up and over. Be ready with hammer, lath and nails. Quickly tack the plastic down at strategic intervals. When everything is under control, stretch it tight and fasten securely, fastening on the ends also. Before commencing with the second sheet, secure the first around the opening of the squirrel-cage fan. Then cut away the plastic that covers the opening itself. Having done this, cover the greenhouse with the second sheet of plastic using the same procedure as for the first. (As a precautionary measure, you might nail down yet a third set of wood lath all around the base and on both ends.)

At this point the two sheets of plastic should be virtually airtight. Turn the fan on. There should be no significant air leakage anywhere in

Unrolling the plastic

the entire greenhouse. (Remember, the fan does not inflate the greenhouse, but only the air space between the two tightly sealed sheets of plastic.) Within five or ten minutes the first sheet of plastic should be pressed tightly against the hoops and the outer sheet should be taut, and billowed out like a huge bubble. If this is not the case, check to see where the air is escaping.

Very little air pressure is needed to inflate the polyethylene. A strong fan may create too much pressure, which can be remedied by restricting the flow of the fan or allowing a little air to escape around the base of the greenhouse. The object is to have just enough air pressure between the two layers to prevent whipping in the wind.

Dependable heat is a must. When the temperature drops down into the twenties or teens you don't want any problems. If the investment is to be kept small, one or two dependable space heaters will work out fairly nicely. For their 1,000-square-foot greenhouse, the Schonbergs first used a Jungers oil heater. The stove pipe went out above the door on the north end. A window fan was used to distribute the heat. Now a Jungers heater is used at both ends. This makes for more even distribution of heat and gives a bit of a safety factor in case one should malfunction and go out. You may find it convenient to go to either gas or electric heat set to thermostats. Whatever the system used, make sure the heaters are vented properly. Some plants are very vulnerable to bad air.

The inflated greenhouse

The interior plan of your greenhouse depends on what crops are desired and on the amount of space needed. A visit to a commercial greenhouse will give you some ideas. David says he chose to keep the plants close to the ground for the simple reason that the greenhouse is bigger close to the ground than it is three feet above. To keep plants off the cold earth, they are placed on a platform of concrete blocks supporting a grill of pipe and wooden lathe. If the greenhouse is only for your own use and does not see many visitors, keep the aisles narrow. The two aisles in David's 16-foot-wide greenhouse give access, with a little stretching, to every flat.

Greenhouse construction can be summarized this way: If you want a well-designed greenhouse with all the head work done by someone else, consult the yellow pages and your bank account. If you can't afford that kind of investment but are willing to do a little figuring, improvising, and construction on your own, you may find David's style of construction a place to begin. Pick up what you can from those who know the business and then set off on your own experiment.

When you can stand back and look with satisfaction on your completed greenhouse, with the plastic taut and already warm and dripping on the inside, it isn't hard to picture it full of strong, sturdy seedlings all ready to transplant. Neither is it difficult to picture ripe delicious muskmelons when the young plants are just beginning to send out runners. In both cases, however, a lot of time, work and skill is required before the dream comes true. Sturdy young seedlings don't grow by themselves. A general knowledge of planting dates, germination techniques, containers, potting soil, potting, watering, feeding, temperatures, and hardening is needed. This is not to say that one has to be an expert to see success. The Schonbergs set up a 12-by-18-foot greenhouse for a nearby elementary school, and for several years the sixth grade class has done a fairly good job of raising and selling potted flower plants and vegetable plants.

Many factors combine to make strong seedlings, and the most important of these would probably be the potting soil. A plant draws its life for weeks from a tiny little cube, and that cube has to be stocked with nutrients.

Another consideration is texture of the mixture. Potting soil must take repeated waterings without becoming gummy, and it must not turn hard when dry. Proper texture encourages roots to grow and intertwine freely. Most commercial potting soil is a combination of peat moss, vermiculite and soil, with chemical plant food. Those who are not committed to organic agriculture will find plenty of literature available for mixing up a good potting soil preparation. Those hoping to avoid chemical fertilizers may need to do some experimenting.

Schonberg has had best success with tomatoes, cauliflower, melons, and green peppers when using straight barnyard manure that is fairly well rotted but not to the point that it has already turned back into soil. Fertile black dirt by itself lacks texture and nutrients; he has experimented with it and was surprised by how poorly it did, as seedlings transplanted into that same soil in the garden did very well. The best results were with half-rotted barnyard manure. Yet even with this nutrient-laden plant food, the small seedlings eventually reached a stage in their development where they simply ran out of food. From a deep dark green, the leaves began to turn light green, and the growth slowed down and almost stopped. By the time the plants were set out into the field, some showed severe stress to the point that lower leaves would dry up and fall off.

David was able to come up with a non-chemical preparation for feeding the deficient plants. After some experimentation he adopted a "somewhat disagreeable but extremely successful" method of dunking the flats in a vat of manure tea every week or two. One part fresh chicken manure containing wood chips was mixed with three parts water by volume. Experimenting with both tomato plants and melon plants on a small scale lest the brew should be too potent, David noticed a marked change within just a few days.

"To our delight, the plants became lush. Not only did they look great, but when the time came for them to be set out into the field they were advancing daily. These plants did not need to reverse their downhill trend before starting to generate some forward momentum, unlike those that had not been fed. They were off and growing from the very first day."

David now uses a dip tank and a drainboard. To avoid moving the flats he may go to a filter system so that the tea can be sprayed on the plants from an overhead reservoir. "At this point we cannot claim any medals for efficiency and we are not beyond making mistakes. Furthermore, manure potting soil and manure tea are not as pleasant to work with as vermiculite, peat moss and chemical fertilizers. Still, we are pleased to think that there is a way to raise strong healthy seedlings without resorting to commercial fertilizers."

Soil that teems with life is a delight to every organic gardener, but too much life in the form of weeds can also kill any commercial venture. This holds true in the greenhouse as well as outside in the field. To minimize the weed problem, guard the barnyard or compost pile from which you intend to take your potting soil. Keep all weeds from going to seed for at least one season before using that material in your greenhouse. You will still have weeds, but few enough to handle.

Apart from potting soil and plant feeding, work is much the same for the organic gardener as for the conventional grower. "It would be worth several chapters to spend a day in a greenhouse visiting with a veteran grower," says Schonberg. "The tips we have picked up in this way have proven invaluable." For one: cover the flats with a layer or two of newspaper while the seeds are germinating to insulate the soil from the hot sun. This keeps the moisture rather uniformly distributed in the flat, and prevents a dry crust from forming over the tiny seeds. As needed, sprinkle down the newspaper.

Experienced growers also cautioned about overwatering—a common mistake of beginners. Once plants such as tomatoes, cabbages, peppers and other vegetable plants have become established, be a little stingy with the water. Let the vegetable plants wilt a bit before sprinkling them. This stimulates root development and holds down the growth of the tops. When ready for transplanting, these plants are usually stout, sturdy, and possess an extensive root system.

The young plants must be hardened to outdoor weather before transplanting them into the field. The trip from the greenhouse to the field gives the plants the double shock of outdoor weather and new soil. The trauma is reduced by introducing these changes one at a time. A week before you expect to transplant into the field, remove the flats from the greenhouse. David believes it is important to let the young plants feel the wind and direct sunlight while their roots are still contained in the familiar surroundings of the greenhouse packs. He is convinced that it is more important to avoid setbacks during this stage of plant growth than one might normally think; a young transplant that just sits in the field for even a week is much more vulnerable to damage than one that never stops growing from the time it leaves the greenhouse. As in all areas of agriculture there are enough unforeseen problems without inviting trouble by failing in the jobs you know can make a difference.

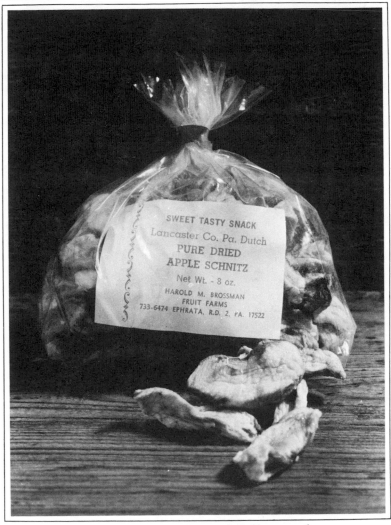

Twenty-three part- and full-time businesses.

Five

32: Market garden: Newport, New Hampshire

FOR SOME GARDENERS, going commercial simply means adding a few rows. For Jerry Jachim and Diana Weidenbacker, going commercial meant buying a 150-year-old farm in central New Hampshire.

The two women haven't chosen an easy life. The surrounding farmland has reverted back to forest, and saplings are to be seen here and there on Heartland Farm's acres. The farm is reached by a dirt road that travels through woodland. At a turn in the road, the woods opens up to a white clapboard farmhouse, attached shingled barn, and a view that makes visiting friends vow to someday buy their own old farms.

But it's a dream that demands total involvement, causing Jerry to wish at times that she could disassociate herself from her work. That's

Jerry Jachim, right, and Diana Weidenbaker

difficult to do, because the making of her dream is all around her: a house that needs plumbing and complete renovation, land to be tilled, produce to be delivered, and books to be read.

Book learning is important to Jerry and Diana because they are seldom in touch with other small-scale growers and they haven't a county agent. But gardening books say little of larger scale methods (most books written for the market gardener went out of print fifty years ago). For example, Jerry looked up a nostrum for earworms, and the time-consuming solution "makes you want to just scream": peel back the top of each ear and squirt a bit of mineral oil. While this is a proven method for a family-sized garden, it is of little use in the truck patch, Jerry feels.

Another hitch in bringing the dream to reality is that beautiful, isolated location; customers have to be lured down the dirt road, which is made difficult by the state's stringent regulations on roadside signs. They've gotten around this problem by painting "TOMATOES" right on their mailbox—a sneaky ploy really, since their mail is not delivered.

This is the two women's first season, and business has been very modest so far. Tilling 2½ acres, they count $300 for four week's sales—not much, considering an outlay of $160 for seeds alone, and a mortgage payment that keeps Diana at her job as a psychologist. Ordering seed was a problem. Jerry said she had trouble finding untreated seed, expecially popcorn. She learned belatedly of Johnny's Selected Seeds, a Maine company that sells seeds especially suited for northern New England weather. These seeds are not hybrids, meaning that seed collected from plants will grow true to their parents.

Sales should be better next year. Word is getting out that the two women at the end of the lane have excellent produce at good prices. Local folks typically are not gardeners, and those that are still come for crops they don't grow, such as pumpkins and cukes for pickling. Many customers are summer residents, and 30 percent or so of all customers are from out-of-state.

At some point, increasing business may warrant hiring a hand— perhaps a picker or help at a roadside stand. For now, however, the business is kept modest both by the hard work and an on-going lack of information. Jerry is concerned with both learning how to create new channels for their crops and finding labor-saving short cuts to ease the strain of fourteen-hour days (Jerry confesses to having made retreats to a nearby McDonald's just to get away from the farm). Jerry and Diana are eager to talk to other small organic farmers, but the opportunities are rare. Not far away, the National Organic Farmers Association (NOFA) held an ill-timed three-day conference in September—peak business days for the women, and they couldn't attend. New Hampshire sends out a marketing newsletter, and they find this a help.

This first year has turned up an interesting customer attitude: people see cheap food as a right, says Jerry. At a time when folks don't blink at spending hundreds for car repairs or heating bills, food shopping has become the last consumer area in which pennies are taken seriously.

33: Mushrooms: Mullica Hill, New Jersey

AMERICANS ARE EATING more and more mushrooms these days; total consumption has risen over 100 percent in the last ten years. That's quite phenomenal when you consider that consumption of all vegetables has risen less than 20 percent in that time. Per capita consumption of mushrooms in the United States currently is about 2.6 pounds, still much lower than that of many other countries, especially those in Europe. Interestingly, fresh consumption has increased some 360 percent in the last ten years. Consumption of canned mushrooms increased only 73 percent in that time.

As a result of the tremendous new consumer interest in this delectable fungus, new mushroom growing operations are springing up in various parts of the country. That's one of the nice things about mushrooms—they can be grown anywhere. Local soil and climate are unimportant because a grower supplies his own. Mushrooms currently are being grown commercially in at least 25 states: Pennsylvania, Delaware, Maryland, New Jersey, New York, Ohio, California, Colorado, Florida, Georgia, Hawaii, Illinois, Indiana, Kentucky, Massachusetts, Michigan, Minnesota, Missouri, Oregon, South Dakota, Texas, Utah, Virginia, Washington, and Wisconsin. Two large facilities are expected to be in operation in Connecticut in 1978.

A recent addition to the ranks of mushroom growers is the Caltabiano family of Mullica Hill, New Jersey. Alfred Caltabiano and his three sons, Alfred Jr., Phil, and Ronald, are apple and peach growers who got into mushrooms just five years ago. Why mushrooms?

Phil explains: "A couple of bad years with our peach crop convinced us we needed another enterprise that would supply income in a more reliable manner. After looking around, we decided on mushrooms as something we could grow during the winter months when our orchard work is at a minimum."

Cultivated mushrooms normally are grown in long houses of wood or cinder block. But instead of going to the expense of erecting new structures, the Caltabianos figured they would simply use the buildings in which they store their apples until sold. One of these is made of block, and other is of corrugated steel. By moving their apples to market as soon as possible, the Caltabianos have the structures free for mushroom growing from November on.

Alfred Caltabiano

The Caltabianos try to get their first mushrooms picked around Christmas and then continue to harvest the next three months. They accomplish this by starting one house ahead of the other. Like many small growers, they produce only one crop a year. This gives time to clear out the houses in advance of the apple harvest.

To make the structures suitable for mushroom growing, foam insulation was sprayed on walls and roof, at a cost of about $5,000 per house. They added hot-water heating systems (hot air is too drying) at about $1,000 per house and circulating fans at $150 per house. Humidity is raised by daily hosing the concrete floors.

The Caltabianos now use the "tray" system for growing mushrooms. For years, mushrooms houses were equipped with permanently installed beds, built one atop the other. All work of filling with compost, spawning, adding casing soil, and harvesting was done by hand in the houses under cramped conditions. The new tray system provides for removable containers which can be mechanically filled outside the house. The trays are handled by fork-lift trucks. The Caltabianos fill portable wooden beds with compost outdoors and then stack them one on top of another in the growing house, where the spawn and casing soil are added. Total cost of the trays was about $6,750, not counting labor; they spent $5,000 for lumber to build some of them and acquired the rest secondhand at $5 each. Because of the continued need for temperature and humidity control, the trays stay in the houses during the harvest period. By stacking their trays nine high, with catwalks at the fourth level, the Caltabianos are able to jam 9,000 square feet of growing area into each building. They get an average yield of 2.5 pounds per square foot, for a total of 45,000 pounds for the season. (Average yield was estimated at 2.9 pounds per square foot in 1976-77. This compares with an average of 1.65 pounds in 1948.)

A publication issued by the American Mushroom Institute in 1970 estimated the cost of growing a pound of mushrooms commercially at 25 to 35 cents a pound, including labor and depreciation. By 1977, however, one commercial grower said that his costs were running about 50 cents a pound.

The average price received by commercial growers selling through brokers for the fresh market averaged 82.4 cents in the 1976-77 season, according to the U.S. Crop Reporting Service. This was 10.5 cents a pound higher than the previous year. Average price paid to the grower for canning mushrooms was 66.9 cents. Prices vary from area to area and from season to season. Prices are higher on the East Coast in summer than in winter because fewer mushrooms are grown due to the need for air conditioning. (Unless, of course, you grow mushrooms in a case where temperature and humidity can remain constant the year around.)

The family business hasn't yet been troubled by disease. Phil attributes this to the fact they are in an area where mushrooms have not been grown before. A combination of pyrethrum and malathion is used to spray flies during harvest.

Because they are close to southeastern Pennsylvania, the nation's largest mushroom growing area, the Caltabianos are able to buy ready-made compost.

The family was aware that mushroom growing is more complex than raising fruits and vegetables, and asked the help of an established grower in another area of southern New Jersey. He taught them many of the fundamentals. They also joined the American Mushroom Institute (Box 373, Kennett Square, Pennsylvania 19348) from which they receive considerable technical assistance. And they attend mushroom seminars sponsored by the Pennsylvania State University.

The Caltabiano's sign doesn't indicate their new line

Most of the Caltabiano mushrooms currently end up at a nearby cannery. But Phil says the family is seriously considering ways to market fresh mushrooms in order to realize a better profit. They grow a strain called "creams" which are highly desirable for canning but aren't as favored for fresh consumption in the eastern states, where strains called "whites" and "off-whites" reign supreme.

It is not likely the Caltabianos will switch to whites when they move to heavier fresh sales, however. Despite the slight price differential in the East in favor of whites, there appears to be a growing interest in creams on the part of eastern consumers. There are devotees who say the creams stay fresh longer and are more flavorful and crisper than the whites. An alert retailer in the Washington, D.C., area charges more for creams than for whites, merchandising the creams as "gourmet" mushrooms. He may well be pointing the way to a whole new status level for creams in the eastern market. Some commercial growers will tell you that creams are more prolific than whites and more disease resistant. And creams are traditionally more popular in the West.

Marketing mushrooms in over-wrap trays of 8, 12, and 16 ounces is becoming increasingly popular because it helps extend the shelf life by a few days—provided, of course, the mushrooms are kept cool. When sold in bulk out of large containers, mushrooms suffer from considerable bruising and lose quality rapidly.

The American Mushroom Institute estimates that the minimum size of a growing establishment required to make a family living is 20,000 square feet of harvest area. Since trays or beds are stacked several high this doesn't mean the building would need to be that large. The institute says the cost of erecting and equipping a building to handle this much growing area would be about $50,000, with an additional working capital of $10,000 to pay for compost, spawn and other expenses.

The Caltabianos are happy with their decision to add mushrooms to their agriculture enterprise. "We've achieved our purpose of adding a crop that helps even out our cash flow," says Phil. "We have profitable work for the family during the winter months and at the same time provide year-around work for some hired help that otherwise would be only seasonal. We've improved our financial situation and brought about greater assurance that we will be able to continue in agriculture and the kind of life that goes with it."

34: Wild shiitake: Davis, California

FRED HOWARD AND his wife, Billie, live in a modest suburb of Davis, California, a sleepy college town and agricultural research center. Their lives had been fairly typical, centered around raising five children, assorted animals, flowers, and vegetables—until Fred, a university lecturer with insatiable curiosity, a penchant for hard work, and a zest for opportunity, discovered the shiitake.

The shiitake, *Lentinus edodes,* is a mushroom grown primarily in Japan, China, Korea and Malaysia. Its mystique is abetted by its multi-sexual nature, a characteristic that has kept this gourmet's prize an essentially wild crop. Japan is a major exporter of the shiitake; the mushrooms are dehydrated and shipped, 80 percent of them to the United States.

"In Japan," says Fred, "the shiitake grows wild, principally on shii trees. The Japanese picked shiitake from the wild shii trees over 1,000 years ago. Two hundred years ago the Japanese began 'managed stand' operations to prevent extinction of the shii tree. Today, a Japanese shiitake grower raises shii trees, cuts them to four-foot lengths, inoculates them with the mushroom mycelium, then returns the trees to their natural habitat to await mushroom growth. About two years later, the shiitake fruits—producing mushrooms."

"They said the shiitake couldn't be grown in our environment," says Fred. "Only two or three people have done it. We built a shed and were astonished to be able to grow it on oak trees, although they are similar to shii trees in composition. From there we moved out of labor-intensive culture to a streamlined bed culture."

Today, the Howards' home is a mushroom factory. Mushrooms are everywhere: in bedrooms and baths, in converted fish tanks, recycled infant incubators, in eight refrigerators, six freezers, in number-12 tin cans, stacked floor to ceiling, and naturally in salads and other dishes.

Every family member has a place in the Mushroom Factory, Inc., the Howards' newly incorporated business. Diana and Karl, recently married, are in charge of production. They prepare the specially balanced growing medium of oak chips, wheat or rice bran, paddy rice, sugar, and water.

"The bulk of our growing medium is largely throw-away," Fred points out. "We buy oak chips by the garbage can full. Rice bran, the most nutritive part of the grain, is milled away when polished rice is produced. California is one of the world's largest rice producers, so the bran is readily available, loaded with nutrients. The shiitake thrives on it."

By providing the optimum growing conditions for shiitake—the process of domestication—the Howards have cut production time from two years to 3½ months.

Once the medium is mixed, the Howards place it in large cans and seal each with an oven plastic cap. The cans are then placed in an autoclave and treated at high temperature under pressure. The medium is inoculated with shiitake mycelium, which Fred cultures himself from vegetative mushroom tissue. This process insures each mushroom is identical, without the possibility of strain variation. Inoculation takes place in cans placed in a sterile chamber made from a recycled fish tank and equipped with an ultraviolet light.

Next, the inoculated container is sealed with plastic, admitting air while discouraging contamination. Each can is then labeled, dated, and stacked on shelves under slightly subdued room light.

After three months, the thin strands of shiitake mycelium are placed in a homemade plastic box, rehydrated, sprayed frequently with water mist, and kept at 70°F (21°C). Mature buds form in several weeks and then, within a matter of days, the shiitake pops out. Each weighs 33 to 250 grams and can be harvested. Fred isn't sure yet how long each log will produce, but his educated guess is two years.

In the marketplace, the shiitake is not really in competition with the standard mushroom, since the Japanese exotic is vital to gourmet

Eastern cooking.

"Nutritionally," says Fred, "the shiitake, like the brown mushroom, is a superior food." Shiitake contains three percent protein, little fat or sodium, is rich in B vitamins (especially niacin) and minerals. In common with most wild edible mushrooms, shiitakes supply more nutrients than the common market mushroom.

The Howards' Mushroom Factory will supply quality shiitake to what Fred describes as the smaller markets, including primarily restaurants and grocery stores specializing in Oriental or gourmet cooking. The Howard's are dedicated to keeping theirs a family-owned business wherein each family member can use his or her particular skills.

In time, Fred will follow his primary ambition, which is to continue wild edible mushroom domestication. Future conquests? The morel, the boletus, the chantrelle, and the truffle.

35: Schnitz: Ephrata and York Springs, Pennsylvania

ELSEWHERE IN THIS book, in Chapter 8, "What Can You Sell?," mention is made of dried apple snacks called schnitz by the Pennsylvania Dutch, who originally made them so they could have apple pie and other apple delicacies during the out-of-season months.

Schnitz has become a good seller at roadside markets in Pennsylvania. Many of the enthusiastic buyers are tourists from all parts of the country, which seems to indicate dried apple snacks would be highly saleable anywhere apples are grown.

One small Pennsylvania apple grower has found that making apple snacks offers a more profitable way of marketing a larger percentage of his apples than selling them fresh. As a matter of fact, he doesn't bother to try to sell *any* fresh. Those that don't go into schnitz wind up

in apple butter or cider. Harold M. Brossman of Ephrata, Lancaster
County, has only 30 acres of apples—not much, judging by the standards of most commercial apple growers, especially in a state where
some orchards cover more than one thousand acres. Harold says most
brokers and wholesale buyers didn't want to bother with his fresh apples because he didn't have the volume to suit them. If they bought at
all, the price left him little or no profit.

So ten years ago Harold got into the schnitz-making business, and
now can hardly keep up with the demand. He is one of only a couple of
schnitz makers in the state who put out enough volume to supply
scores of roadside markets and area retail stores. (Some roadside operators make their own or have them made by a neighbor.)

Harold's schnitz business has progressed to the point he now has

Harold M. Brossman

two stainless steel drying tables, heated by gas. Both can handle the slices from 35 bushels of apples. Every 35 bushels will net about 140 pounds of schnitz.

To prepare the apples, Harold has acquired a second-hand machine that peels, cores, and slices. The machine handles four apples at a time. The slices are dumped onto the drying tables and cooked at 140°F (60°C) for anywhere from 15 to 17 hours, depending on the condition of the apples. The slices are stirred occasionally while drying. He has learned by experience when to turn off the heat, but there have been a few times when he got busy elsewhere and the slices overcooked, making them unmarketable.

After drying, the slices are cooled and stored in steel drums prior to being packed in half-pound plastic bags. Harold finds the snacks keep best in cold storage if held for any great length of time.

Snacks are made all winter long from apples out of storage. When his own apples are exhausted, Harold buys from other orchardists in the area. Both sweet and tart snacks are made. For sweet, he uses mostly Red Delicious, Golden Delicious, and Rome; for tart, he uses Stayman and York. The varieties would vary by sections of the country.

Harold's label emphasises that his schnitz is pure. He uses no additives or preservatives of any kind. Neither does he use citric acid to keep the slices white as they dry. He finds that the word "pure" on his label is a good selling point.

As this is written, Harold grosses about $280 for each 35 bushels of apples. Out of this comes the cost of hired labor, electricity, bottled gas for the drier, and general overhead. He figures he has put about $2,000 into equipment, which is located in a small out-building. Harold employs a half-dozen area women on a part-time basis to handle the work of running the schnitz operation.

To get extra use out of drying equipment, he also does a small business in dried corn. He uses white or yellow sweet corn. His apple butter is made for him by a fellow farmer who specializes in this type of processing. Harold does, however, make his own cider, which is sold without preservatives.

The demand for his dried apple snacks has reached the point where Harold is faced with a major decision: to stay with his present setup or get larger. Expansion would mean more capital investment, more logistics problems, more headaches of all types. A strong advocate of the small-is-beautiful philosophy, Harold Brossman isn't sure whether expansion is the next logical step, despite the extra net dollars it would bring.

While most roadside market operators in Pennsylvania buy their schnitz from an outside supplier, Everett Weiser of York Springs makes the snacks right at his roadside stand. That is, his stand at-

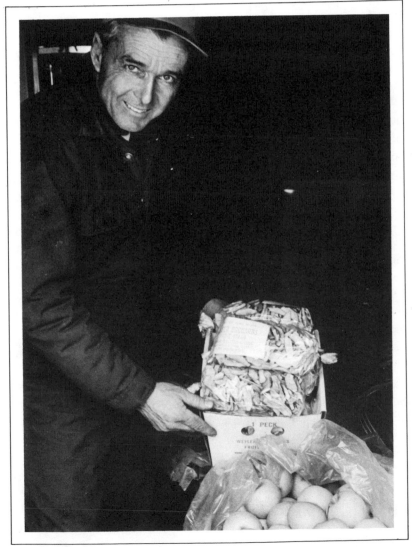

Everett Weiser

tendant makes them, in between customers. Ev himself is too busy with his varied farming enterprises.

The Weiser schnitz manufacturing setup is about as simple as you can get without reverting back to using the kitchen oven, as schnitz was made years ago. Ev uses a four-tray food dehydrator—a lightweight box about 30 inches square that holds an electric heating coil and a small fan to circulate the warm air. A slot in the door admits fresh air.

Apple slices are laid on the trays and dried for a period of seven to eight hours at about 185°F (85°C). They come out when the attendant feels they are ready: some people make schnitz rather soft and rubbery, but Ev's product is inclined to be crisp, or nearly so. This seems to make them extra tasty.

When the snacks are cooled, they are packaged in plastic bags. Instead of using a scale, which would have to be okayed by a weights and measures inspector, Ev simply sells by dry measure—each bag holds one quart. When we weighed a bag we found it came to about seven ounces. This would vary with the dryness of the schnitz. Ev gets $1.50 a bag, meaning about $3 a pound. Since the drier makes about five quarts at a time, he grosses $7.50 a batch.

To prepare the apples, the stand attendant peels them by hand and cores and slices them with a simple device that can be bought in many stores for about $1.50—as it is pushed down over the apple, an inside circle cuts out the core and thin blades radiating out from the center make the slices. The gadget as purchased makes 8 slices. Since these are too thick for schnitz, Ev has done what most farmers do with equipment that doesn't quite fit their needs. He made his own adaptation. To get 16 slices instead of 8, he simply bolted two of the gadgets together.

Everett Weiser says he makes only a small profit on his schnitz, but he charges off the value of the apples, attendant's time, and cost of electricity to run the dehydrator. However, he does feel the schnitz brings customers to his market for other items.

For someone who has more apples than he can readily sell and who doesn't charge off hired help time, schnitz would seem to be a fairly profitable item when made on a small scale. But, as Ev says, the real worth may lie in using schnitz to build traffic to your market.

36: Organic beef farm: Freeport, Maine

IN CONTRAST TO many direct marketers' modest operations is Wolf's Neck Farm, on the coast south of Freeport, Maine. Mrs. L.M.C. Smith and farm manager Charlie De Grandpre oversee a thousand-acre organic beef operation. The farm is idyllic. Manicured fields, hedged with pines, roll gently to the edge of Casco Bay. A tidy New England farmhouse serves as the office, and right next door are the walk-in freezers.

All meat is handled frozen, whether it is sold at the locker door, delivered by truck, or air-shipped. The late Mr. Smith devised a box-within-a-box shipping container. Reusable freezer ice blocks—the sort placed in picnic coolers—are packed around the meat, and long-distance delivery must be by air. As an example, beef is taken to Portland Airport at 7 A.M. and arrives in Florida in time for evening pick-

Charlie De Grandpre, manager of Wolf's Neck Farm

up, still "hard as a rock," according to Charlie. The customer pays the air freight charges, plus a surcharge that covers double boxing, the reusable ice containers, and transportation to the airport at Portland.

Truck deliveries are made monthly to New Hampshire, Massachusetts, and Connecticut. For this service, the customer pays a modest charge per carton.

Meat may be purchased at the farm any day but Sunday, and is also sold at the office of a farm-owned campground that abuts the pastures.

Wolf's Neck Farm currently offers a 42-pound hind-quarter carton, a 42-pound standard carton, a 42-pound ground beef carton, and a 20-pound ground beef carton. Organ meats, stew beef and soup bones are also available, and organic lamb is sold from time to time.

Parasites aren't much of a problem because the three-hundred-odd head of cattle are rotated to different pastures every seven to ten days. Animal health has not been a problem. Cut animals are treated with peroxide. Charlie has tried fly traps, but these mostly catch houseflies. He sends the cattle feed to New Jersey to be tested for contaminants, at $60 per sample. The cattle are slaughtered at a federally inspected house, aged approximately 14 days, then cut, wrapped, flash frozen, and returned to the farm's freezers.

Wolf's Neck Farm is hardly the typical homestead operation. The farm employs three men full-time on the beef operation, plus clerical help year around; in summer, four or five men are hired to put up crops. The beef operation was set up by Mr. Smith as the practice of the

Wolf's Neck Farm

man's beliefs, rather than for need of income. In the fifties he saw a need for chemical-free beef. He also wanted to preserve a few pieces of Maine's open land which was rapidly reverting to forest. Neighboring New Hampshire is now the most heavily wooded of the forty-eight contiguous states, and throughout New England, old farmhouses are crowded on all sides by trees. But today, Wolf's Neck Farm is a beautiful exception.

37: Natural foods store and truck farm: Humansville, Missouri

YOU WOULDN'T ORDINARILY expect to find a well-stocked natural food store in a town the size of Humansville, Missouri.

But then the proprietors of the store, Dan and Paulette Wohnoutka, are not exactly ordinary people. Three years ago, the Wohnoutkas and their three children left the urban sprawl of San Jose, California, and settled on an 80-acre farm near this southwestern Missouri town of 825 people.

The Wohnoutkas had become accustomed to natural foods in California. But in rural Missouri they found that the nearest natural food store was in Springfield, some 40 miles away. Other than the organic produce from their own garden and milk from their cow, the Wohnoutkas could only stock up on natural food products during infrequent trips to the larger town.

"Forty miles is a long way to drive to do your food shopping," says Paulette, "but we wanted to stay with natural foods as much as possible while we got the homestead geared up to produce more of our food supply. It came as quite a surprise to us to learn that the reputation of rural America as a source of wholesome, nutritious food is largely a myth. Some families produce a good part of their food supply organically, of course. But, on the average, rural families are probably

Paulette Wohnoutka, with daughter Sharon and customers   *Jim Ritchie*

no more conscious of good nutrition than a family in town."

During their first year on the farm, the Wohnoutkas often voiced their wish that someone would open a natural food store closer than 40 miles away.

"After talking it over with friends here, we decided that 'someone' might as well be us," says Paulette.

For the first two years, the store was located in a rebuilt guest house on the farm. The Wohnoutkas put in shelves, bins, and a pot-bellied stove, and the guest house took on the flavor of an oldtime country store.

"We started with only $500 worth of inventory—that's all we could afford," recalls Paulette. "But we brought natural foods to rural Missouri. We still haven't earned a lot of money to put into our own pockets, but we have increased the selection of foodstuffs offered to our customers, both from outside sources and from the produce of our homestead."

Interestingly, when the Wohnoutkas first opened their natural foods store, a high percentage of their customers were older neighbors rather than younger people. The Wohnoutkas figure the store reminded the oldsters of earlier days, back when people grew much of their own food and shopped at country stores for the few things they needed to buy. After operating the store at the farm for about two years, and building up a modest business in the process, the Wohnoutkas rented a building in Humansville and moved the store to town.

"The whole experience has been as much an education process as a business venture, both for us and for our neighbors around here," says Paulette. "When we opened the store, we hoped to make a profit, of course. And we also hoped to educate people in proper nutrition at the same time. We've had some success at both."

As the store clientele grew, Dan Wohnoutka spent as much time as he could spare at clearing the land and getting the homestead into production. In time, and in seasons, the family produces more and more of the organically grown food products they market through the store.

Now, they're selling quite a variety of home-grown vegetables, and want to develop a larger truck farming enterprise. Dan is raising some calves to baby beef size for local customers. The family also likes goats and wants to expand that operation, with the milk marketed through the store and also used to raise some of the baby calves. They have several top milking does, and hope to raise top-quality milk goats to sell to families who want to own their private source of milk.

As they acquire capital from the homestead and natural food store, the Wohnoutkas plan to use the money to expand their retail operation to include an organic farm-and-garden supply store.

"It's interesting to note that many people in this region of the Midwest use chemical methods in their commercial farming operations, but garden organically," says Paulette. "We believe more farmers would make use of organic products and practices in their total operation if the products were available. We want to give it a try, at least."

Meanwhile, the Wohnoutkas will continue to work hard at expanding their homestead enterprises and building a bigger business for their retail natural food store. The whole family works together in both the farm and store operations.

"That was our main goal in leaving California, to have a sane life together as a family," says Paulette. "You've got to take a stand somewhere for the things that are truly important in life. Sometimes, taking a stand hurts—we've given up the paychecks Dan earned as a fireman in San Jose. He must work off the farm yet, from time to time, to supplement the income from the farm and the store. But we've gained, on balance, in those things that are important to us as a family."

The folks around Humansville have gained, too. More and more of them are shopping at the Wohnoutka's New Life Natural Foods store as an alternative to walking the glittering aisles of supermarkets.

38: Vineyard and winery: Bucks County, Pennsylvania

WINEMAKING HAS BECOME a profitable home industry for Jerry and Kathy Forest. They first started selling wine in 1974 and expect to make their winery a full-time business in a few years.

The Forests grow their own grapes, and make the wine in the basement of their rural home in Bucks County, Pennsylvania. They started out in 1966 by planting an acre of wine grapes—about 600 vines. Now they have over 10 acres in vines and may soon double that. They made 7,500 gallons of wine in 1977 from 40 tons of grapes.

When they started out, the Forests offered only three kinds of wine—red, white, and rosé—all of them blends of their various kinds of grapes. Now they have enough production to include what are known as varietal wines: wines named for the predominant variety. Federal law requires a minimum of 51 percent of a single variety of grape to name the wine after the grape, such as Baco Noir or Seyval Blanc. The Forests, however, use 100 percent of the grape for which the varietals are named. Their varietals have become so popular that they now account for 75 percent of the family's total output.

Buckingham Valley Vineyards is the impressive name the Forests have given their home industry. But it's strictly a family affair, run by Jerry and Kathy and their three teenage children. They hire a few area kids to help with the harvest and occasionally get a helping hand from friends who want to learn something about winemaking. Otherwise, the work of planting, cultivating, pruning, harvesting, making the wine, bottling it, and selling it is done by the family.

The Forests operate under a state law known as the Pennsylvania Limited Winery Act. It permits operators of small wineries to make and sell wine on their premises provided the wine is made from Pennsylvania-grown fruit. Some other states have similar laws.

The Forests first began making wine for their own use from purchased grapes. They admit their first efforts brought forth something less than prize-winning results. But they continued to experiment and to learn from others, visiting commercial wineries whenever they got the chance.

After the Forests moved into their present home, they set out their first vines. It wasn't long before what had started out as a family hobby began to take on the appearances of a family business. But to make wine in large enough quantities to sell, you need a little more equipment than a home winemaking kit. Jerry is a great scrounger and managed to buy a lot of the needed equipment secondhand. He acquired a used hand-operated press and crusher. He rebuilt a used filter. He made his own labeling machine. He built racks for his aging barrels from the cross-arms of old telephone poles.

The Forests started out using both oak and plastic barrels for their wine. The used wooden barrels came from a whiskey distillery and were charred on the inside. Such charring is said to improve the flavor of whiskey, but Jerry doesn't feel it enhances the flavor of wine, so he scraped the charcoal out. The plastic barrels were manufactured to handle processed food. Jerry managed to get some over-runs at an attractive price. But it appears the plastic gets brittle after a few years, so stainless steel tanks are being acquired as replacements. The Forests now have storage capacity for 12,000 gallons.

The family has spent about $1,400 out-of-pocket for their winemaking equipment. This includes the barrels, press, crusher, filter, bottling machine, corker, pumps and hoses. It also includes $150 for lab equipment required by the federal government for testing alcohol content. The fee for a state license was $250, plus $50 for "filing" fees with the state.

It was found that bottles were unavailable in less than a truckload of 2,400 cases. Since mixed loads of various shaped bottles could not be arranged, the Forests ordered only one type of bottle for all their wines. They see no problem at all in putting both their blends and their varietals into the same shaped bottles. The bottles, by the way, cost about 15 cents each.

Another saving was made at the start by having only three different labels, one for each of the three wines—red, white and rosé. Now they also have labels for each of their varietals.

The Forests started from scratch in acquiring equipment for their vineyard. They bought a tractor, mower, sprayer, post hole digger, and miscellaneous items, totalling about $11,800. They recently bought a second tractor for $4,800.

When it came to planting the vines, costs totaled $1,372 per acre, including labor and care for the first year. For each acre they bought 625 vines at 50 cents each; 210 trellis posts at $2 each; 15,000 feet of number 9 wire, using three strands. They figure land preparations came to $250 an acre. It takes three years for grapes to get into production, so it was necessary to care for them for two more years before the vines began to pay off.

COST OF ESTABLISHING VINEYARD

	1 Acre	10 Acres
Vines @ 50¢ each	$312.50	$3,125.00
Trellis posts @ $2 each	$420.00	$4,200.00
Wire (#9) 3 strands,		
150,000 feet total	$291.60	$2,916.00
Preparation of land	$250.00	$2,500.00

Needed equipment includes tractor, harrow, sprayer, mower, post hole digger, etc. The Forests figure vineyard maintenance labor amounts to 50 hours an acre per year.

The Forests grow only French hybrid grapes. These make excellent wine and do very well in the soils of the area. Good wines also can be made from the labrusca or so-called native grapes, such as Niagara, Catawba and Duchess. The viniferas, such as Johannesburg Riesling and Pinot Chardonnay, are the classics of the Rhine Valley and do well in California, but are only now being experimented with in colder areas. Winter hardiness can be a problem.

The Forests age their wines at least a year before offering them for sale. As at other wineries, large and small, taste samples are offered visitors to their salesroom. Because they believe in doing things right, the Forests use quality wineglasses for sampling rather than the paper cups encountered in some wine salesrooms.

COST OF MAKING ONE BOTTLE OF WINE

Value of juice	$ .60
Sugar & miscellaneous	.05
Bottle	.15
Cork	.03
Label	.02
Capsule (goes over cork)	.03
Total	.88
To sell, add federal and state taxes	.058
	$ .938

Selling price = $2.25
(including taxes)

To help finance the early stages of their wine growing and making, the Forests started selling juice concentrates and equipment for home winemaking, both at their home and via mail order. They still do. Home winemaking kits capable of producing a gallon or so of wine cost only about $10.

Even home winemakers are supposed to register with the Bureau of Alcohol, Tobacco and Firearms, U.S. Department of the Treasury.

By law, you can make up to 200 gallons of table wine for your own use. When you start to sell wine you'll need to be licensed by the federal bureau. You'll also need to check out the laws and regulations of your state, county and local government.

Small vintners like the Forests concentrate on table wines, with alcohol ranging from 10 to 14 percent. These are the only types permitted under the Pennsylvania Limited Winery Act. Fortified wines, such as port and sherry, have a higher alcohol content and are a different ballgame as far as the laws are concerned. Port and sherry also call for more elaborate winery procedures.

Even if you have no room for growing grapes, you may find it feasible to buy the grapes or juice from area wine grape growers. At current prices, you should be able to buy good wine grapes such as French hybrids for about $400 a ton. That's the equivalent of 160 to 170 gallons of juice if you're using a good press.

It's not necessary to make grape wines only. Other fruits can be used. Apple wines are popular and many small vintners make them, including the Forests. In a normal growing year you can get "orchard run" apples from a grower at attractive prices.

"The best way to find out whether operating a small winery is your bag is to start out making wine for your own use," advise Kathy and Jerry. "That way you'll soon get to know whether you are going to be any good at it. Then you can go on, absorbing all the winemaking information you can get your hands on."

TEN ACRES = $68,000

Ten acres of wine grapes made into wine can yield $68,000 gross, the Forests say.

10 acres = 40 tons of grapes (4 tons per acre)
40 tons of grapes = 6,800 gallons of wine
6,800 gallons of wine = 34,000 bottles (5 bottles to 1 gallon)
34,000 bottles of wine = $68,000 ($2 per bottle, sales tax not
included)
$68,000 gross = $38,760 net (not counting vineyard costs).

39: Fruit leathers and soup mixes: Oliver, British Columbia

NETTA AND HOWARD Thompson live on 1½ acres in British Columbia. Though their place is small, they have 25 cherry trees, 16 apricots, 54 peaches, 20 pears, 5 prune plums, 18 apples, 1 quince, 2 walnuts, 2 chestnuts, 2 filberts, and 4 young persimmons. The Thompsons happened upon leather making by way of drying fruit in a more conventional way. About twenty years ago, the couple investigated arrangements other people had for drying small quantities of fruit for their own use. The drying cabinet seemed the best idea, so Howard designed one. Much experimenting was necessary to find the best method of heating the dryer. After much trial and error, they settled on an electric stove oven element.

This first dryer measured 26 inches wide, 26 deep, and 53 high. The heater doors at the bottom were 9 inches high, above which were nine 3-inch drawers, supporting fruit on quarter-inch wire mesh. The dried fruit was so successful and popular that in 1970 they had four more driers custom-made. These are the same measurements but are thermostatically controlled and there are ten drawers in each. One dryer can handle one hundred pounds of fruit.

With so much drier space available, the Thompsons had room to try fruit leather. Fruit leather is not a modern idea. Indeed, native peoples in Canada and many European countries have made leather from berries for centuries. The first variety Howard and Netta tried was apricot. This leather was spread too thin on the drying paper and was tough. The next turned out well, and was cut neatly into two-by-four-inch strips with the idea of putting four or five pieces in a package as a unit. Customers asked for their comments liked the taste and texture but thought the leather should be offered for sale in the full sheet. Later, the Thompsons made pear, apple, cherry, raspberry, and strawberry leathers.

As a test of keeping quality, some of these leathers were stored in the drier room and in kitchen cupboards; mold caused no trouble, but after two or three years the leather got very dry.

For leather making, select good unblemished fruit at the stage of ripeness that is perfect for eating out of hand. Put the fruit through a blender and pour the pulp onto cookie sheets lined with brown paper.

Netta Thompson

Place the cookie sheets into the drier. Remove in 2 to 4 hours depending on the fruit used. After 8 to 12 hours, flip the leather over onto fresh paper and dry again. Flip leather every 4 hours or until it is firm and not sticky to touch. Finally, fold edges of the paper over the leather and stack into cardboard boxes.

Cherries take the most preparation. If you know you will be drying, the fruit can be picked stemless; this doesn't hurt the tree and saves you the trouble of handling the fruit again to remove the stems. The Thompsons have several kinds of cherry pitters, the most elaborate of which is a countertop model with a plunger action. But it takes but one cherry at a time and the pit is inclined to stick. Another model uses a grinding action and has a funnel opening that takes a handful of cherries at a time. This one works well if operated slowly, but you must watch carefully to see that every pit drops out the waste chute. The most accurate (and most time-consuming) is a hand pitter with a plunger action, in which you can see the pits more easily.

Five pounds of cherries produce one sheet of leather—that is nine cups of pureed cherries. Spread the pulp evenly over the paper-lined cookie sheet; the layer should be almost a half-inch thick. Put the tray into the lowest drawer of the drier. After about two hours, slip the tray from under the paper. The fruit should be firm enough to stay on the paper, but it's rather a disaster if you pull the drawer forward quickly when the leather is still loose, so that it all spills out the back. In about four hours, run a knife point around the four sides of the leather to loosen the edges from the paper; edges are inclined to stick to the paper and cause the leather to split as it dries and shrinks.

In another four hours the leather should be ready to flip onto new paper. First put the warm sheet of leather with the paper on a work table. Place fresh paper on top. Hold the entire works together and quickly turn over. Carefully peel off original paper to expose the soft side. Return to the drier. A few hours later test that the leather is ready to flip by lifting one end of the leather and paper to allow the leather to roll back over your hand, each end, each side. If the leather is loose over the entire surface, you can pick it up and flip it over.

It seems best to start the pitting process early in the morning before any other chores. If the leathers are into the driers by eight it would be possible to remove the trays by noon and then turn the leathers onto new paper in the late afternoon. The first flip-over would be the next morning. Cherries take into the third day to dry because the heat must be kept just barely over 100°F (38°C).

Finished leather is about one quarter-inch thick and shrunken to show a border of paper one inch or more all around. Fold these edges over the leather and place the whole into a cardboard box. Use a flat box that will hold six or eight sheets. For long keeping, store in a cool, dry place.

This method works for all kinds of fruit. Only the preparation differs. Apricots are cut in half and pitted; peaches are peeled and pitted; pears are peeled and cored and cut into lengthwise quarters; apples, cut and cored; prunes, cut in half and pitted; strawberries, hulled; and raspberries require no work at all.

Any fruit leather should be pliable, but textures vary. Cherry, apricot and apple, is slightly embossed, while pear leather is very fine-grained and peach tends to be shiny. Berry leathers show the seeds. Pear is the quickest to dry and is very thin and super tasty. Cherry and prune are the slowest to dry and stay thick and chewy.

Howard and Netta have made tomato leather as well. It is excellent for flavoring roasts and steaks. The size of the sheet comes down to about five-by-eight inches and it is hard to believe that this represents five pounds of tomatoes. One customer eats it out of hand. Recently the Thompsons tried zucchini milk leather. It needs to be dried to crispness and turns brown. Zucchini leather is good crumpled into soup or stews.

Fruit leather is especially popular with hikers, skiers, back-packers, and cyclists because it is light to carry and easy to eat. Leathers may be used as dessert in the lunch box, or stashed in the glove compartment; they take very little space, do not spill, smear, or leak, and are good snacking food.

"This business of making leather is fun and interesting and allows you to pick all the fruit at its very best ripeness," says Netta. The Thompsons reserve about one third of the total fruit crop for leathers. Because five pounds of fruit becomes one leather it's necessary to charge at least five times the fresh fruit per-pound price to allow for time and work involved, and this sits well with their customers. "We have customers all across Canada and in Alaska. These are people who used to come here for fresh fruit and whose jobs have caused them to move far away. So they write in their orders in May so that we can mail them what leathers they want as it is ready through the growing season. The customers pay the shipping charges."

To make a big business of leather would involve a lot of driers and help for picking, as well as more work space. Remember that some of the drier space will likely be used for making dried fruit at the same time. Orchardists or fruit growers would have to examine their work schedules, facilities, and interests in deciding if fruit leather is a worthwhile venture.

For the Thompsons, the driers have paid for themselves many times over. The cost of operating is insignificant and the work fits in with other chores during crop season. But the leather making does take time—when time is already divided between farm chores, mowing, irrigating, gardening, canning, pickling, and freezing fruit and produce. "There is no time for holidays or outings," says Netta. "But if you love your work you stay with it."

Even though summer's vegetables do not all mature at one time, you can make soup that incorporates any of your favorites. Netta Thompson's answer is to dry each vegetable at its very best, from early asparagus in spring to late hubbard squash in fall. And don't forget to add herbs for a gourmet touch.

The first time she made it, Netta thought her dried soup mix tasted great, and gave bags of the mix to customers so that they could evaluate it over the winter. "The next season, they came for fruit and asked for soup mix as well. Friends tell friends and soon a good number of people are asking for soup mix in pound lots. So, another easy and profitable sideline was established."

"We didn't know how dried vegetables would be," she says, "so we did a small amount of each kind and tried them as separate vegetable servings. For some kinds, peas and corn especially, we like them dried better than frozen. Then later we put all the vegetables together for soup. We noticed that commercial soup mixes have very small pieces for quick cooking, and the assortment of vegetables is limited. Our vegetable mix has more variety and bigger pieces. So, it requires more cooking time."

Start drying asparagus when it is young and tender. Use male stalks only, no longer than five inches tall, and cut into one-inch lengths. These bits look very stringy and must be dried crisp.

Very small green beans can either be left whole or french cut.

Yellow beans and ramana beans should be french cut as well. Later in summer, collect dry mature beans of all kinds (navy, soy, Swedish brown, black oregon or whatever kinds you have) but use a few of each. Beets tend to darken the soup liquid but beet greens, dried crisp and crumbled, make a good addition. Broccoli can be cut into one-inch pieces and then sliced thin; they are unbelievably small when dry but swell up nicely as they cook. Cauliflower is cut in small florets and the tender leaves roughly chopped. Chop cabbage roughly, using the very greenest leaves. Cucumbers may be sliced if you are using gherkins but are best if peeled, seeded, and cut into lengthwise strips and then into one-inch pieces; use sparingly.

Use green onion tops cut in half-inch pieces. Egyptian tree onions are good for this because they keep their ring shape. Sweet spanish onions are dried when they are mature and then are coarsely chopped. The best carrots for dried soup mixes are the small thinings of less than finger size. Cleaning them is slow but well worth the effort. Slightly larger carrots can be cut lengthwise and big carrots can be sliced or diced.

Tomatoes lose 90 percent of their weight and bulk when dried. For example, 20 pounds of tomatoes become less than one pound—a mere handful of paper-thin sections. They should be peeled for quick drying to keep a good color.

Peas and corn both need to be dried on a cotton cloth, as they would fall through the mesh of your trays. Use very young shelled peas and corn niblets. Zucchini, hubbard and similar squash are cut into about one-inch cubes. Spaghetti squash is cut into thin one-by-four-inch strips so that it can string out as it cooks.

For seasoning and interest, add a small handful of celery leaves or two or three leaves of lovage. You might also try amounts of sweet green basil, oregano, marjoram, a few dill seeds, a couple of rubbed sage leaves, or a touch of thyme. Sweet red or green pepper bits may be considered either seasoning or another vegetable. Dry the biggest part of the pepper as half-inch rings and save for fried or poached egg rings, and cut the rest into half-inch bits for the soup.

To suit hikers and backpackers, put the dry soup mix into a plastic bag; when water is added to make twice the bulk, the vegetables will absorb the water by the end of the day, reducing cooking time. At home, the ideal way to cook the soup is to have the water boiling and add the vegetables slowly, allowing the water to continue boiling; then, simmer to desired tenderness.

Add meat stock at home; on the trail, campers can add one or more bouillon cubes. Try crumbling zucchini milk leather into the soup for a distinctive flavor. The soup may be thickened with mashed potatoes, rice, barley, or alphabet macaroni.

By late September, all the vegetables are dried and waiting in

Netta preparing the dried soup mix

their big brown paper bags, and it's time to put them together in sale-able units. Because of the number of vegetables and herbs involved, Netta has found the smallest suitable amount to be four ounces. The Thompsons first put three dozen one-pound-size flat-bottom brown paper bags on the work table. The vegetables are distributed to each bag in a quantity that Netta describes as "the amount that you can hold in your bunched fingers." The tops of the bags are double-folded, secured with tape, and labeled.

A four-ounce bag will make six to eight quarts of soup. The mix keeps indefinitely in a dry cool place. If not used all at one time, the soup can be frozen and used at a later date.

40: Pick-your-own orchard: Warwick, New York

DAVID HULL RUNS a pick-your-own operation on his 130-acre farm in New York State's Orange County. His location is enviable: while Applewood Orchards is a mere 90 minutes from midtown Manhattan, the land is still very rural, beautiful, and unspoiled his-torically. So, Hull has both proximity to a major population area and a handsome place that people enjoy visiting.

Forty acres of the farm is orchard, the remainder shared by pas-tureland, woods, ponds, and swamp. David grows five varieties of ap-ples: MacIntosh, Cortland, Red Delicious, Golden Delicious, and Rome. Half the trees are semidwarf, and half are grown on standard rootstock.

The property has an influence on the success of a PYO operation, David believes; customers are after not only inexpensive apples, but an experience as well. He suggests it's valuable to introduce several diver-sions to involve the pickers. He points out his home, the oldest in the county, and the barn with its attached solar-heated greenhouse from which plants are sold during the fall season. Customers are encouraged to picnic around a pond located near the PYO parking lot, and the younger members of families enjoy feeding lunch scraps to the Hull's ducks. A flower garden and herb garden are popular attractions. David sells cut flowers, although the herbs are there just for the sensual experience of sniffing. Most popular of all are wagon rides to and from the orchard behind Hull's tractor.

David says a PYO operation is likely to face both advantages and problems. On the favorable side, PYO offers a good way to get around labor problems. "You would think that with so much unemployment in our country that a work force would be no problem," says David. "But picking fruit, although remunerative, is hard work. Few people are willing to work hard for even $35.00 a day, which is the figure a good apple picker can expect to earn." Marketing through pick-your-own also relieves the farmer from the responsibility of many difficult labor-management related problems: labor camp regulations, supply of competent labor, bookkeeping, and cash flow to meet the ever-increasing payroll.

Pick-your-own operators do require labor, but often family members can fit this need, and if necessary a high school boy or girl or retired person can be taken on without much difficulty. Housing of course is not required and fringe benefits are minimal.

David Hull

A second advantage to pick-your-own marketing is that the grower controls his own pricing policy and is not necessarily influenced by wholesale markets. You have to be fair and reasonable in order to attract customers, of course, and should remember you are not only selling produce but a day in the country as well. Try to strike a medium between the wholesale price and the retail price. Few people realize the wide spread between wholesale and retail prices, and are usually satisfied with a price slightly below retail. You also have the option of lowering your price near the season's end to help clean the orchard of windfalls.

All pick-your-own sales are cash, and this means no waiting and hoping that the wholesale commission merchant will send a good check.

With a PYO operation, growers are spared the costly operating expense and investment of a packing house with a large refrigerated storage facility. With inflation, these costs have become awesome.

The containers used for pick-your-own harvesting are less expensive than the cardboard cell and tray cartons used for the wholesale market. David uses a ¾-bushel white vinyl bag with handles. It's strong and not overly heavy to carry. He feels there is still room for research with PYO containers that are strong, sturdy, easy to carry, and which store well.

David finds that the farm producer who enjoys people and can work well with others should enjoy PYO. "I felt advantaged and privileged to meet and converse with our customers. They in turn felt grateful for the opportunity to pick tree-ripened fruit in quantities for canning and freezing at a price lower than they could realize at the retail market; for many families it was simply a social recreational day in the country."

Naturally there are problems associated with pick-your-own, most of them stemming from improper supervision and poor planning. Successful planning and management start with the crop you're going to market. David planted the five most popular varieties. The Malling V11 semi-dwarf root stocks are adaptable to a wide range of soils, and because of their medium size are practical for PYO harvesting. Trees of standard rootstocks are pruned to a height of 15 feet. The lower branches are allowed to flourish. Hull uses organic fertilizers. "I firmly believe this makes a difference in the taste of our apples. And, for our safety and that of our customers, we use as many organic and biodegradable sprays throughout the growing season as is practical and still produce a high-quality product."

As the crop grows to maturity, David starts organizing and planning his advertising and promotion. Over the years the most successful medium of advertising has been three or four large apple-shaped signs pierced by a white arrow. The signs simply state "Pick-Your-Own" in white letters. Other forms of advertising media used in order of importance include word of mouth, newspapers, radio, and free promotion. David coined a new idea for promotion, the "Apple-Thon," a series of events and prizes, such as apple-picking contests, apple dunking, and the like. Ten percent of the farm's gross sales for a weekend was donated to a local charity. Plans for the coming year will include an attractive brochure to help promote chartered bus tours for various clubs and organizations. Hopefully this will help the slower week-day business.

David has experimented with renting out trees. Last year a section of the orchard was roped off and designated the rent-a-tree area. For $25.00 a family could sign a lease, choose their own tree and pick all the apples off the tree that fall. Last year was a heavy crop year and in some instances a tree yielded 18 or more bushels. David likes the idea of Rent-A-Tree. "It allows me to choose my customers. They bring their own containers and the signed lease gives me iron-clad liability protection. I try to keep a budget of 10 percent of expected gross sales for advertising and promotion. If this promotion of the business has been successful, the parking lot should be full throughout the marketing season."

David offers this checklist of potential problem areas that should be given attention:

- Ample space for parking
- Transportation to and from the orchard
- Distribution of picking containers
- Toilet facilities
- Trash removal and clean up
- Convenient checkout counter
- Equitable method of charging by weight or volume
- Handling the cash
- Adequate accident and liability insurance

In the area of customer relations, supervision and communication with the customer are of prime importance. "We have maps of the orchard with directions and a few clearly stated rules that are delivered in a positive rather than a negative way," explains David. "For example we discourage climbing trees and encourage the customer to rent an apple picker pole for fifty cents. The customers actually prefer this to climbing trees. Our direction and information signs are attractive and easy to read and understand. The majority of our customers are really so appreciative of the opportunity to pick their own apples that supervision in the orchard can be kept to a minimum."

David Hull's pick-your-own season generally starts about the first week of September and runs until the first week of November. "The success of our harvest season depends on good weather. I am the first to admit, it's a real gamble, but that's farming. Luckily, PYO harvesters will come to pick in spite of a torrential downpour. Be prepared to stay open despite foul weather and a scattering of customers. If you're a good farmer and merchandiser you'll turn the bad-weather days around to your advantage."

41: Basement processing: Allentown, Pennsylvania

M R. AND MRS. Warren D. Kern are kept busy with their truck farm in spring, summer and fall. They plant and harvest table vegetables, all of which are sold locally in farm stands and stores.

By the time winter comes around you might think they would be ready for a break, but aside from about two weeks Kern spends deer hunting, the couple is kept occupied with canning sauerkraut and chow chow and preparing apple schnitz.

"It's just enough work to keep us busy," Warren says. "Mostly the wife though so she doesn't get in any trouble."

The canning operation is truly a mom-and-pop business. It is done right in the home in the way it was in the old days. Sauerkraut production begins in spring when the Kerns plant the cabbage. The va-

---

This chapter originally appeared in somewhat altered form as an article in the *Allentown Morning Call*.

riety they use runs about eight to nine pounds a head. "This is bigger than the cabbage at most markets," Warren says. "Most people don't want heads this big."

The cabbage is harvested in August and September and stored until ready to be prepared. "It takes about six to eight weeks to cure. You trim it, slice it, stamp it, and put in barrels. We just add salt, nothing else."

After the kraut is placed in the barrels, it is covered first with big cabbage leaves and then a thin plastic sheet. A couple of inches of water are poured over the sheet to keep the kraut compressed so it can work.

After a period the Kerns boil the kraut to stop the fermentation. It is then put in jars and labeled for the market.

"This isn't like store sauerkraut," claims Warren. "They put chemicals in it, let it set two or three days and then sell it."

The Kerns prepare sauerkraut the way their parents and grandparents did it years ago. "When Mother was living," recalls War-

The Kerns at work   *Ken Clauser*

ren, "we used to do it upstairs. Then we built this kitchen in the cellar. But we never expected to do this much. We put up 30 barrels of sauerkraut this year."

About the same time the sauerkraut operation is going on the Kerns make schnitz. When the sauerkraut and apple schnitzing are complete, the Kerns start on the chow chow. This is more involved, requiring green and yellow beans, red and white limas, cauliflower, peppers, pickles, onions, celery, and carrots. The Kerns raise all of the vegetables except the celery, carrots and onions. The chow chow preparation begins when the vegetables are harvested. They are washed, cut up for size, and put in three-pound containers to be frozen until winter.

Comes cold weather, the vegetables are cooked separately, then mixed, seasoned, and put up in jars. The seasoning consists of sugar and vinegar to give the traditional sweet-and-sour flavor. "By the time we're done with the chow chow," Warren says, "it's time to plant lettuce. We plant early. We try to be the first on the market."

42: Christmas trees: Barnett, Missouri

BUD GREEN'S OZARK-GROWN Christmas trees really get around, thanks to his three-pronged marketing strategy. The Scotch and white pines grown on his 120-acre farm decorate Christmastime homes as far away as Garden City, Kansas.

"Last year, we sold a few trees directly, and a few wholesale, but this is the first year we've had a great many trees to sell," says Bud. "So, we designed several market avenues for our product."

Bud's choicest Scotch pines are reserved for local customers who come to the farm to cut the tree of their choice. He does a careful pruning and shaping job on all his trees, and makes note of those that turn

Bud Green   *Jim Ritchie*

out to be prime specimens. These are not cut for wholesale buyers, but are left standing for choose-and-cut customers.

"We sell trees at the farm at the same rate as those sold on lots in town," Bud says. "I know that a lot of Christmas tree growers give a discount for buyers who cut their own trees. But my philosophy is that people pick prime trees and get exactly what they want. They should, at least—they have about 55,000 trees to chooose from. That's why we make no price break for those trees sold here."

Bud currently prices trees at $1.40 per foot, with price step-ups for each six inches of tree height. He charges the same price for those trees he cuts and hauls to retail lots in nearby towns.

"These are trees of my choosing," he says. "And, while I pick first quality trees to retail on the lot, I make the selection. And I charge the same price as for choose-and-cut trees out on the farm."

Bud also sells several thousand trees each year at wholesale. The balled trees are loaded onto semi-trailers and hauled to retailers' lots in cities in Missouri and Kansas.

"A grower who produces very many trees should line up a wholesale outlet for some of the trees, even if his major market is choose-and-cut," believes Bud. "This gives you an outlet for your less-than-perfect trees, gets them out of sight of your regular customers who come to the farm. That doesn't mean that you palm off only ragged, unmarketable trees at wholesale, of course. But any grower will have several trees that are less than perfect in size and shape, and wholesaling gives you a volume market for these trees."

He notes a growing market for potted live pine trees. "A good many people like to buy a potted tree to use at Christmas, then plant the tree as a lawn tree later on. We also rent out potted trees to businesses—banks, stores, and offices—during the Christmas season. We pot the trees in half-barrels and charge a rental fee that is about what a cut tree would cost. The live tree stays fresher, and we do the setting up and taking down."

Bud Green began thinking about merchandising when he started his Christmas tree planting in 1969. He moved from Iowa to the Missouri Ozarks, bought 120 acres of rough land, and planted 10,000 two-year-old pine seedlings. The next year, he planted another 10,000 trees; the third year, 12,000 trees.

"You don't just plant a few acres of trees, then sit back and wait for them to grow to Christmas-tree size so you can clip the coupons. There's a lot of work: pruning and shaping the trees each year, mowing weeds and brush, keeping fire breaks open. And, you have to do something to earn a living while you're waiting on the trees to grow to market size."

At the time Bud bought the land, rough unimproved real estate was available in the area for less money than today. "In 1977, we sold enough trees to recover the initial cost of the land, but since we bought the land in 1969, real estate prices have tripled in this part of the country. It would be harder nowadays to make the first full year's crop pay for the land."

To promote his Christmas tree operation locally, Bud uses most of the conventional methods of getting out the word: radio spots, newspaper ads, and signs along the roads leading to the plantation.

"We also run tours of the plantation for Brownie troops and grade school classes in the weeks before Christmas," he says. "We run hay rides through the place, and the kids have a big time. We also donate trees to elementary school homerooms. It's hard to gauge just what this kind of public relations is worth, but we believe it pays off. We know it's a lot of fun, both for the kids and for us."

Bud puts a great deal of merchandising effort into his choose-and-cut operation. The main attraction is the opportunity he offers customers to drive down the rows of green trees, choose their very own tree and cut it with the saw Bud provides.

"We're in a definitely rural area; the biggest towns in the immediate region are in the 2,000 to 3,000 population range. And, our plantation is off the major highways. We would have more choose-and-cut traffic if we were located near a larger urban area and on a well-traveled highway, where the trees would be in plain view of passing motorists. It's pretty hard to overestimate the value of location in a choose-and-cut tree operation."

For a landowner wishing to start a part-time Christmas tree enterprise, Bud offers several suggestions gleaned from his own experience.

First, it's better to buy land with a Christmas tree plantation in mind, particularly if you'll have a choose-and-cut market, rather than buy land and then decide to grow trees. "We had already bought the land when we decided to grow trees," he says. "If we were doing it over again, I'd try to find land that is better located in relation to major highways and population centers. As it is, our choose-and-cut market is limited, although we have customers come here from as far away as St. Louis [some 150 miles distant]."

Bud suggests a prospective grower first volunteer to help out during the heavy-work seasons at an established tree farm, to learn the finer points of managing trees. "I worked one summer, for free, helping prune trees, just to learn how it's done. I should have worked a few days during the harvesting and marketing season just before Christmas, too. The experience you gain is well worth the time and labor expended."

Lay out a choose-and-cut plantation so that all customers come in one access and go out one exit. This helps control traffic and lets the salesperson meet all customers as they come to cut trees.

Plant one-tenth of the total acreage each year. For example, if you're planting 40 acres to Christmas trees, plant four acres the first year, four acres the second year, and so on. This planting sequence lets trees grow in groups of uniform-age trees. If a customer wants a five-foot tree, he can be directed to the section of the plantation where trees of that size are growing.

A final tip: "A Christmas tree plantation is good use to make of marginal land," believes Bud. "However, your labor and out-of-pocket costs will be high, and it's hard not to get discouraged while you are waiting for the trees to grow to marketable size. You'll have to wait seven or eight years before you harvest your first crop. But once you get the operation rolling on a sustaining basis, it's an interesting business to pursue."

Bud Green's enthusiasm for do-it-yourself buyer–harvesting has gotten him started on another similar enterprise. He recently planted part of his land to blueberries, for a pick-your-own berry operation.

43: Wild bird feed: Bucks County, Pennsylvania

PEYTON L. HINKLE is a New York City native who, with his wife, quit the city some years ago for the country and now makes a

Peyton Hinkle

comfortable living mixing and selling wild bird feed to small retailers within a 75-mile radius of their farm.

Peyton says he has no trouble competing with feed offered by the corporate chain supermarkets because customers soon learn the birds waste little of his quality mix, developed especially for him by an ornithologist. He sells about 500 tons a year.

When they first moved to their farm in Bucks County, Pennsylvania, the Hinkles went into the egg business. They did well enough for awhile, but then came the time when eggs began glutting the market and prices dropped below what it cost the Hinkles to produce them. That meant only one thing—they had to get bigger or get out. They decided to get out, but first they had to come up with some other enterprise that would enable them to stay on the farm and raise their family.

As part of the egg business, Peyton grew corn and other grains to help feed his layers. But he also began growing millet and sunflowers with the idea they would be a worthwhile cash crop. "It wasn't long, however, before I decided I could make out better using these crops in a wild bird feed mix than selling them as unmixed grains," he says. "The idea of wild bird feed came to my mind because so many people I knew were starting to feed the birds."

Peyton made an early decision to go completely wholesale in his selling of wild bird feed. "I did not want to get mixed up with the state government and its sales tax."

After obtaining the special formula for his feed mixture, Peyton had to acquire equipment for mixing and bagging. He managed to buy a used 1½-ton electric feed mixer for $600, including motor. He set this up on the second floor of his barn and arranged to have the mix drop by gravity to the bagging room on the floor below. At the start he manually filled and sealed the bags, which range in size from 5 to 50 pounds. The bags are calculated to increase the quality image of the product. They are of four- and five-mil plastic, heavier than those of most competing brands, and carry an attractive Pennsylvania Dutch design worked out by Mrs. Hinkle. As befits the product's name a distelfink is a prominent part of the design.

After mixing and bagging his first batch of feed, Peyton was faced with finding retailers who would handle it. He loaded his station wagon and went from store to store, mostly grocery and hardware, in nearby towns. This was about 20 years ago and wild bird feed had not become as popular as it is now, so Peyton ran into a certain amount of resistance. Some store operators were skeptical that the stuff would sell, he recalls. But Hinkle kept pushing, even leaving some of his bags on consignment.

At this point, he began to wonder whether he had made the right move by going into bird feed. But two weeks later, he returned to the

stores that had taken on his product and found most of the storekeepers were pleased. Customers who had taken a chance on the feed had come back for more.

Peyton soon found that top quality isn't everybody's bag, so he now offers an economy mix that is directly competitive with other low-priced mixes. He's found, however, that the quality mix outsells the cheaper version by two to one, year in and year out.

When he started out, Peyton grew most of his feed. Now he buys all of it, finding this more economical. Most of his feed comes from nearby feed mills, but he buys sunflower seeds direct from Minnesota and North Dakota, and millet from these states and Colorado. The quality mix includes sunflower seeds, millet, peanut hearts, cracked corn, wheat, oats, and grain sorghum. The economy mix includes fewer sunflower seeds and no peanut hearts. His bags show an analysis for crude protein, fat and fiber. The quality mix has more of each of these.

Peyton's equipment now includes two automatic bag fillers and sealers, one for small bags and the other for large bags. These cost him over $2,500. He also has a couple sets of roller-type conveyors to move bags and cartons of bags in and out of storage.

Because the bird feed business is a seasonal thing, Peyton soon felt the need for another line that would bring in cash the balance of the year and also enable him to give year around employment to his two drivers. As a result, he has become a distributor for a diversified line of nearly 100 products: jams, jellies, pickles, salad dressings, peanut butter, and related items. Some carry his own Pennsylvania Dutch label. Most sales are to roadside markets in eastern Pennsylvania and nearby parts of New Jersey.

Roadside markets are becoming more numerous each year in his area, and prove an important type of outlet. Peyton plans to expand in this direction. At this writing, he was investigating sources of supply for confectionery items suitable for roadside markets. He reasons the more items he can handle on the delivery routes the more he can cut unit costs.

Peyton Hinkle has come to the conclusion that a business either grows or it declines. "There is no just holding the line," he says. "So I've had to decide how fast I want the business to expand. I feel that a gradual expansion is best. But I don't want to get too big. One of the troubles with the country's economy is that a few large conglomerates are in control of most types of businesses."

44: Eel fishery: coastal North Carolina

ALONG THE EASTERN seaboard, people harvest a food that they rarely eat: eel. Charlie Bass of Plymouth, North Carolina, is no exception. His part-time job as eel fisherman nets a modest income, but no food for his table. Throughout tidewater North Carolina, the favored foods are grits, cornbread and chicken. Live eels bring a good price, but are sold to a buyer for export to Europe or Japan.

Fishermen typically pot for eels around another job, making runs to haul in the pots morning and night. It's the sort of part-time work that appeals to the independent country people of the area—outdoors folk who like to work for themselves and shift from one job to another as the season's change.

Not everyone is suited for moonlighting as an eel fisherman. "The real river rats do best," says Leon Abbas, economist with the University of North Carolina Sea Grant Program. They are "wise to water," and even after dark will charge about the coastal plain rivers in their motor boats. A standard commercial fishing license is good below the tidewater point; the state allows fishing in the fresh waters above only by special permit, and this is rarely done.

The eels are caught in pots, cylindrical or rectangular containers of wire mesh. The bait may be fresh fish or shrimp heads. Pots are emptied each day, and the eels await the buyer in a holding pen. Fishermen typically construct their own eel pots and holding pen. Other equipment includes a freezer for storing bait and a depth finder.

How much does a person stand to make over a season of 13 weeks in spring and 13 weeks in fall? Abbas estimates that each pot will yield an average of 2 pounds of eels a day. A 30-pot enterprise would generate 10,920 pounds of eels over 26 weeks, 7 days a week, averaging 4 hours of work per day. Given the going price of 50 cents a pound at the holding site, total receipts would be $5,460.

Before investing in eel fishing equipment, it would be best to visit with other eel fisherman and contact a marine advisory agent for additional information; agents are located at the North Carolina Marine Resource Centers in Manteo, Morehead City, and Kure Beach.

Charlie Bass

45: Sprouts: Whidbey Island, Washington

A LONG-TIME ORGANIC gardener and his wife sell sprouts for a living. Cornplanter and Aster sprout 600 pounds of alfalfa seeds each week. Their greenhouse is on evergreen-covered Whidbey Island in the Puget Sound. They market to outlets in nearby Seattle and Everett.

Cornplanter got into this business in 1975 when a woman asked him to manage her part-time sprout business. At that time the business only made enough money to pay one person a weekly salary of $50. One hundred pounds of alfalfa seed was sprouted each week in gallon jars, all of which had to be rinsed by hand. Cornplanter introduced some innovations and two years later owns a business that employs him and his wife full time. As well as the ever-popular alfalfa, the couple grows a mixture of alfalfa, mung, wheat, fenugreek, and lentil sprouts.

Sprouts are grown in natural conditions under a 30-by-40-foot greenhouse of pole construction, covered by a double layer of plastic. The sprouts are first soaked in five-gallon buckets and rinsed manually. Two days later the sprouts are spread onto three-foot-square racks covered with screens. They are rinsed automatically with a sprinkler system that sprays a fine mist with well water for ten seconds every six minutes; this system was purchased from a greenhouse supply store. Cornplanter believes that plants of all kinds benefit most from natural light, and every rack has full exposure to the sun. No artificial lights are used, and the sprouts develop healthy green leaves.

In this cloudy region of the United States, the Cornplanters have yet to tap solar sources of heat and they instead rely on three wood stoves. Winters in western Washington are mild, but even so there are times when the temperature dips below 20°F (−7°C) and the couple has to stoke the stoves every hour, night and day. In summer the greenhouse is ventilated with fans so that the temperature will stay below 100°F (38°C).

Cornplanter, inspired by the book *The Secret Life of Plants*, treats his growing sprouts to classical music, playing the radio for them and occasionally sitting down at a piano located near the greenhouse. He feels that humans can affect plants in many ways and that it's important to be attuned to plants if one is a farmer. He says he has had a whole crop die after two people had an argument in his greenhouse.

The couple grows two crops a week, and twice a week the sprouts are packaged for delivery. Sunday is their biggest packaging day. Cornplanter and Aster may get up at 4 A.M. and work until 5 that afternoon packaging both two-pound and four-ounce plastic bags of sprouts. These are immediately put in a refrigerated truck for delivery the next day.

Monday's delivery runs visit as many as 40 outlets, including restaurants, natural food stores, and food co-ops. At present, the most lucrative part of the business is sales of two-pound bags to restaurants. Sales to the smaller outlets often amount to less than $4. Cornplanter already has an account with a commercial warehouse, Washington Fruit and Produce, and is attempting to expand to other wholesalers and supermarkets.

Aster and Cornplanter hope that eventually their business will grow to the point that they can hire another worker, and would like to be able to pay someone at least $3.50 an hour. At present, they enjoy being self-employed and selling a healthful product, but caution other people who think that sprouting seeds is an easy way to make a living. It's a seven-day-a-week job requiring regular hours.

The Cornplanters hope to make enough money this year to buy a new tractor and work towards their goal of becoming organic market growers.

46: Fruit butters: Aspers, Pennsylvania

F RUIT BUTTERS ARE well suited to direct selling. They are made easily, usually from fruit that is somewhat off-grade for fresh sale.

And, they are said to be among the most wholesome of fruit sweets, containing a large amount of fruit to a small amount of sweetener—if, in fact, any sweetener at all is used.

In making fruit butters, the whole fruit is cooked until tender and then rubbed through a sieve. Usually, spice and a sweetener are added and the mixture cooked again until it is smooth and thick.

The most popular fruit butter is made from apples and, interestingly enough, it's called apple butter. In some places, however, it may go by the name apple spread. The Pennsylvania Dutch are big on apple butter and insist that the best is made with a combination of fresh apples and fresh apple cider. Years ago the Pennsylvania Dutch made apple butter in huge copper kettles with flat bottoms and sloping sides. But you'll have trouble finding such kettles today; they have become collector's items and sell for several hundred dollars.

Most everyone who makes apple butter—or peach or plum butter, for that matter—seems to have his own secret recipe. That's the case with Robert Kime and family.

Like some other farmers mentioned in this book, Robert and his wife, Cora, figured out one day they ought to be able to make more money processing their output than by selling it fresh at wholesale prices.

One old-time small batch recipe says to boil 4 quarts of fresh cider until it is reduced to 2 quarts. Then add 2.5 quarts of peeled, quartered tart apples and cook until very tender. Put through a colander, add any desired sweetener and spices (cinnamon, cloves, ginger), and cook until thick, stirring to prevent burning. Pour into clean hot jars and seal. This will make 3 pints, so you're getting a ratio of slightly less than 1 to 4.

Apple butter without sugar is becoming a big seller for many roadside market operators. Another popular variation is the use of honey instead of sugar as a sweetener.

Luckily, the Kimes were able to locate a small, custom food processor who wanted to sell out. The equipment was suitable for acid-type foods, such as apples, peaches and tomatoes. It dictated pretty much what the Kimes were going to be able to handle. (High-temperature, high-pressure cookers called retorts are required to cook low-acid foods.) The equipment was hauled to the Kime farm.

Next, the Kimes had to decide on a marketing strategy that would set them apart in the market place. Since they are located in the heart of Pennsylvania's apple country and have 30 acres of apple trees of their own, they decided to specialize in apple butter made the old-fashioned way—cooking the apples in fresh cider. It costs a little more

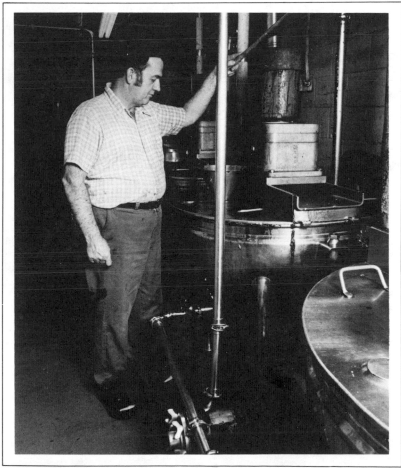

Robert Kime

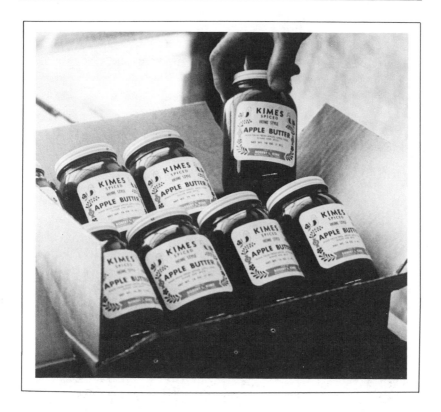

to make this way, but the Kimes claim the process gives their product a distinctive flavor. They also use a secret blend of apples.

In their study of the market, the Kimes saw that most apple butter being sold was of one type—made with sugar and spice. They decided to give their customers a choice of several types. So they make apple butter without sugar, with honey instead of sugar, and with sassafras flavoring instead of spice. They also make it the regular way, with sugar and spice, but find there is an ever-increasing demand for the product without sugar.

Next, the Kimes had to choose their market. To whom were they going to sell? They decided roadside markets and small specialty food stores offered the best opportunity. It was a good choice. Today they have an extensive business supplying such outlets—not only with apple butter, but also with canned tomatoes and freestone peaches, which are also produced on their own place. Their products have the distinction of being "country made," something that has strong appeal for many consumers.

Apple butter production goes on through the winter months, with enough put into inventory to carry through until the next apple harvest. The peaches and tomatoes are more perishable and are canned at once after harvest.

The Kimes have another, related product to offer their roadside market operators and specialty stores: cider. Starting out with a simple manual press, they now operate two rotary presses that can handle as much as 400 gallons at a time. An automated setup permits growers to unload fruit from their trucks directly onto a conveyor belt that leads to the presses. The cider comes pouring out the other end into a huge plastic container. Roadside market operators who have their own apples bring them to the Kime place a couple of times a week in order to be able to sell fresh cider that contains no preservatives.

Except for two women who work full time, the Kime operation is strictly a family affair: the parents, three sons, one daughter, and one daughter-in-law who all work full time, and one daughter who works part time. From its present success, it is obvious the Kime operation could get larger and larger. But the family members have decided they'll hold where they are. They have all the work they want to handle.

47: Goat's milk cheese: Wilton, Maine

"LOCAL GREASER" IS a label one might apply to the young bearded man walking down the dirt road. The long hair, flowing from under an oversized railroad hat, has become the label of the small-town hotrodder rather than the hippy of the sixties. But the spirit of that decade is all about the little hardscrabble farm of James Knebelman.

James left the University of Michigan after two years, despite his distaste for the draft that would thereby hang over his head, and traveled for some time before settling on a farm in Nova Scotia. He had problems in trying to become a Canadian citizen, and so crossed back over the border into Maine. He is happy here, and enjoys a good, easy relationship with the natives, sharing labor and skills. After all, James points out, his simple way of life isn't much different than that of his neighbors. James' history is different—as suggested by the atypical surname lettered on the mailbox—but his path has led to the same place in life.

James and his wife, Celeste, make vegetable-rennet cheese and yogurt from the milk of their twenty-five goats. The cheese sells at $2.30 a pound, the yogurt for $3.30 a gallon, which provides enough income to support the goats and little more. The house, shared with several others, is dark and cluttered. It is perched on a hilly piece of earth, graced by a willow on what once might have been the front lawn.

Cheese making is time-consuming, but gets James around the expense and trouble of getting certified by the state to sell raw milk (although raw milk is sold by several people in the state). The Knebelmans most often make colby, some of it spiced with caraway seeds, cumin (for a spicy, yellow cheese), or sage (popular with the older people in the area, as it was a regional favorite years ago). The colby is aged only a week. Mozzarella, made of smaller curd and less butterfat, can be sold right away. They have made feta cheese, but it was not much of a success. Cottage cheese is made from time to time.

Whey is used in making bread, occasionally to feed a thirsty dog, and as a foot bath to remove corns.

James and Celeste now make around eight pounds of cheese a week, selling five and eating the remainder. They could sell twenty-five pounds weekly, but raising a herd four times the size of the present one is a discouraging thought for James and Celeste—it would simply take too much time and work.

Marketing five pounds of cheese a week is no problem. It is sold at

James Knebelman, far left, Celeste, holding goat, with friends and daughter

the door or through the little co-ops that have sprung up in neighboring towns over the past five years. These co-ops serve a real need, not just for the young people who start them, but for older natives, too. Grocery stores are usually a good drive away; and co-ops offer locally grown produce in a state that trucks or flies in more than 80 percent of its food.

The goats breed once a year, and kids are usually weaned by the mother, sometimes not for ten months. Goats are not raised for slaughter, as all at the farm are vegetarians.

James has given some thought to selling cheese through mail order, perhaps placing an ad in the New Yorker around Christmas. But he's likely to stick to local sales, as he doesn't foresee an increase in production.

48:   Farmstead cheese: Milaca, Minnesota

C HEESE MAKING MAY not be the cheapest or easiest way to get into business for yourself, but it might help small farmers to survive. It's difficult to find any definitive answers, but a concept developed at the University of Minnesota, called Farmstead Cheese, offers hope.

The Minnesota plan takes advantage of new techniques in cheese making as a way of simplifying procedures. One key is the use of a recently developed frozen conventional starter cake.

Dr. Ed Zottola, professor and extension specialist in food science in charge of the Minnesota project, reports that half a dozen farmers in that state have gotten involved under his guidance. All the facts aren't in yet and Zottola is maintaining a cautious attitude, but at least one of the farmers is highly enthusiastic about the way things are going for him.

Ray Baune of Milaca, Minnesota, markets his cheese direct, either to consumers who come to the farm or to nearby grocery stores. He processes 1,500 pounds of milk a day, which ends up as 150 pounds of gouda cheese, made in ten-pound wheels. He gets $2 a pound from consumers who buy an entire wheel, and $2.10 a pound for a portion of a wheel. Stores get a discount. The average for all cheese sold is about $1.75 a pound.

Ray and his wife, Carol, learned cheese making by attending a special course at the University of Minnesota. They make cheese five or six days a week. If they make it an average of only five days this would mean an annual output of 39,000 pounds, or a gross income of $68,250, an average of $1.75 a pound. The equivalent amount of fluid milk would bring $35,100 at a market price of $9 a hundredweight. (Milk prices vary by area and utilization. A higher price is paid for Class I, used for fresh consumption, than for Class II, used for ice cream and cheese. The producer selling to a handler usually gets a "blend" of the two prices based on the amount used for each class.)

The Baunes spent about $35,000 on a special building for cheese making and the necessary equipment (some of it second-hand). Based on estimates prepared by Zottola and his teammates at the University of Minnesota, the Baunes' production costs probably amount to $200 a day; this includes the market value of the milk used, starter, electricity, insurance, loan re-payments, maintenance, packaging, and miscellaneous expenses. Production costs for a year would amount to $52,000 for a five-day week, leaving a net of $16,250, not counting labor and depreciation. This would be in addition to whatever net is derived from the milking operation. Don't forget, the Baunes charge against their cheese operation the going blend price of the milk that is used and sell the balance to the handler.

How much labor is involved in making cheese? Zottola estimates about six hours a day. This includes 3½ hours for processing and the balance for care and handling of the cheese in storage, sanitation and marketing.

As might be expected, the Baunes are very happy with their Farmstead Cheese venture. "It's much more profitable than selling milk and we have no trouble getting rid of all the cheese we make," says Ray. "Our cheese is a far better and tastier product than normally found in the supermarket. Consumers appreciate this and are willing to pay what we ask. They also appreciate that we use no additives or preservatives." The Baunes also are happy about the fact that by making cheese they are more independent of the fluid milk marketplace, with its price fluctuations.

How small an operator can profitably make cheese under the Minnesota plan? As yet, no one seems to know. Zottola points out that the method was originally designed for farmers located in heavy production areas where the market price for fluid milk is relatively low (such as Minnesota and Wisconsin, where a large part of production goes for Class II).

But let's take some Minnesota cost figures and adjust them for a small operation, one with a daily output of 500 pounds of milk from 15 cows. Zottola says start-up costs do not go down substantially for smaller operations. The Baunes' investment of $35,000 for buildings and equipment will be used here. Figuring that all 500 pounds of milk is made into cheese seven days a week and is sold direct at $2 a pound, the yearly gross comes to $35,500. Cheese production costs with milk at $9 a hundredweight would come to $31,536, figuring $86.40 a day. That would mean a net of $4,964, not counting labor and depreciation. If the producer's milk was made under conditions that would qualify it only for manufacturing grade, the net from the cheese would be little higher because of the lower market value of the milk.

These net figures may not be very enticing. But let's consider that the farmer would have created his own market for his milk, leaving him independent of the handler. If he tried to sell fluid milk direct to the consumer he could run into problems. In some states the sale of raw milk is not permitted and the cost of pasteurization equipment can run as high as a small cheese-making plant. Milk used for cheese need not be pasteurized, government specialists say, provided the cheese is allowed to age 60 days at 35°F (2°C). Another point: fluid milk is highly perishable, while cheese can be stored until sold.

Still another point in favor of the small farmer making cheese is the by-product whey, which can be fed to livestock. The Minnesota study figures the value of whey from a 15-cow cheese operation would amount to about $518 in a year's time. Then, of course, there is the value of the manure as fertilizer.

Cheese making, Zottola points out, provides an ecologically complete farm cycle: the cows eat grass and produce milk; the milk is converted to cheese and whey; the whey is fed to swine; the swine manure is spread on the pasture to grow more grass; and the grass is eaten by the cows to start the cycle all over again.

DAILY CHEESE MAKING COST ESTIMATES

15-cow herd producing 500 pounds of milk daily, converted to 50 pounds of cheese a day. Market price of milk at $9 a hundredweight. No depreciation or labor.

Value of milk	$45.00
Frozen conc. starter	3.50
Rennet	.25
Electricity	2.00
Insurance	2.00
Loan to get started	24.65
Building maintenance	2.00
Packaging	5.00
Miscellaneous	2.00
Total	$86.40

49: Dried weeds: Quakertown, Pennsylvania

AS A COMMERCIAL vegetable grower, Robert Thayer hated weeds with a passion. They were a time-consuming, ever-present, costly nuisance. One day he reached a decision. Rather than fight weeds, he'd join them. As a result, he has developed the very profitable business of selling weeds, instead of vegetables.

Robert sells all kinds of weeds—goldenrod, wild yarrow, milkweed, foxtail, cattail, wild oats, and peppergrass, to name a few of the most common. But you'd hardly recognize them when they leave his hands. That's because he dries them, bleaches them, and then dyes them all colors of the rainbow.

Robert is in the business of selling dried plant materials for floral arrangements. Some of the things he sells aren't really weeds, such as

Robert Thayer

corn tassels, okra pods, timothy hay, tame oats, and bearded rye. But all are sold in a form uncommon in the marketplace. They've become decorative. The only easily recognizable items he sells in the dried state are "everlastings," such as straw flowers, which are sold natural—not bleached or dyed.

Who are Robert's customers? Mostly flower shops, specialty shops and roadside markets. He also sells directly to consumers at his farm on Muskrat Road near Quakertown, Pennsylvania.

Robert started out using goldenrod from his own farm. He experimented with other weeds and soon reached the point where he had to look beyond the confines of his own fields. He would spot desirable weeds in someone's field and make arrangements to buy them for a few dollars. Then he'd send in a crew of young people as pickers. They got paid by the pound or by the bundle. Now, Robert has contact with enterprising people all over the country who make a business of locating and gathering weeds for him. In addition, he flies all over the world looking for the unusual but useable in weeds.

Despite its present size, Robert's business still is a relatively simple one in terms of equipment and buildings. The setup could easily be duplicated on a small scale by anyone with an outbuilding or two, and with very little cash outlay.

He is willing to reveal some of the secrets of his business. First, the weeds or other materials must be picked in the green, or immature, state and then hung in a shelter to dry—usually for a week or ten days, depending on the weather. Then they are bleached in a 35 percent solution of hydrogen peroxide, dried again, and dyed. (Some are left in the bleached state for contrast.) Thayer uses regular clothing dyes, similar to those for household use, but in a more concentrated, commercial state, sold in large quantities.

The dyeing is simplicity itself, at least so far as the mechanics are concerned. Robert uses small steel drums about 30 inches high and 18 inches in diameter. Each drum holds a different color of dye solution. When a particular color is to be used, it is heated to the boiling point by the application of a direct flame against the side of the drum (Robert uses a weed burner).

A bunch of bleached dried material is dipped into the hot dye for 15 to 20 seconds by a person wearing gloves and holding the bundle by the stem end, which doesn't go into the solution. When the dyed ma-

terial has dried it is ready for use. The colors include bright red, orange, yellow, blue, and green.

Most of the materials have stems anywhere from 12 to 30 inches long. The bundles are made up of a dozen or so plants and are sold this way to the volume buyers. For direct sale to consumers, smaller bundles are made up and inserted into plastic bags.

Some buyers, wholesale and retail, want arrangements already made up. So Robert hired several people to make up arrangements in various sizes and combinations, using a variety of containers that includes woven baskets and plastic hanging baskets.

One of the nice things about Robert's type of business is that it can operate the year around. The busiest time is when the green weeds are gathered and brought in to dry, but from then on the work of bleaching and dyeing can be carried out over a period of months.

Robert cautions that you can't dry and dye just any old weeds. Generally, they should have showy characteristics and possess fairly sturdy stems. They also must be what Thayer calls durable—able to stand up to the business of drying, dyeing and handling without falling apart. He has found, for instance, that Queen Anne's lace (wild carrot) doesn't work out very well.

Even in the case of such cultivated crops as corn, rye and timothy, he has found that certain strains are more desirable than others. Some have stiffer stems than others. Old-type timothy with a long head is preferred over strains with short heads. Bearded rye makes a better looking item than other forms. When it comes to corn tassels, he finds that Silver Queen, a relatively new hybrid white sweet corn, isn't as good as other types for his purposes.

The need for certain desirable weeds has reached the point where some actually are being cultivated. Robert grows his own peppergrass, for instance. Other favored weeds are being grown for him in other parts of the country. College agronomists do a double take when someone like Robert asks them for the best way to grow weeds.

He is forever on the lookout for unusual plants that will widen the variety of arrangements. Besides dried okra pods, he handles the unicorn plant (proboscidea), whose fruit is shaped like a bird four to six inches long. It is grown in the Southeast. The dried fruit is mounted on a thin stem for use in arrangements.

Dried flower arrangements are not something new. They've been popular for years. But recently there has been an expanding market. Retailers of all sorts find they move well and are very profitable.

Robert's weeds and other dried plants are in demand and a ready market exists for them. He no longer seeks out markets. He just waits for the buyers to come to him.

All of which means a big, growing market for the main ingredients—just plain old weeds.

50: 'The largest organic grower in Maine': Canton, Maine

THE SIGN IN front of Richard McCollister's house proclaims him the largest organic grower in the state of Maine. The farm he and his son Benjamin work has been in the family since 1874.

But Richard hasn't always been a farmer. For years he worked as an aircraft and tool designer in Ohio. When he came back to his native area, Benjamin returned with him, having had too much of the "plastic-perfect" world. "I don't see how people can live there," says Benjamin, pointing west.

As is true of many market gardeners and home processors, the McCollisters traded the prospect of good-paying, nine-to-five jobs for a measure of independence: the freedom to choose where to live, what hours to work, and what authorities to answer to. For a time, Richard and Benjamin ground up their own wheat berries and made bread— but when they found they had to get a $20 processed food license in order to sell in Lewiston, they gave up the sideline rather than pay the fee.

So, they now turn their grains into flour with a 2¾-horsepower mill, and sell the flour at a nearby farmers' market. They've given some thought to putting up the flour in five-pound bags bearing a fancy label, and then selling through regular supermarkets. But a problem is pricing—determining just what to charge to allow for overhead and

Richard McCollister

something extra for labor. Says Richard, "I don't believe a small operator can say 'it costs us 56 cents to grow this bag of flour.' " He suggests
that even if bags, seed and gas could be accounted for, it would be discouraging to try to attach a decent amount for labor. "You'll never
make your labor costs, not by the hour." Add an hourly wage comparable to what he could be earning back in Ohio, and the flour would be
priced right out of the market. Another problem in pricing is that
"there's no place to go to get a comparable price." The McCollisters are
not selling run-of-the-mill flour, but an organic, whole product, and
really have no competitors to match.

Some of their customers care that food is organically grown, while
others don't—about sixty and forty percent, respectively, depending
on the crop. The local customers happen to appreciate organically
grown potatoes, for example. Most of the McCollisters' sales are at the
stand in front of the house. They've learned that a variety of crops is
needed for maximum sales, that it's best to have at least two or three
vegetables available throughout the season. One reason a variety of
offerings is important is that a good number of people they sell to have
their own gardens. The vagaries of northern New England's weather
mean that only experienced home growers come through with certain
crops—for example, most gardeners have trouble with tomatoes that
don't ripen, and come to the McCollisters' stand. A note of caution
from Benjamin: with a number of crops to worry about, it's awfully
easy to lose focus, working too hard on one item that may turn out to
have insignificant sales.

If the short, frost-chased seasons are tough on vegetables, they're
also tough on bugs. McCollister and son have few pest problems. They
plant their potatoes in nine rows to two of bean and have little trouble
from potato bugs, while the big commercial fields right across the road
are protected by frequent spraying throughout the season. Ladybugs
are the McCollisters best allies. Luckily, these beneficial beetles
somehow aren't harmed by all the spraying, and come to help out on
the organic side of the road in great numbers. This season, however,
nature's timing was a bit off and the ladybugs arrived early, before
there was much to eat. Their numbers dwindled while the potato bugs
flourished. But the pests spent most of their time on the weak plants
found in poorer parts of the field, just like books on organic growing
claim they will.

The McCollisters have made goat's milk cheese but, like the Knebelmans (Chapter 47), find it very time-consuming; aside from tending the herd and milking, it takes four hours to make a batch of cheese. The cheese is waxed with a combination of paraffin and vegetable oil. There is a good market for cheese curds, known locally as "singing cheese" for the way the rubbery curds squeak against the teeth. The curds are simply drained and kept loose, and then are sold unaged at the Smithville auction.

Might the McCollisters develop their cheese sideline into a full-time business? They've thought about it, calculating that a 20-goat operation, making nothing but cheese, could bring in $5,000 a year. It would be a labor-intensive business, but enough cash could be generated to permit a fair existence if the cheese makers grew most of their own food.

This past season, the young couple in the following profile contracted with the McCollisters to grow an acre of soybeans for a commercial tofu business. The crop never came to fruition, thanks to deer that nibbled the young plants as they reached three or four inches high. The deer returned when the soybeans made another try, keeping the field looking "like a mowed lawn, two inches high all across," says Benjamin.

51: No Moo Dairy: South Portland, Maine

A LIVING ROOM tofu factory sounds like a novelty. It may remain a novelty, too, as Judy and Peter Beane see it, for there is talk in the wind of a huge tofu factory soon to be built in Boston.

Not long ago, tofu (also known as soybean curd) had been an esoteric Eastern food found only in the more authentic Chinese and Japanese restaurants. But with an increased interest in vegetarianism,

Peter Beane making tofu in his living room

and with the publication of *The Book of Tofu,* by William Shurtleff and Akiko Aoyagi (Autumn Press, 1975), the manufacture of tofu is on the verge of becoming big business. As it is now, health food stores and restaurants typically get packaged tofu from good distances. And so it is that the Beane's No Moo Dairy remains a small business, not thriving well enough to support the couple.

Peter has been working for a roofer of late, while Judy makes four or five batches, or about 200 pounds, of tofu a week. She delivers the tofu in a van to a natural food co-op in town, and to the nearby Maine

Turnpike, where eight or so groups of upstate co-op people stop on their monthly produce runs to Boston. The Beanes make no direct sales, and do not sell at their door, as the city would then want them to be licensed. As it is, the street they're on is residential, and so the business will be moved into a natural foods store in Portland.

It was *The Book of Tofu* that first interested Judy and Peter in producing the food for sale. Although the business isn't going great guns, Judy still enjoys the independence a home industry permits.

The equipment consists of a Vitamix 300 (a small kitchen blender that handles a day's worth of beans in 15 or 20 batches, a very time-consuming process), a big cauldron heated by an ancient gas Majestic candy stove, a simple stainless steel box in which the soy milk is expressed from the cooked beans by means of an ingenious jerry-rigged press, a wooden tub in which the soy milk is curdled, and pans for pressing whey from the tofu.

The beans are soaked for up to nine or ten hours, depending on the beans used. The soy milk is boiled three times, then allowed to simmer ten minutes. A mesh football jersey with the arms sewed up is used for straining the pulp from the milk. Judy tried a Japanese pressing sack made for the purpose, but the holes are too big for the tiny pulp particles, thanks to the industrious little Vitamix. And it's because the Vitamix chops up the beans in such small pieces that an experiment to use the pulp was to fail. The Beanes bought a large dehydrator to dry the pulp so that it could be used in preparing a hamburgerlike mix, but the pulp fell through the dehydrator's screens. Judy does make a mix, nevertheless, but because it must be kept frozen for storage, it is put up in one-pound bags. The mix sells to natural foods stores for 60 cents a pound. She also sells a dressing of blenderized tofu, onion powder, cayenne, oil, vinegar, and tamari.

Tofu is an ideal product for a local cottage industry because of the modest overhead and the nature of the product—it is perishable, having a shelf life of but a week or ten days. Also, the homemade product is preferable to commercial tofu that may be adulterated with MSG and preservatives. Commercial tofu may also be made from calcium sulphate instead of the traditional nigari, which is derived from sea salt and is fairly expensive. The chemical gives a higher yield, meaning that more water is held by the tofu—meaning less food for your money.

The Beanes sell tofu in bulk at 30 cents for a block that varies in weight from 8 to 11 ounces; pieces were once weighed individually, but this proved time-consuming. Stores then put the tofu in plastic bags. Prices must be as low as possible, as health food distributors can sell their mass-produced product very cheaply. Luckily the local co-ops and stores would rather buy tofu from a small Maine concern than an out-of-state company.

The price of soybeans has doubled in the 1½ years Judy and Peter have been making tofu. Last spring they were able to buy a ton of beans for $300, or 15 cents a pound plus shipping; the price through distributors is now over 30 cents a pound. Nigari has gone up in price, too, and now costs about $35 per kilogram.

52: Tempeh: Houma, Louisiana

UNLIKE TOFU, THE manufacture of another soybean food, tempeh, has yet to be commercially exploited. Most active in large-scale production of this Eastern food are members of The Farm, a large spiritual community based in Tennessee. A California branch of The Farm manufactures tempeh, as do John and Charlotte Gabriel of Houma, Louisiana, who are former residents of the Tennessee community.

Charlotte now makes batches of fifteen pounds a day, for her own use and to give to friends. But she and her husband plan to go into commercial production of 50- and then 150-pound batches. Small batches, up to 6 pounds, can be made in a foam picnic cooler, heated by a light bulb. But the humidity and heat in Charlotte's Louisiana home provide the proper atmosphere, so she can set the tempeh right out on the kitchen table, covered only by a plastic sheet. (Recent room temperatures have ranged from the low eighties to an ideal 88°F [31°C].)

Culture is purchased from The Farm, and is propagated in a bulb-heated picnic cooler. The necessary split soybeans aren't available locally, and are also purchased from The Farm. John Gabriel is now adapting a large, commercial insulated box—used to keep restaurant food hot—into a tempeh incubator, and will replace the existing heating unit with either a light bulb or a smaller unit. Who will buy such an exotic food for as much or more than they'd pay for hamburger? Vegetarians and others interested in alternative diets, surely, but Charlotte believes tempeh will also appeal to people who now buy flesh foods but are concerned with cholesterol and food additives found in meat. To facilitate its use, Charlotte plans on making up the tempeh into round burger shapes, as well as selling it in blocks.

53: Crabs and oysters: Wingate, Maryland

AT 4:30 EACH morning, Calvert Parks sets out in the *Dorothy Lee,* a 45-year-old drake-tail craft common to Maryland's Eastern shore. From April through the end of September he catches crabs, paying out two half-mile-long lines to which are tied pieces of eel at three-foot intervals. The line is then hauled in and crabs hanging from the bait are knocked off, then sorted by his wife, Nancy. Cull crabs—those missing appendages—are sold to canneries that pick the meat out. The biggest crabs, called Jimmies, end up at restaurants and beer places in Baltimore. Soft-shelled crabs, or peelers, are the most valuable, and are frozen in plastic bags. A middleman may meet Calvert out on the water and pick up part of the catch.

He works his lines until the afternoon heat makes the crabs go for deeper water, then makes a delivery to a packinghouse in his pick-up.

Through the winter, Calvert goes hand-tonging for oysters. Oyster tongs are like long scissors, with a rake at the end. The catch is picked up by trucks and taken down into Virginia, although Calvert

Calvert Parks

Carl Doney

will sell them to customers at the dock. Recent cold winters make this wet work uncomfortable, and cut into his income when he can't safely navigate through the ice.

Carl Doney

Crabbing and oystering involve long hours and hard work, for a wage that is less than spectacular. Asked why he stays with it, Calvert Parks first says, "You hate to be a quitter if you start." But he admits to getting satisfaction out of challenging the weather on Chesapeake Bay.

His father and uncle both made their living the same way. Another uncle built boats, but the last drake-tailed cedar craft left the dry dock in 1956. Calvert has no sons to follow him, but his son-in-law is leaving a city job to return home and go out on the water.

INDEX